Private Investigation in the Computer Age

Private Investigation in the Computer Age

Using Computers to Revolutionize Your Work and Maximize Your Profits

Bud Jillett

Private Investigation in the Computer Age:
Using Computers to Revolutionize Your Work and Maximize Your Profits
by Bud Jillett

Copyright © 2003 by Bud Jillett

CONTENTS

A Word about Computer Literacy IX

A Word about Privacy X

Introduction 1

SECTION ONE: THE TRADE 3

   Chapter 1: What We Do 5

   Chapter 2: The Trade in the Computer Age 17

   Chapter 3: Becoming a PI in the Computer Age 21

SECTION TWO: THE TOOLS AND TECHNOLOGY 25

   Chapter 4: So, Where Are the Computers in the Computer Age? 27

   Chapter 5: The Internet 35

   Chapter 6: Computer Monitoring and Surveillance 55

   Chapter 7: Squeezing Clues from E-Mail 71

   Chapter 8: Computer Forensics 81

   Chapter 9: Lie Detection 89

   Chapter 10: Graphology 103

SECTION THREE: TIPS, TRICKS, AND TALES 109

   Chapter 11: The Very Personal Computer 111

Chapter 12: Better Business Bureau 115

Chapter 13: GPS 117

Chapter 14: Lip Reading 121

Chapter 15: Heir Finding 125

Conclusion 131

Bibliography 133

Appendix 1: Sources 135

Appendix 2: Geographical and Chronological Distribution of Social Security Numbers 137

Appendix 3: Private Detective Licensure 155

ACKNOWLEDGMENTS

I would like to acknowledge the following people for their contributions to this work. In no particular order, they are:

Kyle, without whose expert advice on the Internet, web programming, and networking, much of this book would not have been possible.

John, Jenna, Jookie, Bella, Guido, and Spot, for being the perpetual hosts of "sausage night" and keeping me fed so I could concentrate on writing.

Charlie, Nathan, Sarah, and Stimpy for the recreational foxhunts and hosting Sunday and Monday football events (complete with sausages, of course) and the 2001 New England Patriots Super Bowl party.

Steve and Paula, for the use of their condo so I could get this manuscript started, potatoes, the occasional rat-tail file, and sugar for my coffee so I could write in the morning.

My family, for not inquiring too deeply about what I was writing these past 18 months and just leaving me to do it.

I would like to thank my editor, Jon Ford, who helped transform my original manuscript from what some might've called a decent first draft into the finished product you now hold in your hand. He worked with great care and diligence, continually complimenting the work, even when it required major changes and rework. Many of the changes directly resulted from Jon's expert input and clever solutions to managing the presentation of the material within. Jon never complained, nor refused me any indulgence. He was a pleasure to work with.

The person whose name appears on the following page is very special to me. No work of mine would ever be complete without my acknowledging the impact she has had on my life. In fact, no work of mine could ever have been completed without her. She told me years ago that I could do this, and has been my source of inspiration ever since . . .

Lisa.

A WORD ABOUT COMPUTER LITERACY

Though this book is not entirely about personal computers, some passages assume the reader has basic desktop computer knowledge. This means you know how to turn on a computer and find your way around it. To get the most out of this book, you should also know what the Internet is and how to log onto it.

If you are not comfortable with the foregoing, there are many books and courses available to the beginning computer user. A short "adult ed" course in basic computers should be more than enough to get the beginner through this book.

A WORD ABOUT PRIVACY

Privacy. Many young investigators balk at the word's mere mention. "Privacy?" they say. "Excuse me, but I'm a private detective and I have a job to do. Besides, if you have nothing to hide, you don't need privacy."

A truly seasoned detective, however, knows the gross naiveté of that statement. We send society—and our profession along with it—barreling down the proverbial slippery slope if rookie detectives approach the craft from such an unfortunate perspective. A professional detective diligently defends a citizen's right to privacy; if not for noble reasons, then at least because his business depends on it.

For example, evidence obtained by violating a suspect's privacy rights is useless. A crafty detective might catch a perp red-handed by scanning the cell tower behind his apartment, but the evidence would be inadmissible in court because he violated the law to get it. Furthermore, any information garnered by following leads generated during an illicit phone tap would also be thrown out of court. Our crafty detective's license would be meaningless because he violated the licensing statutes. In breaching his ethics, he will have destroyed his integrity as an investigator. Whoever hired him would surely never do so again.

Besides, as I said above, investigating is a craft, just as acting is a craft. But is Sally really an actress if all she succeeds in is traveling to California to perform in a string of porn flicks? No. She must work at her craft, taking acting lessons, attending workshops, and auditioning for meaningful roles. So an investigator is not much of an investigator if he simply stoops to the perp's level to build a case against him. The craft of our profession requires using the higher functions of our cerebellum to gather information *legally* so it will be *useful* when it is needed. We thereby preserve our integrity so we may work (and sleep) again and do our part to keep society from becoming a cesspool.

Spend a short time in this business and you'll find cesspool enough out there. Our industry pursues deadbeats, bail skips, wife beaters, child molesters—you name it. I am of the firm conviction that we should not add to the cesspool by blindly infringing on people's rights. It is our duty to remember that most people are innocent, and we thrive because of the many good people who hire us to find the few bad ones. It would be unfortunate to thank those good people by taking liberties with their liberty.

Let's keep our industry clean.

WARNING

Read this now! I am putting this here so I do not have to clutter this book with warnings, caveats, and legalese.

The investigative tools, methods, and ideas discussed in this book may be governed by various local, state, and federal laws. A warrant may be required before using any of these tools, methods, and ideas on a third party. The author, publisher, and distributors of this book expect that the reader will seek legal counsel before testing or implementing any of the tools, methods, or ideas presented herein.

The author, publisher, and distributors of this book disclaim any liability from any damages or injuries of any type that a reader or user of information contained in this book may incur from the use or misuse of said information. It is presented *for academic study only.*

INTRODUCTION

If the types of tools we use in our everyday lives define the "Age" of mankind, then we have transcended clearly and unarguably into the Computer Age. What does this mean for private investigators and the detective industry? That's what this book is about.

Whether you're a novice PI, a veteran gumshoe, or simply an individual intrigued by the private detective industry, you've undoubtedly noticed that the advent of the Computer Age has affected it—in some ways more than others. Even if you can't say exactly how, you surely have some vague sense that the industry has been forever changed by the proliferation of desktop computers and the Internet that links them together.

The success of today's investigative agencies is largely dependent on their ability to rapidly and effectively incorporate this latest technology into their business. That's not to say that traditional door knocking and pavement pounding is passé. Any well-rounded detective must be adept in these areas. But if you think your agency can get by relying solely on traditional investigative practices, you'll soon become intimate with the inner workings of the Chapter 11 bankruptcy procedure.

The key here, again, is well-roundedness. Today's successful PIs will not only need a facility for pounding the proverbial asphalt, they'll also need, among other things, an agility to surf inner and outer cyberspace. After all, how can you catch a cyberstalker if you don't know how to trace e-mail headers? How can you find child pornography on your perp's hard drive if you don't know the system level

commands to recover deleted data?

This book will be your resource for doing all of that and more.

Private Investigation in the Computer Age is divided into three sections: "The Trade," "The Tools and Technology," and "Tips, Tricks, and Tales." In section one, we'll discuss the perennial roles of detectives and how the Computer Age requires us to approach dynamically our traditionally static functions. In section two, we'll discuss the burgeoning arsenal of detective tools and new technology proffered by the Computer Age. Although new school and Computer Age tips and tricks will be strewn throughout this text, section three will highlight some choice goodies that I thought deserved their own section and also relay some tales from my early days in the business.

• • • • •

Expert and novice computer users alike will note just how fast the Computer Age is moving. Some aspects of it are moving more predictably than others. For example, in 1970 Intel Corporation predicted its computer chips would double in speed and efficiency every year. Intel was right, and the computer industry has benefited greatly. Less predictable was the advent of the Internet, now more commonly known as the World Wide Web (although technically, the web is only a part of the Internet). People and companies, unsure of their place in this new age, hop on and off the web faster than commuting New Yorkers change subway cars.

Therefore, Internet (web) addresses

mentioned in this book may have changed by the time you read this. Large corporations may have bought out some addresses; other addresses may have disappeared forever into cyber-oblivion. When you come across an address, or web "link," that is no longer current, consider it an early exercise in detective work by locating a current one!

SECTION ONE

THE TRADE

CHAPTER 1: What We Do

"What we are concerned with here is the fundamental interconnectedness of all things."
—Douglas Adams' Dirk Gently

Though the Computer Age offers private investigators new tools and opportunities, what we do is fundamentally the same as it ever was and always will be. What *has* changed, and will continue to change, is how we do it.

Let's face it: locating is locating, documenting is documenting, and security is security. For example, to conduct a surveillance, a detective has to set up operations, remain unseen, gather information, interpret it, form an opinion, and relay his findings to the client. Whether the client is King George III or a modern-day housewife makes little difference. The difference is that George's court investigator did not have the option of scouring the server-side e-mail directory of his suspected perpetrator. Had he had the option and failed to use it, he would have been beheaded and replaced with a more thoroughly equipped courtier. So, you can think of the modern-day Chapter 11 process as a Georgian beheading. The more thoroughly equipped courtier is the competing detective firm that knows the difference between a modem and a moat.

Table 1.1 is a general list of PI services that might be offered to the public by a firm in general practice (as opposed to one specializing in forensics or messy divorces). You will notice that the services fall into three categories. Why would that be? Well, it's sort of like a Snickers bar. No matter how you slice it, you're going to get peanuts, nougat, and chocolate. And no matter how you subcategorize or slice up (or, as some ad brochures do, *puff up*) a given private detective service, you'll find that it all boils down to three basic functions: locating, documenting, and security.

What about surveillance? It's in there. Surveillance is a part of documenting and/or security, depending on the job. What about countermeasures? Well, you *locate* the bug and the person who put it there, *document* the evidence for court, to provide your client a sense of—you guessed it—*security*. Some agencies have different words for these three things—skip tracing, mapping, detail work—but it's all the same stuff.

Any firm advertising all of the services listed in Table 1.1 would be a very well-rounded firm indeed. But this is a general service list, not a typical one, and it is by no means exhaustive. Rather than discussing each service in detail, I'll expound a bit on each of the broader categories and highlight a typical service or two that I think exemplifies it.

LOCATING

Of the three primary facets of investigation, locating is often the most rewarding. There is nothing like the feeling you have after finding someone or something you've searched long and hard for. For this reason, I make a point to sprinkle my workweek with a liberal dose of locating. Hopefully, I can close at least one case by Friday and go into the weekend with a sense of fulfillment.

Generally, your firm will get calls falling into two broad subcategories of locating: people and property. I find (in Massachusetts, at least) that most people calls will be for missing teens and most property calls will be for automobile repossessions. Let's explore

TABLE 1.1
General PI Services

Locating		Documenting			Security
Known Subjects	Unknown Subjects	Fraud	Domestic	Commercial	
Missing Persons/Runaways	Heir Finding	Worker's Comp	Adultery	Accident Reconstruction	Bodyguard
Heir Finding	Cyberstalkers	Insurance	Divorce	Background and Asset Checks	Identity Theft Detection and Prevention
Skip Tracing	Hackers	Welfare	Child Abuse Neglect/Molestation	Handwriting Analysis	Alarms, Burglar, Fire and Medical
Automobile Repossessions	Homicide	Social Security (SSI)		Surveillance	Backstage Activity Monitor
	Theft, Larceny, Embezzlement		Spousal Abuse	Insurance Investigations	Event Security
			Neglect of the Elderly	Crime Scene Analysis	Computer Security and Data Extraction
	Prowlers			Store Detective	Countermeasures (Bug Detection)
	Peeping Toms			Corporate Plant	Personal Protection
				Political Corruption and Malfeasance	Construction Site Monitor

these two topics to get a feel for what locating generally entails.

Missing Persons

The most common call your detective agency will get that fits this category will involve "missing" teenagers. More often than not, the teen has run away from family troubles and is not so much missing as totally fed up. After going to the police, the family was probably left with a gnawing suspicion that the cops planned to let the case solve itself and thus they have come to you.

In these cases the police aren't all wrong. They are very busy, have limited resources, and know that, in fact, most of these situations do eventually solve themselves. But the parents who knock on your door do not know this and are convinced that their little girl (she'll always be their "little girl," teenager or not) is going to find enlightenment only after hitting bottom on the sidewalk of some red-light district. Again, this will almost never happen. All the same, we have to consider that you've hung out your shingle to make a buck and, as dull as this case might sound, it is now your job to solve it.

To solve this case, a good detective would conduct a sympathetic and detailed interview of the parents, paying particular attention to the circumstances surrounding any recent arguments that may have erupted over their differences with the runaway. Any siblings or other peer cohabitants (friends, cousins, exchange students, etc.) would be interviewed, preferably out of the house and definitely without the parents being present. Our detective would be open to subtle signs that the siblings might be hiding something or may have otherwise been confided in. They are never pressured for information in the beginning because this will only delay things. First you must gain their fragile trust—they, too, may feel oppressed in the household and may be considering a midnight move. Siblings of runaways tend to be more forthcoming as time goes on and their own concern for their missing brother or sister grows.

The experienced detective reading this might say, "Yeah, yeah, I know. But how has the Computer Age changed all this?" Well, years ago if a sibling had been confided in, there was usually an agreement that the runaway would be out of contact. "I just can't take mom and dad anymore so I'm leaving. I'll miss you, though. You were always a good sister. I'll be okay, but I can't tell you where I'm going because I don't know yet. I won't be able to call you." While obviously it didn't always happen this way, that was a fairly typical pre-Computer Age last exchange between a runaway and a trusted sibling.

The Computer Age conversation is fairly similar—with one glaring exception that could help you solve the case quickly and thereby convince the parents that your $2,500 retainer was justified. The conversation is more likely to contain the word "e-mail" and statements like "I'll be on AOL under a new s/n [1] at the usual time."

That's not to say that Computer Age siblings are stupid enough to leave incriminating e-mails on the computer or to chat with their runaway brother while mom's making egg salad sandwiches 10 feet away (though I did have a case where something not too dissimilar did occur). Most teens today are actually quite diligent about deleting e-mails and hiding the chat window under the Word document entitled Senior Biology Project. But as you'll see in the "Tools and Technology" section of this book, there are Computer Age tools the detective can use to monitor a person's activity on the computer.

Automobile Repossessions

Automobile repossession is fun, exciting, and rewarding. Successful repossessions help keep loan interest rates low and the automobile industry moving. It is a quirk of the law that no states (at least none that I know of at the time of this writing) require automobile repossessors to be licensed private detectives. This is because you are not finding or investigating *people*, and most state PI licensing laws are structured around the act of looking into the location, habits, and whereabouts of people or other legal entities such as corporations. Most states, in fact, do not

TABLE 1.2 State-by-State Auto Repossession Requirements		
State	**Licensing/Requirements**	**Recovery Type**
Alabama	None	Self-Help
Alaska	None	Self-Help
Arizona	None	Self-Help
Arkansas	None	Self-Help
California	Repo license	Self-Help
Colorado	Bond only	Self-Help
Connecticut	None	Self-Help/notify police
Delaware	None	Self-Help
D.C.	Repo license	Self-Help
Florida	E/EE license per Chapter 493	Self-Help/except mobile homes
Georgia	Insurance certification/business license	Self-Help
Hawaii	Licensed as collection agent	Self-Help
Idaho	None	Self-Help
Illinois	Cert. to operate for hire from Commerce Commission	Self-Help
Indiana	None	Self-Help
Iowa	None	Self-Help
Kansas	None	Self-Help
Kentucky	None	Self-Help
Louisiana	Occupational license	Debtor must sign voluntary surrender.
Maine	Debt collector's license	Self-Help
Maryland	Collection agency license	Self-Help
Massachusetts	None	Cannot recover from property owned or leased by debtor.
Michigan	Collection agency license, bond	Self-Help
Minnesota	None	Self-Help
Mississippi	City and county business license	Self-Help
Missouri	None	Per contract, which must be in hand at repo time.
Montana	None	Trip permit if removing from county lines.
Nebraska	None	"Peaceful repossessions permitted."
Nevada	Repo license	Self-Help
New Hampshire	None	Self-Help

State	Licensing/Requirements	Recovery Type
New Jersey	None	Self-Help
New Mexico	Repo and "Warrant for Transportation Services" licenses required	Self-Help
New York	None	Self-Help
North Carolina	None	Self-Help
Ohio	None	Self-Help
Oklahoma	Tow vehicles must be licensed	Self-Help
Oregon	Registered as Collection Agency per ORS 697.031	Self-Help
Pennsylvania	Licensed and bonded	Self-Help
Rhode Island	None	Self-Help/notify police
South Carolina	None	Self-Help
South Dakota	None	Self-Help
Tennessee	None	Self-Help
Texas	None	Self-Help
Utah	None	Self-Help
Vermont	None	Self-Help
Virginia	None	Self-Help
Washington	State registration	Self-Help
West Virginia	None	Self-Help
Wisconsin	None	Debtor must sign voluntary surrender.
Wyoming	None	Self-Help

SOURCE: Time Finance Adjusters, The Official Guide 2001–2002.

NOTE: Other laws and regulations may apply.

KEY:

Self-Help—Means the lien holder (usually the auto dealer) or his repo agent may take it upon himself to remove the vehicle from the debtor's property without involving the police. This assumes there is no "breach of peace" in the process. If an altercation ensues, such as the debtor displaying arms or standing in front of a tow truck, then the dealer or his repo agent must involve the police or a sheriff to complete the repossession.

Notify police—Means the lien holder must notify the police before, after, or within a specific time period following the repo; varies by jurisdiction.

require repossession agents to be licensed at all. Therefore, becoming a "repo man" is an excellent way to start an investigative agency before you have an actual license. Be aware, however, that some states require repossession agents to be registered as debt collectors and may require a bond. As of this writing, the strictest states for repo men are Florida and California. For a state-by-state listing of requirements, see Table 1.2.

So, how does my detective license fit into my repo activities, you might ask? For one, car dealers are more likely to choose you as their repossession agent if they see by your PI license that you are generally experienced as a finder. A license also gives you advertising power. For example: *"As a licensed private detective agency, our locating experience helps keep 'chase fees' to a minimum."* You see, most auto repo agencies want to know where the vehicle is up front, preferring to simply recover the vehicle from a known location. If they have to "chase" the vehicle, they charge more.

As a licensed private detective wearing my repo hat, I've always considered it my responsibility to find the car, so I do not charge a chase fee. Of course I take any and all information the dealership has in its file. But if the car isn't conveniently parked at the subject's place of employment, [2] then that is where my fun begins. For this reason, my agency often gets the tougher repo cases. Of course there's nothing stopping me, as a licensed private detective, from charging a higher rate than an unlicensed repo man, so some income that may be lost by not charging for so-called chase fees I recover simply because I am trusted as a licensed professional.

DOCUMENTING

Documenting gigs also fall into two subcategories: people and events. Most people

calls will be for background checks, and most event calls will be insurance investigations (unless you're known for crime scene analysis or some other specialty).

Background checks are further subdivided into criminal histories and asset checks. (See Table 1.3 for a detailed list of specialized background checks you can perform for a paying client.) You can already see where checking into a person's assets can eventually turn into a locating gig. For example, if you learn that a bankruptcy filer owns a boat, the bankruptcy trustee who hired you will probably give you the job of finding the boat. So if documenting sounds boring to you, keep in mind that it often leads to more rewarding jobs. In the following section, we'll explore background checks to get a good feel of what documenting gigs generally entail.

Background Checks

As its name implies, a background check involves researching a subject's history. The subject is usually an individual, but it can also be

TABLE 1.3 Specialized Background Checks	
Service	**Notes**
Incarceration history	Easier to obtain than criminal records. Can get free of charge from many states.
Sexual offender status	Readily available, thanks to Megan's Law.
Motor vehicle records/Driver history	On-line, or direct from many states.
Divorce	Probate court, state vital statistics office.
Inheritances	Probate court.
Name change	Probate court.
Tax records	Local, good way to see if subject pays his bills.
Real estate holdings	Register of Deeds.
Education	
Military	
SSN	
Internet addresses owned	WhoIs servers (see Chapter 7, *Squeezing Clues from E-mail*).
Previous addresses	Old paper or CD-ROM phone directories.
Better Business Bureau	Free on-line search: www.bbb.org.
Traffic court	

a company. Background facets can range from a simple verification of employment history to a full-fledged investigation into primary and secondary schooling, all licenses and jobs held, driving and criminal record, and a complete list of all known present and past consorts, each with its own follow-up check.

A good detective flags gaps in a subject's background, such as a year off from school, an extended time between jobs, or time spent out of the country. This allows the client to direct follow-up questions to the subject during subsequent contacts or hire the detective to do further investigation.

A client who requests this service of a private detective is usually doing so as a preventive measure and has reserved judgment of the subject pending your report. In fact, your report is often the deciding factor in whether the subject gets an important job or is deemed legitimate enough to a diligent fiancée. A background report is very powerful, and the detective must exercise the utmost care and accuracy in its preparation. It's better to omit something than to expound on unreliable or incomplete information.

The subject, either directly or by implication, has given your client a certain set of facts and you are hired to check them out. The advantage here, of course, is that you have at least one known starting point. Even a mal-intended, disreputable cad will have to be honest with his fiancée (your client) about some facet of his reality, such as his birthplace and upbringing. It's your job to get his birth certificate, check his school records, and look for inconsistencies in his story.

Since the September 11, 2001, terrorist attacks, private detectives have been kept very busy with background investigations. This is good if you're a detective, but when you take off your detective's cap and become an ordinary citizen, the privacy implications are horrific. If we're not careful, pretty soon you won't be able to buy lighter fluid or fertilizer without submitting to a background check. So, as always, when I am hired to do a background check, I maintain strict professionalism and the utmost respect for a citizen's right to privacy. It always

feels good to weed out a bad guy—especially when you've played by the rules in doing so.

Criminal Histories

Unless your client orders a complete background investigation, there is usually a specific set of facts he or she would like verified. Did the subject really work at a certain software company? Is it true the subject has never been married? But if a client orders only one facet of a background check, it will invariably be a criminal history.

Criminal histories are requested by companies and skittish fiancées alike. A town wouldn't hire a guy to drive a school bus if he has prior DUI convictions. A debutante would not entertain a gentleman who earns his money illegally. But how do they dig up the dirt? They hire a detective agency that includes criminal history as part of its background investigation, that's how. In fact, a good Computer Age marketing strategy is to advertise that you include a criminal records check in the subject's home state with all background investigations. This automatically gets the client past that stage and wondering, "Okay, what else can I order?" Reason being: criminal records checks, as you'll see if you don't already know, are inexpensive for us detectives to perform.

In the old days there were two popular ways to get a subject's criminal history. Either you knew a police official who didn't mind sharing information with you, or you went through the same channels as everyone else: you ordered it from the state. Today both methods are still available, though police officials are becoming more and more hesitant to share information with private detectives, even ones they know well. Most states allow you to order a person's criminal history for a nominal charge (Screenshot 1.1. is a sample form from the Commonwealth of Massachusetts), and more and more states are allowing you to order one on-line for slightly more.

Suppose a given subject lived in three or four states during his adult life. He could've gotten into criminal trouble in any of those states, and writing to each one for information can get to be

REQUEST FOR PUBLICLY ACCESSIBLE MASSACHUSETTS CORI

It is lawful to request this agency to provide a copy of another person's <u>publicly accessible</u> adult conviction record. For the adult conviction record to be "publicly accessible" the person whose record is requested must have been convicted of a crime punishable by a sentence of five years or more, or has been convicted of any crime and sentenced to any term of imprisonment, and at the time of the request:

1.   is serving a sentence of probation or incarceration, or is under the custody of the parole board; or
2.   having been convicted of a misdemeanor, has been released from all custody or supervision not more than one year; or
3.   having been convicted felony, has been released from all custody or supervision for not more than two years; or
4.   having been sentenced to the custody of the department of correction, has finally been discharged therefrom, either having been denied release on parole or having been returned to penal custody for violating parole for not more than three years.

<u>Directions</u>: Please fill this request form out as completely as possible. The more information you are able to provide, the more easily this agency will be able to process your request. A <u>non-refundable</u> processing fee of $25.00 is charged for <u>each record</u> requested and must be included with your request(s). There will be no exceptions made to this rule. Only checks or money orders made payable to the Commonwealth of Massachusetts will be accepted. A self-addressed, stamped envelope must also be enclosed with your request(s). Walk in requests or faxed requests will not be accepted. Requests will be processed in the order in which they are received. Mail all requests to: the Criminal History Systems Board, 200 Arlington Street, Suite 220U, Chelsea, MA 02150, ATTN: CORI Unit.

All requests must be typed. Requests containing any illegible identifying information will be returned. If you are making more than one request, please copy this form and fill in the requested identifying information accordingly.

1.

Last name	First name	Middle initial

Maiden name	Alias

Date of Birth (MM/DD/YY)	Social Security Number

2.

Last name	First name	Middle initial

Maiden name	Alias

Date of Birth (MM/DD/YY)	Social Security Number

Screenshot 1.1. Sample of a criminal history request form from the state of Massachusetts.

time consuming, not to mention having to research each state's ordering and pricing policies first. A good Computer Age solution to this dilemma is to use an on-line search service.

The least expensive on-line criminal records search I've been able to find is criminalscreen. com, which as of this writing charges a flat $12.95 for each county or state search. Why would you pay $12.95 for a county search when you can get the whole state for the same price? I thought you might be wondering about that. Some states require a subject's consent before releasing his or her criminal record. As a detective, you will often want to perform criminal records searches without the subject knowing about it, so written consent is out of the question. However, all 3,100+ counties in the United States consider criminal histories to be public records. This offers a convenient loophole around the state's requirement.

Other on-line search services offering criminal record checks include:
- americandatabank.com
- USsearch.com
- criminalusa.com
- backgroundsusa.com

More search services go on-line every month. Your best bet is to use an Internet search engine such as google.com, hotbot.com, or altavista.com to find one offering competitive rates.

Asset Checks

The world is full of potential clients dying to know what the other guy has. Former business partners, bankruptcy trustees, attorneys, but most of all spouses in the throes of divorce want to know what cards the other half holds. They call in detectives to dig up real estate holdings, life insurance equity, bank accounts, stocks, mutual funds, IRAs, safe deposit boxes, big toys such as boats, even unclaimed money.

Years ago a detective would have to tail a suspect for a while or raid his trash to find out where he banks. Still valid methods, but the Computer Age offers something that will greatly reduce your exposure to maggots and half-squeezed ketchup packets: information

clearinghouses, also known as information resellers. These outfits have access to just about any information on a person that can be accessed. Asset searches are among their most popular services; they are also among their most expensive, upwards of $400 depending on the search.

Personally, I never order anything from an information clearinghouse unless it offers a "no hit, no fee" policy. A good clearinghouse, to keep itself honest, must offer this or at least a reduced fee, such as $75 for a complete asset check that turns up nothing. But its profits will increase proportionally to the accuracy and completeness of its records, since you'll still have to pay $300–$600 even if a search turns up a bank account with two cents in it. This incentive is your assurance that the company is doing all it can to keep its records up to date.

I have dealt successfully with many information clearinghouses over the years. Source Resources is a fairly decent outfit. (My only complaint is that they completely ignored my repeated requests to be interviewed for this book.) In general, I've found that smaller information resellers will work harder for you. They are hungrier for repeat business and generally embarrassed to charge you if they don't get a hit. I'd suggest developing a close relationship with a small reseller, especially if you happen to have one local to you.

SECURITY

As I mentioned in this book's introduction, security is the third basic function of private detective work. I noted in a general sense how locating and documenting—the bread and butter of our industry—provide security to our clients. But private investigation skills can also be applied to the vast, peripheral, but still related field commonly called "security."

The security industry encompasses many types of professions, including home security technician (e.g., alarm systems, specialty locksmithing), security guard (e.g., malls, rock concerts, and related events), and even countermeasures expert, where you work for paranoiacs with plenty to be paranoid about (corporate executives with trade secrets, high-ranking government employees, etc.). But perhaps the most obvious—though often misunderstood—security field where private investigation skills can be applied profitably is bodyguarding.

In the real world, there are few clients who can support even one full-time bodyguard, let alone a coordinated team of them. It works out that the ones who can afford personal bodyguards are also the ones who need them most, usually celebrities, big-time executives, and other people in the public eye. The ultimate security, of course, is to be the president of the United States and to have an entire taxpayer-paid team of security guards (i.e., the Secret Service) dedicated to the task of keeping your ass safe from overzealous egg-tossing protestors on up to deliberate gun-toting assassins.

Bodyguarding gigs are not easy to come by. In order to break into the field you have to build a reputation, and this takes time. You will not start out with celebrities, of course. If you really want to get into this line of work, you need to make some connections. Even low-key bodyguarding gigs go mostly to former law enforcement and military personnel. The more important (read: *richer*) the client, the more elite the cop or soldier assigned to protect said client will likely be. Your brother-in-law-the-beat-cop might be able to moonlight as security for the local rock band or during heated city council meetings, but Fortune 500 CEOs, mega rock stars, and the like are going to turn to former members of big-city SWAT units, the FBI, Secret Service, U.S. Navy SEALs, even the U.S. Army's super-secret Delta Force who have turned to offering their professional experience and skills on the private market.

Bodyguarding in the Computer Age

Since the first terrorist attack on the World Trade Center on February 26, 1993, the security industry has witnessed a rise in market demand for so-called bodyguards. Many of you may be aware of this demand and think that bodyguarding is a quick way into the private detective or security industry. This is dangerous thinking, as you will soon see.

With the advent of the Computer Age and its associated techno bells and whistles, one might be led to believe that every facet of our industry must march lockstep into some inevitable technological change. With the availability of nearly invisible headsets, palm-sized night vision gear, encoded digital voice and data transmission, and on and on, a Computer Age bodyguard wannabe might feel that just because he is familiar with these devices, he's been handed the golden key to a fascinating and exciting career. But as stated in this book's introduction, the base aspects of our industry have really remained unchanged. Yes, in order to survive, our industry must roll with Computer Age changes, but we must also be careful not to jump before such changes are necessary. Roll, yes; jump, no.

Young detectives must remember that all the cybergadgets in the world are not going to spare you the inconvenience of real-world training and experience—especially when human lives are at stake. In the so-called bodyguarding profession, we are dealing with precisely that: saving human lives. Obviously, our industry cannot afford to take this subject lightly. In my opinion, nobody should.

Perhaps not a result of the Computer Age but nevertheless a fact that has come into being with it is the evolution of the very term "bodyguard." Over the past couple of decades, industry professionals have become more comfortable with and accustomed to the terms "executive protection specialist" or "personal protection specialist." My personal feeling for the reason behind this evolution is that Hollywood has too often portrayed bodyguards in an unrealistic manner in films, at the very least creating a stereotype and at worst creating a potentially deadly misconception in the public mind.

Computer Age bells and whistles have their advantages for sure, and anyone considering a career as an executive protection specialist should consider the fact that the following devices and others like them are playing an increasingly important role in the field:

- Discreet—in fact barely visible—headsets, which are quite handy when working with an assistant or if you're lucky enough to be part of a team
- Microprocessor-controlled coded entry systems to keep your clients safer at night
- Face-recognition security cameras and entry systems
- Entryway and handheld metal detectors
- Night vision devices
- Computer-monitored infrared and laser perimeter protection
- Motion-sensitive lighting systems

If you're working with a well-known celebrity who's plagued by harassers or stalkers, a Computer Age detective can even use computer-assisted demographic profiling to gain an idea beforehand of who in a crowd is likely to be a problem. But don't think for a second that having everything in the above list is going to make you a good, or even marginal, executive protector.

In fact, the new preferred term of "executive protector" is pointedly derived to show that being one goes far beyond the stereotypical dark-suited, wide-chested, sunglasses-wearing stereotype of a mere "bodyguard." There is certain training one must acquire, certain life experience one must have.

Below are two quotes from a book you must buy if you are serious about learning what's really required for a career in the executive protection field. They are taken from *Executive Protection: A Professional's Guide to Bodyguarding* by Benny Mares (Paladin Press, 1994).

On page 6, Mr. Mares writes:
"In reality, the professional protection specialist is a capable person who blends into the circumstances and is noticed only if necessary."
On page 7, he writes:
". . . as long as there is boredom, the bodyguard is doing the job successfully."

I quote these here because I know most new investigators reading this section would have a completely opposite image of what the executive protection field is all about. Mr. Mares' book will show you that it involves appropriate dress, proper etiquette in social circles, speech awareness, and other things you may not have considered, such as first-aid skills. CPR and the various Heimlich maneuvers are a bare minimum for anybody entering this field. Can you imagine what your reputation would become if your client *died* because you didn't have the knowledge to save him from choking on a pretzel? Along with basic first-aid skills, an executive protector would do well to enroll in a defensive driving program to complement other executive protection training or courses.

An executive protector must be prepared to fit in with assignments, whether your client is an avid mountain climber, sea-goer, or horseback rider. Naturally, you have to be with your client in order to protect him. If you cannot keep up with her when she goes out for her morning jog, you will not get the job.

Mr. Mares' book will help dispel other common misconceptions about this field. Most would not expect that a working knowledge of unarmed combat is at least as important as prior related law enforcement, government, or military experience, or that a working knowledge of weaponry is a distant second to unarmed combat skills. In fact, many of the best executive protectors in the business do not routinely carry weapons. Because you will be close to your client at all times, unarmed combat skills will be the ones most often called upon. For example, what do you do if a "fan" appears to be stumbling toward your celebrity client? Well, the stumbler might be just that: a fan—maybe a drunken one. Do you want to go to prison for the rest of your life for shooting a drunken, stumbling fan? Conversely, an apparent stumbler might be a clever attacker. You, as a professional executive protection specialist, are in no position to discount this possibility. Suddenly, out of nowhere, a seemingly incidental event becomes a life-and-death quandary that you must be ready to handle in a split second. At the end of that second lies the rest of your career.

Exactly how to handle such situations is beyond the scope of this book, but keeping with the above example for just another minute, let me just say this. Until you see a weapon or some other sign of potential battery against your client, your only choice is to use enough physical force to keep the potential attacker from reaching your client's body. The law allows you to use "equal and opposite force"—doing more that that could land *you* in prison. The foregoing demonstrates the need to properly educate yourself in this field before holding yourself out to the general public as a so-called bodyguard.

Unless you are a former Secret Service agent or Navy SEAL, you should consider attending a respected professional training institute such as Executive Security International (ESI, at www.esi-lifeforce.com). Alternatively, you could apprentice under the wing of an experienced, established executive protector.

Some detectives in general private practice might wonder how their existing status and skills could help them expand into the executive protection industry. Firstly, many PIs are former law enforcement officers, which gives them a leg up when it comes time to socially engineer themselves into this sometimes cliquish field. Also, the background-checking skills of an experienced PI would come in handy for a bodyguard detail that will need intelligence on specific threats, from a lone celebrity stalker to a terrorist group operating near a client company's overseas facility. In fact, ESI offers a specialized training course called "Protective Intelligence and Investigation."

Though the foregoing section is not one of this book's longest, it offers a lot to think about for those of you interested in the executive protection field or the security industry in general. It also demonstrates the need to balance good old-fashioned common sense and training along with our industry's eagerness to compete in the Computer Age. Above all, it shows that a person's perception of a seemingly straightforward field such as bodyguarding can be greatly distorted due to unfortunate and widespread media-propagated misconceptions. We are reminded of the serious nature of our industry and the need to remain vigilant in our professionalism, especially in the face of various stereotypes that society might create for us.

ENDNOTES

1. Net slang for "screen name."
2. Why place of employment? In Massachusetts you cannot repossess from property rented or owned by the debtor without special warrants.

CHAPTER 2: The Trade in the Computer Age

"Man is still the most extraordinary computer of all."
—John Fitzgerald Kennedy

Private investigators aren't simply gumshoes anymore. The Computer Age has changed everything. Not only has the computer given detectives new ways to solve civil and criminal cases, it has also opened up entirely new investigative fields. Today, detectives are being asked to catch cyberstalkers and cyberspies, pedophiles who seduce children on-line, authors of computer viruses, and network hackers, among others.

We are hired by companies concerned with information security. (Are their customer databases safe from hackers looking for credit card numbers? What about their trade secrets that are stored in shared network hard drives?) Parents want us to decrypt encrypted e-mails found on their child's computer. Organizations and individuals want us to find the author of the virus that nearly destroyed them. Data mining—gathering and storing information about people's on-line buying habits—has become an industry unto itself.

Here's a case that demonstrates one way computers have affected our trade. It's a true case from my files. I have changed the names and locations to protect my client.

THE CASE OF THE CYBERSTALKER

In early 2000 I received a call from a client whom I'll call Skip. He was concerned about continued unwelcome e-mails he'd been receiving, one to two per week containing explicit pictures of homosexual adults engaged in various sex acts. Skip's main concern was the sheer volume of the e-mails.

What kind of individual would anonymously go to such lengths to send this stuff to him? He was also concerned that a potentially unstable person knew how to get hold of him. What else did this person know? His address? Phone number? Hangouts?

The e-mails appeared to be sent by different people, but it was obviously the same person. The sender simply used a different name and "reply to" address, which was always cleverly forged. Skip had tried to reply to the e-mails, but they always came back as undeliverable. My challenge, then, was to determine the source or sources of the e-mails and from there draw a conclusion as to who in Skip's life would be sending pornographic photographs from the given source or sources.

It seemed simple enough at first to trace the e-mails, but when I did, they turned out to be coming from one of the biggest Internet service providers (ISPs) on the East Coast. This particular ISP had thousands of dial-up numbers [1] on the eastern seaboard, and Skip's harasser could have been using any one of them. I did not see this as a total loss, however. After all, the harasser's location was already narrowed down to east of the Mississippi River.

I am not being facetious. When you begin a case in which you are searching for a perpetrator, narrowing down his location to any extent is good—especially in a cyberstalker case. A good cyberstalker or hacker can mask his location so as to appear to be coming from anywhere in the world at any time. (At this point, some of you may be wondering how I was able to learn even this much. We will get to that in Chapter 8.)

Once I learned that the ISP had countless dial-up access numbers, I notified my client and told him that the case could get expensive. I would have to call the ISP and convince them I had a legitimate reason for wanting to know the exact dial-up location a particular e-mail was sent from. This is not impossible, but because ISPs do not want to incur liability for any reason, they usually remain tight-lipped about such things until a lawyer or the cops become involved. After all, if an ISP were to give me information, how do they know I won't use that information to track down a person and gain revenge or something equally nasty? They don't. The ISP will, of course, review the abusive e-mails, do their own in-house investigation, and terminate the abuser's account. But remember, my client wanted to know who the abuser was. This left me back at square one.

My client did not wish to incur the expense of calling in an attorney and asked if there were any other options. I told him to keep forwarding me the e-mails on the off chance the perpetrator changed ISPs.

For the next two weeks Skip kept forwarding me the abusive e-mails and, as was expected, the perpetrator continued using the same ISP. But interestingly enough, one of the e-mails originated from an unexpected backbone in the ISP's network (again, all this will be explained in Chapter 8). You see, even though we were dealing with a very large ISP, I was always able to derive the general source of the e-mail—they usually originated up in Maine. Then, all of a sudden we got one that originated on the Boston branch of the ISP's network. I called my client and asked him if he knew anybody who normally lived in Maine but had occasion to be in Massachusetts on the day this particular e-mail was sent.

Skip knew in an instant who the perpetrator was. Case closed.

CLIENT REPORTS IN THE COMPUTER AGE

In the old days, when you completed a case you showed your client some pictures, played a cassette tape, maybe even a video, handed over a report, and gave an oral presentation. Now you can package all this together in a multimedia presentation such as PowerPoint and provide it to your client for his private viewing on his personal computer.

Imagine a presentation where the computer text of your report states the time and manner in which your subject left the apartment—and right next to that paragraph is a picture or movie clip of the subject exiting the door. Good, solid reporting.

Next your report states that your subject drove 20 miles to a shipyard loading dock to make the drop. You have a picture of him sliding an unknown character a wad of cash. Roll the audio. Your client's PC speakers crackle:

"$10,000 like we said. When will it be done?"

"Soon."

"Will you call me?"

"You'll know."

"One in the head so it's over quick, right? I don't want her to suffer."

"She won't feel anything."

By compiling evidence into a PowerPoint file, you also maintain a convenient, organized record of how you can present the evidence to a jury if the case ever goes to trial. This is a big-time savings in time and effort. Usually, by the time a case ever gets to trial, you've completely forgotten it. If you receive a surprise call to testify from the attorney you did the work for, your mind will likely be completely preoccupied with a new case. Before computers, you'd have to spend an entire weekend going through boxes of material in order to remember what you did, why you did it, and what you intended to prove by doing it. With PowerPoint, you simply view the presentation a few times to get your mind back on track. Everything's already laid out for you, your client, and the jury. Nice.

WEB PRESENCE

Business entities from every industry are realizing the competitive importance of establishing a presence on the web. A consumer who's had positive experiences buying books over the Internet is likely to use it to search for a private detective as well. If you don't have a web site established, your firm is completely out of the running for this prospective client's business.

Some detective firms have noted this trend and have tried to compete by merely establishing a web page with their company name and phone number on it. But a web site is not just a token listing that invites potential clients to contact you by traditional means. Such is not a web site; it's an electronic yellow pages ad. It will only succeed in making the potential client angry for wasting his time. A person who is comfortable with the web and has taken the time to find you expects to be able to use e-mail to communicate with you immediately. They expect your web site to give them the details they would otherwise have to call you up and ask you about. What kind of cases do you handle? What are your qualifications? Are you licensed? Bonded? Insured? With whom? What are your fees? If someone likes what they see, do you have an on-line questionnaire they can fill out to get the ball rolling?

I'm not saying you have to be waiting at your computer to receive and respond to e-mails immediately, but the potential client has something he wants to get off his chest. If you don't have a way for him to do that, he'll keep surfing the web till he finds a more web-friendly firm.

I can hear you old schoolers grumbling at this, but why rail against it? A web site is an extremely effective and comparatively inexpensive advertising means. Also, having a web presence lends itself more easily to expanding your business. Your site could have links to on-line information databases, in effect making you a reseller for paying subscribers. On the more involved end of the scale, you could set up an on-line store to sell gadgets your customers might need, including caller ID modules, off-hook indicators, DTMF decoders, room monitors, motion-sensor lighting, privacy books, keystroke recorders and computer data loggers for concerned parents . . . the list goes on and on. You can have links to articles about you and

your firm pertaining to cases you've solved, press releases, interviews you've done, transcripts of important cases you've testified in, open letters to legislators, books you've written . . . another list that goes on.

This, my friend, is today's trade in the Computer Age. Like it or not, it's evolving and will continue to do so.

So, now you're sold. But how do you go about setting up a web site? You employ the services of a web host. Fortunately, the increase in web-hosting competition has driven prices down. I established a web site for a total capital outlay of $108. At the time of this writing, my web host, PowWeb.com, was offering web-hosting services for $7.77 per month. I paid for one year in advance plus a $15 domain registration fee. [2] If you pay a year in advance, PowWeb gives you another two months free, so you really get 14 months.

Other web hosts offer similar packages and incentives. But what do I mean when I say web host? Well, technically, you don't need a "host" to have a web site. You could buy a few thousand dollars worth of equipment, lease a dedicated T3 connection from your friendly phone company for about $1,400 a month, pay the phone company a few thousand in setup and wire-run charges, register an available domain for around $35 a year, hire someone to set it all up and maintain it, and that's it—you have your very own web site. This is precisely what I would do if I had $1,400 a month to spare and believed that having my own web server would somehow be an advantage to me. Right now, neither of those things seems to be true.

A web host is someone who does all of the above, except they spend tens of thousands on equipment and lease much higher capacity lines from the phone company, paying a minimum $30,000 a month for the privilege. To be profitable they divide their servers' disk space into smaller parts, where they "host" people like me. For the moment, I'm fine with that arrangement.

Assuming that you, too, would be fine with a web-hosting arrangement, you can be on-line within hours after signing up. And since you can sign up with a web host on-line, you can be on-line within hours after making the decision to have a web presence. Usually, within 48 hours or so, your domain name will ripple its way across the Internet's domain name servers Internet-wide, and if someone types in www.yourdomain-name.com, they will be taken to your web site.

What will they see when they get there? Well that's up to you. If you do nothing, they'll see a test page put there by your web host. And here's where I have to draw another line in this text. To get web pages on-line, you first have to be able to write them, which means knowing, at a bare minimum, hypertext markup language, more commonly known as HTML. You then have to be able to use file transfer protocol, or FTP, to get the pages onto your area of your host's web server. Going into HTML and FTP is beyond the scope of this book, but if you think you want to go it yourself or if you have a bit of experience already, I will make the following suggestions:

- Read a good HTML book such as *HTML for Dummies.*
- Check out htmlgoodies.com for lots of neat design tricks.
- Find WS-FTP or similar FTP software to get your pages on-line.

If you don't want to get involved in creating your own web design, there are plenty of companies looking for the chance to do it for you. Some outfits are very expensive, specializing in on-line retail, shopping carts, and credit card processing. Since a detective agency doesn't really need that level of service to get started (though you may eventually decide to expand and sell books, gadgets, and so forth, as outlined above), I would suggest hiring an independent web designer, preferably a young student, who won't charge you too much and will be more flexible in listening to your ideas.

I'm lucky. I have a son fitting the above description. You may also be lucky enough to have a family member or child prodigy neighbor willing to help you out at a fair price. If not, ask if you can put up an ad at your local high school or college. Many such institutions have bulletin boards for this purpose to help students earn spending money.

When giving a young student his foot in the door (saving yourself a few bucks is, of course, of secondary importance), you will need to pay close attention to how he works. He might know how to code the pages, but you want to make sure the look and feel of your web site appears mature and professional and not like, well, a student did it. Also, young students (and even seasoned professionals) sometimes cannot resist the desire to show off. Don't let whomever you hire give into this temptation by letting them add all sorts of blinking, revolving, and flashing graphics to your site. All such unnecessary bells and whistles will only annoy savvy web surfers, not to mention the fact that more complicated graphics will show up on fewer computers, leaving many visitors to your site with inexplicably empty spaces on their screen. This will only make them nervous and certainly not foster any confidence in your firm.

ENDNOTES

1. For those of you who don't know, a dial-up number is the actual phone number your computer dials to log onto a particular ISP. Because people don't want to pay long-distance charges or wait long for an Internet connection, large ISPs provide hundreds or even thousands of numbers local to the areas they wish to serve.

2. You refer to your web site by its domain name rather than the cryptic sequence of numbers the Internet actually assigns to it. Special Internet servers called "domain name servers" (DNSs) keep track of this information so you don't have to. For a more detailed explanation, see the "Using Traceroute" section in Chapter 7, "Squeezing Clues from E-Mail."

CHAPTER 3: Becoming a PI in the Computer Age

"Every man at the bottom of his heart believes that he is a born detective."
—John Buchan

Perhaps you are not yet licensed as a private detective but would like to become one. If you've stuck with me thus far, by now you're probably wondering how to go about it. The answer depends on which state you live in. For example, New York and California have fairly stringent requirements, including education and testing. Vermont requires fingerprinting, a background check, and good credit in addition to its minimum eligibility requirements. Colorado's licensing statutes were declared unconstitutional by its supreme court and were thrown out altogether. A few other states have never had licensing requirements, though local business licensing statutes may apply.

States that enact licensing laws usually do so to protect the public from inexperienced or fly-by-night agencies that might take their money but lack the ability to conduct an investigation properly. Legislators are concerned that an unregulated detective industry will create a breeding ground for unsound or illegal investigative practices (unauthorized wiretaps, invasions of privacy, etc). My personal belief is that a consumer should do his or her own homework before hiring an investigator or any contractor, for that matter. The more consumers that take this simple, responsible step, the less laws we will need to regulate our lives.

Though usually enacted to protect the public's interest, private detective licensing laws are following the same trend as other laws in this country. That is to say, they are getting stricter as individual freedoms continue to disappear at an alarming rate. My recommendation for the as-of-yet unlicensed? Get your license sooner rather

than later. Find your state's requirements and follow them to the letter of the law. If your state's licensing agent denies you a license, you sue the licensing board.

Why would they deny you if you followed the rules? Sometimes a licensing agent simply won't like the looks of you. Maybe he married the wrong woman. Maybe he's having a bad day. What's less often said about license denials is that there exists in many states a good-ol'-boy network, and they weed out newcomers simply by denying licensure. Since most people give up once the all-mighty bureaucrat says "no," the good-ol'-boy network is preserved. But if you have followed your state's licensing laws to the letter and have met all the requirements, you'll have a solid case to take to court. Since the board knows that no court will uphold their agent's unreasonable denial, they will save face by "granting you a hearing." You then show up at their hearing and they will give you your detective license—after explaining, of course, that you did not complete one of the lines on the application quite properly and this was the reason for the original "confusion."

So, what are the requirements to become a PI? Most states require some or all of the following:

- A clean criminal record
- Three to five years of related experience (e.g., law enforcement, working for another detective)
- Evidence that you are a person of good moral character; usually three or four signed statements or letters of reference
- A good credit report or three or four letters

of credit from people you've done business with

- Fingerprints
- Passport photos
- Educational requirement, often waived or reduced for those who've studied law or criminology
- Test requirement, usually based on the education requirements, if any

Let's look at my home state as a typical scenario. Massachusetts requires three years' related experience and three people to testify via written statement to your character. If you work for a detective for three years, you can then apply for and receive your license. We can thank the Licensed Private Detective's Association of Massachusetts (LPDAM) for pressuring the state to make some changes to its licensing statutes, including a more than 50 percent reduction in application and renewal fees. Massachusetts now verifies employees of all licensed private detectives, so a person can no longer become licensed simply because he knows the right person.

If you wish to become licensed, send out resumés to detective agencies in your area. Let them know what experience you have in the field (if any), that you're very interested in learning more about the trade, and that you're willing to work hard starting out on the ground floor in order to gain this experience. Hopefully, you will sooner or later impress someone and get your foot in the door. Once you are employed by an agency, you then begin earning the "related experience" time requirement many states have. Usually this is two to five years.

The dates of your related experience will become a matter of public record because each year the detective who hired you must send the state licensing board a form that lists all of his employees. This is done to prevent detectives from writing fraudulent letters of reference for their friends, which state that so-and-so has worked for me for X number of years and is therefore eligible to apply for his own license. In our Massachusetts example, you can use this public information three years later when

applying for your license, assuming you've met the other requirements as well. (See Appendix 3 for the full text of the Massachusetts Private Detective Licensing Law.)

What if you have immediate access to detective work through a good connection but aren't licensed to do the work? One solution is to form a corporation and hire a licensed private detective to chair your Board of Directors. This is a perfectly legal relationship, and if you are an employee of the corporation, you can apply for your license after three years (again, this is in Massachusetts; other states may differ).

I've seen corporations place ads for detectives for exactly this reason. Such ads often state that "active participation is not required" by the licensee. I would not recommend this approach for several reasons.

- No decent detective would allow his name to be used in this way.
- It violates the spirit of the law and encourages stricter legislation.
- You *want* the licensee's participation. He's the one who can keep your corporation on track and make sure it's operating within legal parameters.
- Admitting "active participation is not required" is admitting that the intended relationship is a sham, leaving the door open for a prosecutor to dismantle your corporation.

A better route is to bring in a good detective and pay him well to oversee the business. That way your company will develop a good reputation. New marketing venues should be brought before the Board of Directors so the chairman (the licensed detective) can offer his insight and the board can make an informed decision. Speaking from experience, this is a rewarding roll for a licensed private detective. If you approach candidates properly, you should not have trouble finding someone to fill the job.

Sometimes you can find a detective willing to take on the job by searching the Internet. Type your keywords (such as Massachusetts, Detective, Chairperson, Corporation, or the quoted phrase

"Massachusetts Private Detective Seeks Employment") into a search engine. You can also check Monster.com for resumés.

If none of the above options appeal to you, keep in mind that you could always set up shop in a state that has no licensing requirements. If your business's due diligence occasionally takes you into a state *with* licensing requirements, it's unlikely that that state would interfere. They would not want the liability involved—what if they keep you from finding a key witness and a murderer goes free and kills again? However, if you establish yourself in one state to avoid the licensing requirements of the state where you routinely conduct your business, you will probably be prosecuted under your state's licensing laws.

The book *Requirements to Become a P.I. in the 50 States and Elsewhere* by Joseph J. Culligan is a good quick reference guide to the various state licensing requirements. In addition, many states have their licensing requirements on-line, which you should be able to find by doing a keyword search.

There you have it: the good, the bad, and the ugly. If your hopes of becoming a private detective have dimmed at all after reading this brief chapter, they need not have. Just remember to take one step at a time. Cut no

corners, follow the laws, and you'll have your license before you know it. If you're worried that the Computer Age will push legislators to tighten restrictions after you begin your journey, then document everything. Write your state secretary's office explaining that you understand your state's private detective licensing practice and have therefore made a career decision to work at XYZ Detective Agency so that you may become licensed after the required number of years. Ask for a response to verify that you've understood the law correctly, and save the letter they send you.

If legislators later increase restrictions, you can argue that you are eligible for licensure under the old requirements on which you relied to make a life-changing career decision. Article I, Section 10, of the U.S. Constitution, which prohibits states from passing ex-post-facto laws, may apply—it is the guiding principle behind the so-called grandfather clauses attached to most statutes that potentially affect existing contracts, permits, uses, etc. In my opinion, any increase in restrictions cannot apply to a person who has already documented setting out on a certain career path. Lawyers will, of course, argue about this, but such arguing costs money, and the state would probably grandfather you in if you have decent documentation.

SECTION TWO

THE TOOLS AND TECHNOLOGY

CHAPTER 4: So, Where Are the Computers in the Computer Age?

"The computer is only a fast idiot; it has no imagination; it cannot originate action. It is, and will remain, only a tool to man."
—American Library Association

Is the Computer Age's effect on the private investigation industry limited to how the Internet has changed it or how the all-mighty personal computer (PC) has imposed itself upon us? Not by a long shot. That would be like saying the universe is limited to what our telescopes can see of it. While the Internet and PC are certainly two significant inventions, they do not define the Computer Age and therefore cannot be the sole players in how our industry will evolve through it.

The word "computer" has evolved as rapidly as the industry itself. In the beginning it referred to towering monoliths in sterile, air-conditioned rooms, looming in an endless rank of the unknowable, while clipboard-bearing men in white lab coats frittered about. It later came to mean a useful box sitting on one's desk at home or in the office. Once science found a way to include most of the computer's central processing on a single chip, the word "microcomputer" was invented . . . and that signified the true dawn of the Computer Age.

"Microcomputer" refers to the integrated circuit (IC, or computer "chip") responsible for the mathematical processing of information bits. The actual piece of silicon that does the work is about the size of a fingernail. Any operation of your desktop computer is handled at some level via a central microcomputer. Your PC is really just a hard-working sliver of silicon with a whole bunch of stuff attached to it.

Today microcomputers—now more frequently called "microcontrollers" [1]—can be found just about everywhere: your TV, radio, CD player, automobile, oven, microwave,

heating system, fridge, you name it. In fact, for every computer you see on a desk, there are probably 10 more nearby that you don't see.

Let's look at me. I'm sitting in my living room as I type this. I have on my lap, appropriately enough, a laptop computer. I'm not going to count the computer in my office or the one in the guest room. I'm not going to count the carcass of my now passé 20 MHz Wang that I've kept for testing DOS programs or the 33 MHz Packard Bell that I can't even give away. We all know there are personal computers everywhere, new and old. So where are the others?

Well, about four and a half feet in front of my big toe is a 23 inch Phillips/Magnavox television set. If I so choose, I can turn it on and program all the local analog signals bristling its antennae. I can program it to turn off in an hour. I can turn on the VCR above it and program it to record *Nova* tomorrow night or three weeks from now. I can program it to record *60 Minutes* on Sunday so I can watch it in 45 minutes by fast-forwarding through the intro, commercials, and "coming up" and "next time on *60 Minutes*" segments.

To the right of the entertainment center is a Monitor heater. It's off now, but in the winter I program it to turn on high at 5:00 A.M., lower itself to 70 degrees at 6:00 A.M., and lower itself again to 60 degrees at 10:00 A.M. when the sun keeps the room warm the rest of the day.

Around the room to the right is the base for my 900 MHz digital spread spectrum cordless phone with built-in digital answering machine. I can program it . . . I can program the cell phone

TABLE 4.1 Facets of the Private Detective Industry Affected by the Computer Age		
Facet	**Old Age**	**Computer Age**
Advertising	Yellow pages.	Web site with credit card processing.
Bookkeeping	Dome bookkeeping organizer or hire an accountant.	Peach Tree, MS Money, and Quicken make accounting easier so we detectives can concentrate on detecting.
Clientele	Local person knocking on your door.	E-mail prospect from halfway around the globe.
Communication	Radio transmissions the subject may be listening to.	Secure digital cellular and satellite phones.
Copies	Carbon paper, 24-hour copy store.	Scanner and laser printer.
Document transmittal	U.S. Mail, 2–4 days.	Fax, e-mail attachment, 1–2 minutes.
Evidence, Biological	Fingerprint.	DNA.
Evidence, Material	Tire track.	E-mail server routing stamp.
Fly on the wall	Phone tap with nearby, manned listening post.	Automatic PC Data Logger with e-mailed log file, viewable from anywhere, anytime.
Gigs	Runaway teen.	Cyberstalker.
Help	Local apprentice.	Web guru 3,000 miles away; confer via e-mail.
Interrogation	Perp claims coercion and goes free.	High-definition cameras and digital audio capture everything.
Jurors	Pot luck.	Computerized demographic juror selection allows attorneys to create their "dreamy jury."
Keys	Easy-to-pick locks or dials.	Coded keypad entry and card scanning systems.
Letter writing	IBM Selectric and correction tape.	Voice-type into word processor with auto-format and spell check.
Monitoring	Local monitors with camera switchers.	Monitor premises via web from halfway around the globe.
Networking & Connections	Local LE connections, if you were lucky enough to have them.	Own your own reseller gateway. PI chat rooms and newsgroups.
Overhead	Long-distance charges, postage.	E-mail saves on long distance and postage.
Photography	35mm camera w/ telephoto lens.	Digital camera with software zoom.
Questioning	Take a witness' word for it.	Computer-assisted polygraph. Graphology software assists in analyzing written statements. See Chapter 10, "Graphology."
Recordings	Phone coil pickup to tape recorder.	Directly from modem to hard drive.
Searches	Phone book or suit up and hoof it to the courthouse.	CD-ROM and on-line searches from your home, naked in bed, if you'd like.
Telephone	Wire-line and long distance carriers.	Cellular, satellite, Internet switchboard.
Undercover work	Store detective.	Pose as impressionable teen in chat room to catch pedophile.
Video	TV camera and two-way mirror.	Pinhole camera hidden in pager.
Witnesses	Eyewitnesses, close friends.	Chat room buddies and moderators.

Facet	Old Age	Computer Age
X marks the spot	Rudimentary list of compass directions and distances.	Handheld GPS takes you right to their hideout every time.
Yellow pages	Office full of city directories.	CD-ROM and on-line access to yellow and white pages, e-mail directories, and more.
Zoom lens	Expensive optical accessory.	Digital and software zooms allow blowups and crops of key photographs.

next to me . . . I can program the microwave in the kitchen to . . . I can program the coffeepot . . .

Program, program, program. Sounds like a computer word, doesn't it? Well, that's exactly what you're programming when you use these household appliances: a computer. A micro-computer, yes, but a computer nonetheless. They are changing the world. I don't even want to think about how many computers are in the Oldsmobile outside that has been running on only two cylinders lately. I suspect one of the on-board computers is causing the problem.

For the most part, though, computers do not cause problems for us humans. They help us. That's why we make them. And the little buggers are changing the private investigation industry in ways you may never have even noticed. Just for fun, I decided to come up with an A–Z list (Table 4.1) of how a computer (microchip or otherwise) has changed some facet of how PIs conduct their daily business. I wondered how long it would take. Okay, so maybe I got goofy on a few, but the table took me no more than an hour total.

So you see, the Computer Age does not just mean the PC and the Internet. Computers are entrenched in almost every aspect of our daily lives. The Internet could fizzle out tomorrow, the world could suddenly lose interest in PCs, and the Computer Age would still be in full swing. Why? Just as most people predict that the desktop PC and the Internet will soon be fully and truly embedded in our daily lives, microchips already are. In fact, they have been for decades. They affect every industry, including—as the following sections will show—ours.

RF TRANSMITTERS

You can readily see that a microchip is exceedingly powerful. And it's small. These two attributes combined do our industry many favors.

What if you wanted to build a very small room bug that transmits via radio? In the old days, you'd need transistors. Though transistors are tiny, putting enough of them together to build an RF (radio frequency) transmitter with audio pre-amp, modulation stage, and enough amplification to allow for a stabilized oscillation . . . well, the device begins to approach the size of a transistor radio—not easy to hide. Today, chip-sized operational amplifiers and phase-locked loop circuits allow operatives to build tiny yet highly stable transmitter circuits. The pros use these powerful Computer Age building blocks to custom-engineer stealthy audio and video transmitters tailored to any given situation.

Not handy with a soldering iron? Well then, how 'bout a factory assembled crystal-controlled video transmitter, 1" x 1" x 1/4", that will transmit any standard composite video source up to one-eighth of a mile for $140. Try ramseykits.com and check out catalog number C2001. While you're there, check out C2000 for a $100 version that'll fit under a quarter and broadcast up to 300 feet.

PEN REGISTERS/DTMF DECODERS

Depending on how long you've been in the business, you'll refer to a Touch-Tone™ recorder either as a pen register (old school) or a DTMF [2] decoder (modern term). If you're not in the business, then you may not even know what I'm talking about. A pen register/DTMF decoder is a device that an operative can attach to a phone line to record all digits dialed from any Touch-Tone phone using that line. For example, if you were to hook up a DTMF decoder to your phone line, it would capture and store every number you dial, including phone numbers, bank account numbers, and passwords.

Why would a detective need such a device? Let's say you have a warrant to place one of these devices on the phone line of a suspected terrorist. You want to know who's calling him and who's leaving messages on his voice mail. You can call the voice messaging center and punch in your subject's phone number, but—wouldn't you know?—the darned system insists on a pass code. If you have a DTMF decoder on your subject's line, then it's fairly easy to figure out which digits represent his pass code. Once you have this, you can retrieve his messages anytime. If he and his consorts think the system is safe from prying ears, you may be surprised to hear how candid and incriminating some of the messages can be.

With the information captured on your DTMF decoder, you can do reverse lookups of every phone number your subject dials to see who he's calling. Where is he calling? What area codes? What country codes? The DTMF decoder records all.

How has the Computer Age produced better DTMF decoders? Well, in the days when it was called a pen register, a good one might hold 100 digits tops, and if it lost power before you could retrieve it, you'd find a completely erased memory bank. Even though most phone numbers were a mere seven digits back then, the average pen register was good for about 10 to 15 phone calls, which meant you had to go back often and check it. And they were bulky. One such unit sold by Radio Shack was the size of a modern-day answering machine and needed to be plugged in!

Today's microcontrollers come fitted with thousands of bytes of memory space. It's not uncommon for a Computer Age DTMF decoder to have a storage capacity of between 510 and 2,048 digits. If the power goes out? So what—today's microchips have nonvolatile memory, which means the power can go out for a hundred years and the information is still preserved. The expanded memory capacity means you don't have to risk daily exposure at the target site retrieving your data. The decoder can easily store a week's worth of numbers, maybe even a month's worth if your subject doesn't use the phone much. Plus, today's DTMF decoders are much smaller. Recently I saw one with LCD readout that was the size of a pager.

Because today's DTMF decoders are products of the Computer Age, the information stored in some models can be downloaded to—you guessed it—a personal computer. The ability to download the gathered numbers to a PC in a readily usable file format represents not only an immense time savings but also a powerful tool. The Computer Age detective need not transcribe and catalog handwritten notes. Furthermore, he can employ his spreadsheet's data-sorting routines to glean patterns in the dialed numbers that may otherwise go unnoticed. Perhaps our detective is skilled enough to generate a quick-and-dirty pie chart showing how often certain numbers are dialed. What if such a chart showed the subject's breakdown of office calls as follows:

Supplier A:	30%
Supplier B:	20%
Buyer A:	20%
Buyer B:	20%
Wife:	2%
Wife's sister:	8%

What may have originally been considered a few innocent calls to Auntie Roxanne suddenly stand out once the detective can quickly and easily manipulate the data. Of course the subject may have been calling his sister-in-law to plan a surprise birthday party for his wife that month, so some actual old-school detective work will still be needed before you jump to conclusions.

If you have basic skills in electronics, you can build room bugs, DTMF decoders, and other goodies yourself. You can purchase excellent books like *Electronic Circuits and Secrets of an Old-Fashioned Spy*, *The Basement Bugger's Bible*, and similar titles from Paladin Press. *Poptronix* magazine is another useful resource, with an equally useful web site: www.poptronics.com. As a professional, it is your responsibility to first determine the legality of building and using such devices. In many cases, using these devices on a third party, even employees, will require a court-issued warrant. Consult your attorney before purchasing, building, or using a DTMF decoder or any surveillance device, for that matter.

PINHOLE CAMERAS

Years ago, security cameras were big and bulky and usually set up in the open. Sometimes this still isn't a bad strategy; a visible camera can be a powerful deterrent, as evidenced by their use in banks and convenience stores to prevent robberies. But folks in the PI industry began to come across situations where cameras were better off hidden. Because of the size of early cameras, "hiding" one usually meant placing it behind a two-way mirror or inside a decorative enclosure through which only the camera lens would be visible.

You may recall department and larger drug stores of the recent past that had long, narrow mirrors running along the top of one of their walls. It didn't take long for thieves to figure out that security personnel were peering at them from the other side. Good thieves simply kept their bodies turned away from the glass and did their deeds quickly.

To cover a wider area, department stores hung "decorations" from the ceiling. You've seen them before: huge, inexplicable, orange and black globes dangling from a 1 inch wire high above the floor. The decorative pattern always seemed to end in a black dot pointing in the direction of the jewelry department. Again, it didn't take long for crooks to learn the real function of these ugly contraptions.

The advent of microchip-based pinhole cameras has made things much more difficult for today's would-be filches. Today, a camera can literally be located anywhere and almost invisibly. Facing such security capabilities, an ill-intentioned person is rendered paranoid, and Computer Age detectives and security professionals have learned that paranoia is the best deterrent to shoplifting.

Wal-Mart stores have implemented one of the best paranoia-based security systems of all time. It's a simple recording that periodically interrupts the music over the PA system with a soft-voiced announcement stating, "Security: please scan departments seven and nine. Security: please scan departments seven and nine." Any petty thief about to place four of his favorite CDs into the pocket of his baggy overcoat will abandon the notion upon hearing this "security alert." Combined with a few actual pinhole cameras in high-risk areas, it is a great way for department stores to reduce shoplifting losses.

Not only has the Computer Age changed the size of our video cameras, it has also made possible the following:

- High resolution
- Color picture
- Wireless transmission

X10 2.4 GHz Wireless Video System. Shown here are the camera module, transmitter, receiver, and motion detector. Properly set up, when the detector senses motion it will trigger VCR recording of the target area.

- Automatic turn-on (time or motion tripped)
- Recording to inexpensive, widely available medium (VHS tape via household VCR)

Thanks to the Computer Age, even the casual home user can have a wireless security system in place that begins recording to the family VCR as soon as motion is detected in the target area. A basic, inexpensive system is available through X10.com. For other sources of pinhole cameras and related security and investigative tools, see Appendix 1.

CELL PHONES AND TRANSCEIVERS

The most famous cartoon detective, Dick Tracy, wore a watch that somehow allowed him to communicate with his comrades. Science fiction? It certainly *was.*

Today's cell phones are shrinking with every new model that hits the market. Nextel already has a system in place where you can use your cell phone as a walkie-talkie. It's only a matter of time before you'll be able to strap it to your wrist. Did Tracy have voice messaging? Alpha-numeric paging? Call waiting? In many ways, the fantasy of Dick Tracy has been surpassed by the reality of the Computer Age.

No longer do you need bulky radios, which transmit on easily overheard or intercepted frequencies, to communicate with your surveillance team. If you don't want to incur calling charges, you don't even need to use cell phones. Several companies now manufacture personal FM transceivers that can broadcast up to a mile on private sideband channels. These channels are smaller, quieter, have less static, and are much less likely to be overheard than standard

frequencies. If you're conducting an extra-vehicular surveillance, they are easy to carry around. They have a very short (3–4 inch) antenna and can be easily concealed. Radio Shack markets a line that works very well.

A WARNING ABOUT NANOTECHNOLOGY

The Computer Age is shrinking everything. Pretty soon you won't know whether it's a clump of mud on your carpet or a room bug. Think I'm kidding? Medical science already has a pill you can swallow that takes pictures and measurements of your insides. The pill broadcasts the vital data to a doctor waiting by a radio receiver. (Hmmm. A pill-sized video transmitter . . . now what would we detectives want with such a device?)

Pills like this and tiny robots that perform similar tasks fall under the Computer Age realm of nanotechnology. Remember my "Word About Privacy" at the beginning of this book? Some of you may have wondered why a detective would take such a strong stance. Well, with nanotechnology, it's only a matter of time before

Radio Shack Personal FM Transceivers. I purchased this pair for under $150. Quiet, efficient, easy to conceal, and you can wear it on your belt if you have to leave your vehicle. Each of its 14 channels has 38 "quiet" channels allowing you to choose from 532 private communication lines. Other features include channel lock, call button, headset hookup, ability to charge batteries without removing them from the unit, and a monitor button to override auto-squelch for weak signals.

one of our elected officials decides it's a good idea to plant a "smart chip" underneath the skin of all newborns. After all, it's small, unobtrusive, and can store information about the child, from his Social Security number to any genetic predisposition to criminal behavior. Great stuff for detectives to know, of course, but do you want a microchip implanted in *your* child's head?

If you think it can't happen, keep in mind that 100 percent of the first Continental Congress never for a second thought each U.S. citizen would someday be issued a nine-digit serial number at birth. Also keep in mind that people long believed Dick Tracy's radio watch to be pure fantasy.

ENDNOTES

1   Microcontroller, microcomputer, microchip, micro-processor—people use these terms interchangeably.

2   Dual Tone Multiplexed Frequency, referring to the fact that each tone is comprised of two subtones.

CHAPTER 5: The Internet

"My favorite thing about the Internet is that you get to go into the private world of real creeps without having to smell them."
—Penn Jillette

In 1957, the Soviet Union launched the world's first artificial satellite, Sputnik, to show the world their technological superiority. Shortly thereafter, President Dwight D. Eisenhower established the Advanced Research Projects Agency, known as ARPA. ARPA's mission was to research the scientific frontier in the hopes of putting the United States back on top of the technological heap.

ARPA was well funded. Space travel research was, of course, a priority. But the agency's overseers also wanted to research another emerging technology: computers. ARPA used some of its funding to help such universities as MIT, Berkeley, UCLA, and Stanford to develop mainframe computer systems. By the mid-1960s, a man named Bob Taylor, who oversaw ARPA's computer research division at the Pentagon, was able to communicate separately with each of the mainframes via telephone lines.

After a while, Mr. Taylor realized it was a hassle to have to switch between computer terminals whenever he needed to talk to a different computer. Not only did he need to use a different terminal, but each university had its own communications protocol, adding another layer of inefficiency.

Mr. Taylor asked his boss for a million dollars to fund his idea to link all the computers together and get them speaking the same language so they could all share information. At first the universities were dead set against sharing their valuable computer time with other universities, failing to see the benefit in being able to access data on other computers around the country. However, ARPA, with its hundreds

of thousands of dollars in annual funding, eventually won the argument.

ARPA drew up bid specifications, and BB&N in Cambridge, Massachusetts, won the bid to build the ARPANET. BB&N (now BBN Technologies) was founded by three men named Bolt, Beranek, and Newman. It was and still is a technology company. However, its environment is so intellectually charged that it is often referred to as "Cambridge's Third University." (For more information on these pioneers of the Computer Age, visit their web site at www.bbn.com.)

The early BB&N scientists came up with a system called "packet switching" to send data across telephone lines in short bursts rather than tying up the lines in dedicated connections. By October 1969, a computer at BB&N in Cambridge and another one at Stanford University in California were set up with routers (then called Interface Message Processors, or IMPs) and the first ARPANET message was sent. The message was "LO." Well, it was supposed to be "LOGIN," but the system crashed after the "O" was sent (a sign of things to come, perhaps). A few hours later the technicians got it all sorted out, and the ARPANET was officially born.

For the next two decades, the ARPANET remained an obscure network used by universities, governmental bodies, and computer geeks. It took the widespread availability of personal computers in the mid-1980s, the advent of e-mail, and the end of the Cold War to bring the ARPANET, now known as the Internet, to where it is today: an unstoppable force that is penetrating daily human life and virtually every industry on the face of the earth—including ours.

Like television, the Internet is here to stay. It's an integral and intimate part of people's lives, and if we detectives are to do well at our craft, we must understand how criminals use this new technology and where incriminating evidence may become lodged in it. If you don't learn how to ride this bear, the next computer geek who turns 18 and decides to get his detective license will put you out of business in short order. Though you may have resisted, you must now become a computer geek yourself—or at least learn a little nerdiness. What the hell: for effect, throw on a white-collared dress shirt and button it all the way to the tippy top till your eyes bulge ever so slightly.

SEARCH ENGINES

So far in this book I've made numerous references to the Internet's research and finding capabilities. You may have already plopped this book facedown next to your reading chair, ran to your computer, and logged on to the Internet to experience the wonder for yourself. After a half hour of clicking off pop-up ads and backing out of "page not found" error messages, perhaps you stormed back to your chair and booted this book against the wall.

If so, you have just learned the first lesson in Internet 101: If you don't know how to use it, the Internet can be frustrating. Even after you learn how to navigate the Net, you'll realize another of its frustrating aspects: it's *big!* If you're not careful, you could end up wasting valuable billing hours sifting through reams of information not quite pertinent to your needs.

In a book I did early in my career, I referenced the Internet as a good alternative education source and my editor red-penned in the margin: "information overload." He was right. Still is. But one could argue that a dictionary is also information overload. Let's face it, you'll never use all the information in even a pocket dictionary. However, few would argue that if you know how to look up a specific word, a dictionary can be a very powerful tool indeed. That's how I feel about the Internet.

So how do you "look up" things on the Internet? You use a search engine. A search engine is simply a web site that has the function of indexing other web sites. Instead of you having to locate and search through each of these sites for whatever information you require, a search engine does it for you by scouring its index and instantaneously providing you with a list of references and URLs.

Like knowing how to look up a word in a dictionary, you have to know how to use a search engine properly in order for it to be effective. When you visit a search engine site, you will find a search box into which you can type what you are looking for. If you'd like to look up a great gift idea for your dear, sweet mama, phrasing your search the right way is a very important step. For example, if you go to one of my favorite search engines, www.altavista.com, and type in "sweet mama," you're likely to find a lot of things you wouldn't dare show your mother, much less wrap up for a Mother's Day gift. But if you type in "Mother's Day gift ideas," you're likely to find exactly what you're looking for.

AltaVista is not the most popular search engine, but I like it because it is a global Internet data mine, in my opinion. If the info you want is anywhere on the Internet, AltaVista will dig it up. The problem is, it might also dig up 4,321 seemingly appropriate "hits" to your search terms, and the information you require could be embedded anywhere in 400 pages of results. So here are some quick search tips that will help you use AltaVisa and most any other search engine.

First off, when you use a search engine that is noted for returning a lot of results, such as AltaVista, you more often than not want to narrow your search. The first step to doing this is to choose your search terms carefully. For example, if you want information on the specie of turtle commonly known as the Red Eared Slider, you would not want to type only the word "turtle" into the AltaVista search engine. If you do, you will get way too many irrelevant results. You will do better to type in Red Eared Slider.

If you do this, however, you'll note that AltaVista will also return irrelevant results containing the terms Red, Eared, and Slider along with various combinations of these terms as they appear on web pages across the Internet. When you are looking for something this specific, therefore, it's generally best to put the search terms in quotes. Type into the search box "Red Eared Slider" and you'll get far fewer results, but most all of them will be relevant to your search.

But what if you wanted to find a specific turtle author you'd heard about whose first name escapes you? You remember her last name is McHenry. If you type this in, you will likely get too many irrelevant results to wade through, including every citation for someone named McHenry who's ever been in the news, done something notable, or created their own web site. [1]

So how do you solve your problem of finding the Ms. McHenry who writes good books about turtles? You could do what's known as a "Boolean search." There are several Boolean search devices, and they each allow you to narrow your search in different ways. One of the most common ways to narrow a search is to use the Boolean command "AND." On AltaVista, this command is invoked by typing it in all capital letters without any quotes around it. So to find the Ms. McHenry that writes about turtles, a good search expression would be:

McHenry AND turtle

Notice how I kept "turtle" singular. This will return all pages containing both the character strings "McHenry" and "turtle." Since AltaVista searches by character string rather than whole word, a web page containing only the words "McHenry" and "turtles" (notice the plural) will also show up in your results. This is because the character string "turtle" appears within the word "turtles," and AltaVista does not search for whole words unless you specifically tell it to.

What if it turns out that there just so happens to be a thousand marine biologists with the last name McHenry, they all have web sites that contain the word "turtle," and you still get too many results? Well, Boolean commands can be invoked in lengthy search expressions. In other words, you can have as many ANDs as you want. So, to narrow your search further, you could use the expression:

McHenry AND turtle AND author

Such a search would likely pull up any page about the author you were searching for.

Other Boolean search commands and their functions are:

- OR—The search results will contain any of the search terms. Both terms will not have to appear together on one site (which AND gives you) to generate a hit.
- AND NOT—The search results will exclude a certain term.
- NEAR—Finds two words (character strings) near each other on a web page.

Some very quick examples:

If you want to find out about seals or porpoises, you would simply type:

seals OR porpoises

If you want to find out about the band Morphine but not the drug morphine, you would type:

Morphine AND NOT drug

This will help keep your results limited to the band and not the drug.

If you'd like to find web pages that contain the words "private detective" near the word "licensure." You would type:

"private detective" NEAR licensure

Notice how you can still use the quotes with the Boolean command.

Note that Boolean queries can be as complex as you need them to be. Here is one example of a complex Boolean query that will help you define a very narrow search.

"First Church" AND NOT "of Christ"
AND NOT Nazarene AND NOT unitarian
AND (Oregon OR Wyoming)

Use parentheses to group Boolean commands together. For example, if we hadn't used them in the last example, the search engine would not know whether we were ORing Wyoming to Oregon or to the entire preceding phrase. You can see where a complex Boolean search can be useful if you're digging for a very specific subset of a topic that would normally return bushels of data.

Overly narrow searches are another problem. The problem is less common but potentially more insidious because you may unnecessarily restrict yourself to a mere fraction of the information available to you. For example, if you wanted to learn about President Nixon and typed in "Richard Millhouse Nixon," your search will indeed return relevant results. But if you typed "President Nixon" or "Richard Nixon," you'd have more results to choose from. I use this for example purposes only to show how you can overly limit yourself. It's likely that any of the above searches will return a great deal of data simply because Richard M. Nixon was a very famous man.

So far we've discussed general search engines, using AltaVista as an example. There are also specialized search engines that search the Internet for certain types or sources of information. Let's have a look at these and how they might be used in the context of an actual investigation.

Specialized Search Engines

While AltaVista searches the web site content of the entire Internet, there are certain things it is not geared to. For example, while it may return relevant information found in certain on-line discussion forums, it is not really geared to searching these forums. Nor are AltaVista and other general search engines geared to searching newsgroups. For those who don't know, newsgroups are special on-line forums where people with similar interests share information and ideas. A private detective can get a lot more information from newsgroups than just the information shared by their subscribers, as you'll soon see in this subsection's example case. Other specialized search engines are

mentioned elsewhere in this book, but here I'd like to talk about discussion forum and newsgroup search engines.

Google is a very popular general search engine, probably the most popular at the time of this writing. Google has a separate search page that contains a very powerful newsgroup search engine called Google Groups. You can go to www.google.com to get there or go directly to the page by going to groups.google.com.

So, now that you know what newsgroups are and how to search them, why would you even want to search them? Well, think of the ways old-school PIs used to catch so-called "skips," or people otherwise hiding from the law. A popular method of catching a good hider was and still is to trace him by his interests. Many a skip has been brought to justice because he couldn't live without his *Ellery Queen Mystery Magazine*. Obtaining the new subscriber list from Penny Publications and checking it lead by lead still is a great way to find your suspect. Well, searching newsgroups is a Computer Age method of doing the same thing.

Now let's put this in the context of an investigative search. From interviewing his former neighbor, you know your perp, who's skipped out on his alimony payments, can't live a day without partaking in his favorite hobby: backyard rocketry. You think you know all there is to searching the Internet, so you go to www.altavista.com (www.av.com for short) and type in:

"Perp's Name" AND rocketry

For some reason you get no hits. The Internet has failed you!

Well, not really. You're on the right track, but this is a situation where you're better off using a specialized newsgroup search engine.

Let's say your perp's name is Anthony and in rocketry competitions he registers as "Blastin' T." Wherever he's hiding, you know he's trying to find a rocketry club. Now let's try the search again.

Go to groups.google.com and query hobby rocket newsgroups for "Blastin' T." Within seconds a link to the following message pops up on your screen:

From: blastin_T (blastin_T@jillett.com)
Subject: Local rocketry groups
Newsgroups: rec.models.rockets
View: Complete Thread (208 articles) | Original Format
Date: 2003-09-21 04:26:01 PST

Hi All:

Does anybody know of any rocketry groups in the Rocky Mount, NC area?

All help appreciated,

Blastin' T

Obviously, this is a very good lead on your subject. At this point you could do some rocketry research to familiarize yourself with the topic and begin a dialog with Blastin' T to try to wheedle out of him exactly where in the Rocky Mount area he resides.

The foregoing was a fictitious account of how a detective might use one specific Internet tool to help solve a specific case. But you want to develop general Internet search skills that you can apply across a broad range of your caseload. For starters, you might be wondering, "Isn't there a list of tools that I can check out and learn to use on my own?" Well, yes and no. Let me explain.

I will soon share with you a number of Internet resources for private investigators, which I strongly encourage you to investigate and learn to use. The problem is that the Internet is constantly changing. Though most of the tools I discuss should still be in service when you read this book, you might find that some have become available to paid members only. You might find that others have changed their focus in the hopes of appealing to a broader market. You might indeed find that some have packed up their wares altogether, opting for the safer and more profitable venture of selling carbonated sugar water to hyperactive children. The point is, the Internet is still a volatile marketplace and probably will remain so for a long time to come.

To show how fast the net is changing, let's look again at my above example. To begin your search for a hobby rocket nut, some of you with Internet experience may have thought to go to dejanews.com, at one time the leading Internet clearinghouse for newsgroups. But try to go to dejanews.com or deja.com and you'll find that these excellent search engines are now groups.google.com. This is actually a happy development. Firstly, if you type in deja.com or dejanews.com, you are seamlessly redirected to the Google Groups main page, a neater and more user friendly site than the original deja.com main page. Also, Google does not require you to register or log in, and you can read and post to newsgroups right from the Google page. The search results pages are easier to read, and Google eliminates duplicate entries, saving you the hassle of clicking through to the same message twice (or three or four or more times, as is the case with other search engines). Of course, by the time you read this, some or all of these facts may have changed.

As we explore some of the more noteworthy Internet search tools below, study the examples to see how each tool might be used in your daily casework. That way, if the company sponsoring the tool should go out of business or change its direction, you will still understand the theory behind using that particular type of search method, thus enabling you to use your skills elsewhere on the Internet.

Information overload, as my old editor said? For sure. But if you can navigate that overload of information, you can find some pretty specific details about some pretty specific types of people. Imagine finding incriminating evidence about a marine biologist turned drug dealer because your search turned up a 20-year-old university paper he published in which he mentioned how a certain migration path for rite whales would make an ideal smuggling route for Columbian cocaine. The Internet makes it possible.

NUMBER PLEASE?

There are lots of reasons why a detective might have a subject's name but not his or her phone number. This used to happen to me all the time when I was doing heir finding investigations. The state's microfiche files would give me a name and last known address, but since in most cases the person had moved (which is probably why they lost their money), I had no phone number at which to reach them. (More on this in Chapter 15, "Heir Finding.")

Perhaps you're doing a missing persons gig and the subject's coworker told you, "I know she was occasionally involved with some dude from California—Arlo Dingleberry—but I don't think she's seen him in a while." Well, it would sure be nice to get hold of Mr. Dingleberry, but when you call directory assistance at 555-1212, the nice lady says she can't look up the name without a city. The fact that long-distance information can cost upwards of $1.95 per call—whether you locate the correct number or not—is also a downside to traditional number finding tactics. This can get very expensive for a detective who needs this sort of service on a daily, if not hourly, basis.

Fortunately, the Internet can once again come to the rescue. Let's begin with a basic, straightforward phone number search.

For the time being, anywho.com gets my top rating for phone number, address, and nearest neighbor searches. It is the birth child of AT&T and, at the time of this writing, claims more than 98 million listings. Anywho.com can even help you generate a map and directions right to your subject's door. It also offers another neat trick that I'll tell you about in the next section.

Anywho.com's phone number search page is less picky than the directory assistance lady. You need not enter a city, although a state is required. So in our case, we'd select California (CA) as the search area and enter the last name Dingleberry. You could enter the first name as well, but what if Mr. Dingleberry has listed his phone in his wife's name or simply listed it with his first initial, "A"?

Click on the search button and you're on your way. That's all there is to it. Either you'll find Mr. Dingleberry using this method or you won't. If you don't, go back and look for him in surrounding states (Oregon, Nevada, etc.) or in other states where you think he might be. If worse comes to worse, you can simply search one state at a time until you find him. Maybe you won't find him, but you'll find others with the same last name whom you can call and interview

to determine if they're related and know anything about his current location. You get the idea.

REVERSE SEARCHES

Remember the other neat trick from anywho.com I mentioned? That neat trick is called the "reverse lookup"—that is, you type in a phone number and get a name and address. To consider why this might be useful, let's look again at our example.

Instead of giving you Mr. Dingleberry's name, what if your subject's coworker said this: "I don't know where she took off to. She called here a week ago, though. I wasn't here, but the waitress who took the call said she sounded really confused. She left this number. I tried calling it, but it just rings and rings." The coworker gives you the phone number.

Obviously it would be real nice to know the address and owner of that phone number. Go to Anywho.com and use their reverse lookup engine. Once you have the address, you can use the neighbor-lookup function to generate lots of leads. Interview the neighbors. See what you can dig up about any newcomers or strangers who may have passed through the area. One of them might be your missing person.

OTHER INTERNET PEOPLE FINDERS

There are countless resources to help you find people on the Internet. Some cost money, some don't. I list a few in Table 5.1, but you can find more by conducting keyword searches in your favorite Internet search engine.

The book *Find It Online: The Complete Guide to Online Research* by Alan M. Schlein (Facts on Demand Press) is a great resource. The information in Table 5.1 and much more is included in Mr. Schlein's book.

The book also covers some very interesting tools to find specific groups of people. For example, www.alumni.net, formerly www.infophil.com/World/Alumni, is a resource to help locate individuals associated with international universities and alumni associations. This could be helpful if your subject has led a

TABLE 5.1	
People Finders on the Internet	
People Finder	**Comment**
http://people.yahoo.com	Pretty good white pages utility. Better for looking up e-mail addresses.
www.infospace.com	Features similar to Anywho.com. Has a good government number lookup database, phone books from other countries, and more detailed directions in its mapping feature.
www.switchboard.com	Good resource for phone directories and e-mail addresses.
www.whowhere.com	E-mail address finder that works in English, French, and Spanish.
www.theultimates.com	Searches simultaneously the above-listed resources in much the same way Dogpile.com searches several search engines at once.
www.worldpages.com/global	Phone book access to more than sixty countries.

scholarly life or is a big booster of his alma mater, especially if he is not necessarily hiding and is the type of person to join or form associations.

UNLISTED NUMBERS

Years ago, getting an unlisted phone number from a telephone company operator was difficult at best. Today, it's damn near impossible to get an operator to give you an unlisted number over the phone. It can be done, but the overhead a detective needs to invest in order to get the number makes it financially unfeasible to routinely con operators out of unlisted numbers. They eventually catch on to you anyway, no matter how many different voices and ruses you've managed to perfect over the years.

The Internet, at least for a while, will give you a chance to rest your funny voices and incredible tricks. People finder databases compile their information not only from telephone company records but from diverse sources. Remember when you sent in the registration card to that new digital camera you bought last year? If you put your unlisted phone number on that card, it could easily end up in an Internet people finder database.

Your chances of getting an unlisted phone number off the Internet increase significantly if you use a fee-based company specifically geared toward the investigative industry. The outfit www.altseek.com, formerly www.discreetdata

systems.com, seems to be worth a try. As always with the ever-changing Internet, it might be worthwhile to run a "how to get unlisted phone numbers" search on altavista.com or google.com to see what new companies are out there.

Finally—and this is actually one of my favorite ways of getting unlisted numbers—check old phonebooks and old CD-ROM databases. Just because someone has an unlisted number today doesn't mean that phone number has always been unlisted. Often, people switch to an unlisted number without ever actually changing the number! Some do it in the heat of the moment with an "I'll show them!" attitude after receiving their eleventh telemarketing interruption during dinner. Others think that their number magically disappears from existence once it becomes unlisted. It doesn't.

ON-LINE CORPORATE FILINGS

An enterprising con man may have tried his hand at legitimate enterprises before deciding that working for a living was not exactly his bag. Such a person may have left a paper trail for you to follow, and thanks to the Computer Age, the beginning of that paper trail may be easier to find than you think.

Let's say Bilk Ewe Construction Company took a $25,000 deposit from an elderly lady ostensibly in preparation to construct a dormer addition on her Cape Cod-style home to

The Commonwealth of Massachusetts William Francis Galvin - Public Browse and Search   Page 1 of 1

---

[x]

The Commonwealth of Massachusetts
William Francis Galvin

Secretary of the Commonwealth
One Ashburton Place, Boston, Massachusetts 02108-
1512
Telephone: (617) 727-9640

Public Browse and Search - Entry Screen

Help with this form

○ **Search by Entity Name** *(Name of: Company, LP, LLP, LLC, etc.)*

   Name: [ ]   **Type of Search** | Begins With ▾ |

- -

○ **Search by Identification Number** *(FEIN, Trust ID, etc.):* [ ] *(must be 9 digits)*

- -

○ **Search by Filing Number:** [ ]

- -

◉ **Search by an Individual** *(Officer, Director, etc.)*   **Type of Search** | Begins With ▾ |

   First Name: | Steven | **Middle Name:** | p | **Last Name:** | jobs |

- -

Display | 25 ▾ | **names per page**

[Search]   [Clear]

© 2001 - 2002 Commonwealth of Massachusetts
All Rights Reserved

Help

Home Business Entities U.C.C. Trademarks Contact Us Help

Screenshot 5.1. You can research public information for corporations, trusts, and other business entities by visiting your state secretary's home page. In this case, we are researching Massachusetts corporations at www.corp.sec.state.ma.us. You can search by entity name, EIN, or individual officer or director by scrolling down.

The Commonwealth of Massachusetts William Francis Galvin - Public Browse and Search - Micros...

File   Edit   View   Favorites   Tools   Help

Address   http://corp.sec.state.ma.us/corp/corpsearch/   Go

2 Records Matched Your Begins With Search for Last Name: Jobs, First Name: Steven (Page 1 of 1)

Individual's Name	Position Held	Individual's Address	EntityName	Identification Number (FEIN, Trust ID, etc.)	Old Identificati on Number (O FEIN, Old Trust ID, et
JOBS, STEVEN P.	PRESIDENT	900 CHESAPEAKE DR.,REDWOOD CITY, CA 94063 USA 900 CHESAPEAKE DR.,REDWOOD CITY, CA 94063 USA	NEXT SOFTWARE, INC.	770085823	000344392
JOBS, STEVEN P.	PRESIDENT	1001 W. CUTTING BLVD., RICHMOND, CA 94804 USA 1001 W. CUTTING BLVD., RICHMOND, CA 94804 USA	PIXAR	000638636	00000000C

New Search

Screenshot 5.2. Using the online form shown in Screenshot 5.1, I scrolled down and entered "Steven P. Jobs" to see what one of my all-time heroes has been up to these days.

accommodate her granddaughter and new grandson-in-law. Two weeks went by and construction had not begun. Worried, your client called Joe Bilk, owner of Bilk Ewe Construction Company, and found that the phone number had been disconnected.

After you were hired to find Mr. Bilk, you asked your client if she'd paid by check. She had. In fact she'd just gotten the check back in her bank statement yesterday. You ask to see it. Turns out that your client wrote the check out directly to Mr. Bilk. This was done at Mr. Bilk's request, probably because he knew his bank would not cash a check made out to a "Bilk Ewe Construction Company" unless he had a business account in that name. The second problem for our con man was that his name

wasn't even Joe Bilk. The check indeed had a signature on the back purporting to be that of a Mr. Joe Bilk, but the check had been signed over to a Dewey Fleecem, our con man's real name.

On a hunch, you go to your state's on-line corporation division and search for "Fleecem." At this point I must interject that not all states have their corporate filings on-line, though in the future I expect most, if not all, will. In Massachusetts you can search by corporate name, employer identification number (EIN), officer name, director name, and filing number. Furthermore, the corporate and officer name searches do not have to be spelled exactly, which could come in handy if Mr. Fleecem had poor handwriting. If that's the case, you can do what's called a "Begins With" search (see Screenshot 5.1). If the signature on the check had been illegible to the point where you could only make out Fleec, this feature would come in very handy indeed.

Referring to Screenshot 5.1, you'd scroll down and click the bottommost radio button next to "Search by an Individual" (Officer, Director, etc.). You would then type in the name of the person you are looking for; in this case Dewey Fleecem. Press the "Search" button and, if you're lucky, you will receive an on-screen listing similar to that shown in Screenshot 5.2.

In my example, I sincerely doubted that a search for a "Fleecem," much less a "Dewey Fleecem," would turn up anything. Instead, I typed in the more likely name of Steven P. Jobs, visionary and cofounder of Apple Computer and a man who is forever on my all-time heroes list. Click on any of the companies listed for more information about it. As you can see by the results in Screenshot 5.3, Mr. Jobs has registered his California corporations as foreign corporations in Massachusetts, as is required if he expects to do business within its borders.

Had this been Mr. Fleecem's report, you can already see how you would've accessed a wealth of information. You have his state, city, address, zip code, EIN, and the names and addresses of other officers and directors of the corporation. It's important to note that you'd have all this information even if the corporation had been dissolved years ago. You can click through to order annual reports and other corporate filings, which will contain even more information. Also, a foreign corporation must designate a "registered agent," which is a person or domestic entity upon whom legal process can be served in the event somebody wants to sue the company. You can see where a simple corporate filing check can generate dozens of leads for you to follow up on.

DEEDS REGISTRIES

Let's say you're working a deadbeat-parent case. Your client is a woman whose ex-husband owes her more than $50,000 in back child support. The government's social services bureau is working with the woman, but we all know what that means. It means she has to scratch and claw her way through every conversation with the bored bureaucrats, most of whom see her as just another case in their overloaded files. Good news for you is that social services has found the man via its database sharing with the Social Security Administration. They've attached his pay for the maximums allowable under the law to cover support, plus pay toward arrears.

Typical case so far, right? So what's your client's beef?

Well the government case reviewer determined the man should pay $115 a month toward arrears. This means he'll be "caught up" in 36 years, by which time his unsupported child could be a grandparent!

You're probably still saying, "Okay, Bud, still a pretty typical case. Why did my firm get a call from this woman?" Well, the woman, fortunately for you, is very intelligent and knows that her ex-husband has assets he is hiding. If she can prove he truly owns the assets, she will have a much better chance at convincing an attorney to circumvent social services and sue him directly for the back child support. Unfortunately for you, the ex-husband is also reasonably intelligent. Perhaps he's an accountant or an attorney himself and knows how to hide assets.

Here's the thing about people who hide assets, however. They hide the asset because they want to keep it for themselves. An obvious statement, but let's look closely at the second half of it: *they want to keep it for themselves.* Very few hiders will put the asset into another's hands without maintaining *some* hold on it. That is to say, this guy most likely did not simply hand over the asset to his new girlfriend. Even if he did a judge could undo such a move, but for this case, let's assume he's the typical person who wants to keep control of his asset. This means that somehow, someway, he has recorded his ownership interest.

But the hider has a problem. He has to maintain ownership but not allow his ex-wife to find it. You've been through the routine. You've probably cracked a few corporate shell game cases in your time, and you believe the lady. She's provided you with evidence or at least a convincing story that the ex-husband owns, let's

The Commonwealth of Massachusetts
William Francis Galvin

Secretary of the Commonwealth
One Ashburton Place, Boston, Massachusetts 02108-
1512
Telephone: (617) 727-9640

PIXAR Summary Screen

Help with this form

Request a Certificate

The exact name of the Foreign Corporation: PIXAR

Entity Type: Foreign Corporation

Identification Number (FEIN, Trust ID, etc.): 000638636

Old Federal Employer Identification Number (Old FEIN): 000000000

Date of Registration in Massachusetts: 12/07/1998

The is organized under the laws of: State: CA   Country: USA   on: 03/22/1991

Current Fiscal Month / Day: 12 / 31   **Previous Fiscal Month / Day:** 00 / 00

The location of its principal office:
No. and Street: 1001 W. CUTTING BLVD.
City or Town: RICHMOND   State: CA   Zip: 94804   Country: USA

The location of its Massachusetts, if any:
No. and Street:
City or Town: State: Zip: Country:

The name and address of the Resident Agent:
Name: CHRISTOPHER PERRY
No. and Street: 61 CRESCENT ST. #6,
City or Town: NORTHAMPTON   State: MA   Zip: 01060   Country: USA

The officers and all of the directors of the corporation:

Title	Individual Name First, Middle, Last, Suffix	Address (no PO Box) Address, City or Town, State, Zip Code	Expiration of Term
PRESIDENT	STEVEN P. JOBS	1001 W. CUTTING BLVD., RICHMOND, CA 94804 USA, 1001 W. CUTTING BLVD., RICHMOND, CA 94804 USA	
TREASURER	UNKNOWN	N, ONE, N, ONE,	

business entity stock is publicly traded:

The total number of shares and par value, if any, of each class of stock which the business entity is authorized to issue:

Class of Stock	Par Value Per Share Enter 0 if no Par	Total Authorized by Articles of Organization or Amendments Num of Shares Total Par Value	Total Issued and Outstanding Num of Shares
No Stock Information available online. Prior to August 27, 2001, records can be obtained on microfilm.			

Consent	Manufacturer	Confidential Data	Does Not Require Annual Report
Partnership	X Resident Agent	X For Profit	Merger Allowed

Select a type of filing from below to view this business entity filings:
ALL FILINGS
Amended Foreign Corporations Certificate
Annual Report
Annual Report - Professional
Articles of Consoldation - Foreign and Unregistered Foreign

View Filings   **New Search**

Help

Screenshot 5.3. Click on any of the companies listed in Screenshot 5.2 to get more information about it.

say, half a condo on Atlantic Avenue in Boston with more than enough equity to pay his arrears, your client's lawyer, and you.

You take the case. You figure it's a straight-ahead financial shell game. Once you put the pieces together, your client's attorney will be able to present the sham arrangement to a judge, who will most likely find for the plaintiff if you do your job properly.

What does this mean? It means you have to find the beginning of the paper trail. Usually you do this by starting at the end of the paper trail. In the old days it meant a lot of walking—first to the secretary of state's office to look up business entity filings and articles of incorporation, then to the local registry of deeds to do research there. If you came up cold, you'd have to drive to the next county's registry of deeds to see if your subject had migrated. There you might come up cold again. It was a bitch, to put it bluntly.

By the early '90s, many of the deeds and probate registries were at least computerized, which saved some walking and driving time. It was possible, for instance, to check both the North and South District Deeds Registries for Middlesex County in Massachusetts from the same terminal inside either registry. Soon thereafter, larger registries offered electronic BBS (bulletin board system) access to filings. [2] These services were usually available to Realtors, attorneys, and private investigators, and the registries charged hefty monthly fees for the privilege of accessing the public data in this way.

As the World Wide Web slowly supplanted private BBSs as the world's preferred method of interconnecting its computers, governmental bodies could no longer turn a blind eye to the inevitable. People around the world who went "on the web" tacitly expected to have access to information at no cost. Elected officials, such as the Register of Deeds, were therefore pressured to please their electorate and put their records on-line for access by taxpayers at no cost. As a result, pavement pounding has been greatly reduced for private detectives.

So in our example, you go to the web site for the Suffolk County Registry of Deeds and look up the condo where your client's ex-husband

now lives. The unit appears to be owned (judging by the most recent deed that pops up) by a common-law trust called "I'm Keeping My Daughter's College Money Realty Trust."

You pull up onto your computer screen the image of the deed and look for the words "under Declaration of Trust," sometimes abbreviated u/d/t. The language of the deed will go on to say when the trust was dated and, more importantly, where it was recorded, e.g., "recorded in the Middlesex (North District) Registry of Deeds in Book 444,222, Page 25,678."

Here's where the Computer Age saves you time. Instead of having to drive to Middlesex County, you simply click your mouse to it and you're there in seconds. Pull the document in Book 444,222, page 25,678. Pull the image file. Yep—it's a Declaration of Trust eight pages long.

You hope to see the girlfriend named as trustee but, alas, the man is too smart for that. Instead the language reads:

"Know all Men by these Presents, that It, Keeping Daughter's Money Limited, a Corporation duly organized under the laws of the Commonwealth, does hereby declare that It is Trustee hereunder . . ." blah blah blah.

You flip to the back page to find an officer's signature. Not the ex-husband's, not the girlfriend's, but at least you got something. Turns out Joe Schmoe, clerk, has authorized the instrument.

The Computer Age saves your tire treads once again. You click over to the secretary of state's home page and click on the Business Entity link. For the hell of it you search under the trust name first to see if it ever bothered to file the required annual report. No filings show up. This is good evidence for your client's attorney—it shows that the trust is not doing business properly and is probably a sham.

Next you search for the corporation. You find the corporation was organized a month before it became trustee of the trust. Who organized it? Well, the articles of incorporation will provide a clue. You learn—without ever leaving your computer keyboard, mind you—that your client's ex-husband is the president of this corporation and that the corporation originally issued 200 shares of stock. The last annual report would have told you who owned that stock, but you've already determined that no such report exists.

At this point you already have a pretty good case for your client's attorney. The fact that her ex-husband is the president of a corporation that has issued stock is strong circumstantial evidence. The fact that the corporation doesn't bother to file its annual report—as is required under the law—shows that its officer the ex-hubby is flouting the law and not living up to his fiduciary duties as a director of the corporation. Since the Board of Directors is now the body responsible for administration of the aforementioned trust, it should have had a meeting appointing an agent to act on its behalf to oversee the corporation's responsibility as trustee. Under the law, all of this information should be in the minutes books of the corporation. You can almost bet that no such books exist. Your client's attorney could file the suit and subpoena the corporate minutes books. You will then know who the corporation's appointed agent is. If no minutes were ever taken (likely), that's more evidence that the corporation is a sham, and the ex-husband/president of the corporation will be held financially accountable.

So you can see, by knowing that more and more deeds registries are going on-line, and by combining this knowledge with other pointers in this book, you begin to get a very real idea of how a Computer Age detective will always be one step (in truth, several hundred steps) ahead of his old-school counterpart. You can expect to see more probate records and vital statistics registries going on-line in the near future. Keep in mind that any governmental body that holds public records and is overseen by an elected official is under pressure to make information freely available on-line. If one such set of records is not yet on-line, keep checking back regularly. Call the office in charge on occasion and let them know you expect a web presence if they expect you to vote to re-elect their candidate. Remind them that we are in the Computer Age.

BANKRUPTCY RECORDS

Throughout the late 1980s into the new century, bankruptcy filing has become almost fashionable. So many cases have been filed, it's always worth checking to see if your perp is in the system. Thanks to an automated telephone information service known as the Voice Case Information System (VCIS), you can do a quick search using your touch-tone phone. The search costs nothing, and many districts have an 800 number, so you won't even incur long-distance charges.

But there are dozens of court districts throughout the United States. How do you access the VCIS for the one you need? One of the most user-friendly Internet tools at your disposal—a standard search engine. Simply go to google.com, altavista.com, or whichever engine you prefer, search for "VCIS" and the district where you know or believe the filing may have been made. A good search engine will return the URL for the proper court district's web site, which will contain detailed instructions on where to call and how to proceed. As an example, VCIS information for bankruptcy court for the Western District of Wisconsin can be found at www.wiw.uscourts.gov/bankruptcy/vcis.htm.

Depending on which division you call, the VCIS will give you all or some of the following:

- Case number
- Debtor's full name
- Social Security number
- Filing (i.e., chapter 7, 11, or 13)
- Filing date
- Reported assets (usually none are)
- Attorney's name and phone number
- Presiding judge
- Status of case
- Discharge date
- Close date

While all of this is useful, a person's Social Security number is the key piece of information you are after. The Social Security number itself contains telltale information (see below), and with it you can more easily conduct other searches, such as bank account searches and asset checks. Bankruptcy jurisdictions differ, and some will withhold a person's Social Security number,

TABLE 5.2
Social Security Number Area of Issue

The first three numbers of the SSN show where it was issued. Use this table as a quick reference to determine an SSN's area of issue. For example, any SSN beginning with 010 through 034 was issued in Massachusetts.

001-003	New Hampshire	362-386	Michigan	650-653	
004-007	Maine	387-399	Wisconsin	525, 585	New Mexico
008-009	Vermont	400-407	Kentucky	648-649	
010-034	Massachusetts	408-415	Tennessee	526-527	Arizona
035-039	Rhode Island	756-763 *		600-601	
040-049	Connecticut	416-424	Alabama	764-765	
050-134	New York	425-428	Mississippi	528-529	Utah
135-158	New Jersey	587-588 *		646-647	
159-211	Pennsylvania	752-755 *		530	Nevada
212-220	Maryland	429-432	Arkansas	680	
221-222	Deleware	676-679		531-539	Washington
223-231	Virginia	433-439	Louisiana	540-544	Oregon
691-699 *		659-665		545-573	California
232-236	West Virginia	440-448	Oklahoma	602-626	
232	North Carolina	449-467	Texas	574	Alaska
237-246		627-645		575-576	Hawaii
681-690		468-477	Minnesota	750-751 *	
247-251	South Carolina	478-485	Iowa	577-579	Dstrict of Columbia
654-658		486-500	Missouri	580	Virgin Islands
252-260	Georgia	501-502	North Dakota	580-584	Puerto Rico
667-675		503-504	South Dakota	596-599	
261-267	Florida	505-508	Nebraska	586	Guam
589-595		509-515	Kansas	586	American Somoa
766-772		516-517	Montana	586	Philippine Islands
268-302	Ohio	518-519	Idaho	700-728	Railroad Board **
303-317	Indiana	520	Wyoming	729-733 *	Enumeration at entry
318-361	Illinois	521-524	Colorado		

NOTE: The same area, when shown more than once, means that certain numbers have been transferred from one state to another, or that an area has been divided for use among certain geographic locations. Any number beginning with 000 will NEVER be a valid SSN.

* New areas allocated, but not yet issued.

** 700-728 Issuance of these numbers for railroad employees was discontinued July 1, 1963.

though most will provide it. Again, the web site will tell you if the number is forthcoming.

I've provided some useful charts that can help you derive a good deal of information about your subject while incurring little or no expense. If, for example, you're investigating a subject who has filed for bankruptcy protection and you were able to derive his Social Security number by searching the VCIS, you can use Tables 5.2 and 5.3 (and Appendix 2) to figure out where and when the number was issued. Knowing where a number was issued may lend clues as to where a given subject grew up, generating more leads for you to check out. Even if the information you gain is not directly helpful in a particular case, a paying client is always impressed to see it included in your report.

ON-LINE MAPS

In the pre-Computer Age days, figuring out where to go was often easier than getting there. I suppose this was especially true for me, cutting my PI teeth in the Boston suburbs. I had to buy a new road atlas every year because inevitably, through repeated use, a dirt-smeared, dog-eared copy was guaranteed to be missing the very page its index directed me to at a crucial moment. I was reduced to rolling down the window and asking for directions at every one-way street. So much for remaining clandestine.

Good riddance to all that.

The Computer Age has given us on-line maps, MapQuest (www.mapquest.com) being a prime resource of yours truly. Ruse and wheedle my subject for just the tidbit of info I need, punch a few keys on my PC keyboard, and my printer spews out detailed directions, complete with all road names and turns between my location and my subject's. It even computes the distance and estimates my travel time. MapQuest is especially helpful on long-range gigs, where you will no longer need to rely on a folder full of old, torn, fold-out maps collected from every gas station across the country! If I'm feeling a bit giddy and feel like taking a peek at my subject's tenement rooftop, heck, I can even get an aerial photo of it. MapQuest has hooked up with GlobeXplorer. com to provide this service. You can, of course, order zoomed-in higher resolution images if you need them.

You still need the old-school tricks, though, to get the key info first. The Computer Age isn't going to do everything for you, at least not in the near future. So, let's pick a ruse, do some wheedling, and see where we end up. Here's a trick from the old school—actually a good one for doing automobile repos.

I'm drawing from my own experience and using a debtor who is a part-time Realtor as an example, but you can adapt this technique to other people and situations. If you've done this kind of work before, then you know that different ruses work best at certain times of the year. I call this one my "July ruse" because it works great during vacation season.

The facts of the case are these:

• Subject has missed his last four auto loan payments.
• Subject sells real estate part time.
• Subject knows the dealership is trying to repossess his car.
• Subject rides with a friend to work.
• Subject leaves his car hidden or at home, knowing that in his state, the law prevents a repo agent from coming onto his property to get the car.

Before reading the below conversation, realize that this ruse operates on the premise that most people, especially those in the service and sales professions, are not only naturally chatty but are usually excited about an upcoming vacation. With little prompting, they will spill the most outrageous level of detail about their plans, even to a complete stranger. It's your job to direct the conversation so they open up. Be careful, though, to keep from being too forward and possibly arousing suspicion. Subtle, innocent prompting is the key here.

You begin by finding one of your subject's real estate listings and calling his office. Ask to speak with the "listing broker" to assure the office administrator does not assign you to a subagent. Once you have the subject on the line,

TABLE 5.3
Social Security Number Highest Group Issued for Given Area (as of 10/31/02)

The Social Security Administration issues SSNs in groups. For example, the first group of MA SSNs issued was 010-01-xxxx. The SSA issues the groups in a certain order. First odd groups 01 through 09 are issued. Then even groups from 10 through 98. After they issue the last number from group 98, even groups from 02 though 08 are issued, followed by odd groups from 11 through 99. Because the SSA issues SSNs in a predictable pattern, you can often discover a fraudulent SSN if the middle digits indicate a group that has yet to be issued. Use this chart to determine the highest group issued for a given area.

001	98	002	96	003	96	004	04	005	04	006	02
007	02	008	86	009	86*	010	86	011	86	012	86
013	86	014	86	015	86	016	86	017	86	018	86
019	86	020	86*	021	84	022	84	023	84	024	84
025	84	026	84	027	84	028	84	029	84	030	84
031	84	032	84	033	84	034	84	035	68	036	68
037	68	038	68	039	68	040	04	041	04	042	04
043	04	044	04	045	04	046	04	047	04	048	04
049	02	050	92	051	92	052	92	053	92	054	92
055	92	056	92	057	92	058	92	059	92	060	92
061	92	062	92	063	92	064	92	065	92	066	92
067	92	068	92	069	92	070	92	071	92	072	92
073	92	074	92	075	92	076	92	077	92	078	92
079	92	080	92	081	92*	082	92*	083	92*	084	92*
085	90	086	90	087	90	088	90	089	90	090	90
091	90	092	90	093	90	094	90	095	90	096	90
097	90	098	90	099	90	100	90	101	90	102	90
103	90	104	90	105	90	106	90	107	90	108	90
109	90	110	90	111	90	112	90	113	90	114	90
115	90	116	90	117	90	118	90	119	90	120	90
121	90	122	90	123	90	124	90	125	90	126	90
127	90	128	90	129	90	130	90	131	90	132	90
133	90	134	90	135	11	136	11	137	11	138	11
139	11	140	11	141	11	142	11	143	11	144	11
145	11	146	11	147	11	148	11	149	11	150	11
151	11	152	11*	153	11*	154	08	155	08	156	08
157	08	158	08	159	80	160	80	161	80	162	80
163	80	164	80	165	80	166	80	167	80	168	80
169	80	170	80	171	80	172	80	173	80	174	80
175	80	176	80	177	80	178	80	179	80	180	80
181	80	182	80	183	80	184	80	185	80	186	80
187	80	188	80	189	80	190	80	191	80	192	80

193	80	194	80	195	80	196	80	197	80*	198	80*
199	78	200	78	201	78	202	78	203	78	204	78
205	78	206	78	207	78	208	78	209	78	210	78
211	78	212	65	213	65	214	65	215	65*	216	63
217	63	218	63	219	63	220	63	221	96	222	94
223	95	224	95	225	95*	226	93	227	93	228	93
229	93	230	93	231	93	232	49	233	49	234	49
235	49	236	47	237	99	238	99	239	99	240	99
241	99	242	99	243	99	244	99	245	99	246	99*
247	99	248	99	249	99	250	99	251	99	252	99
253	99	254	99	255	99	256	99	257	99	258	99
259	99	260	99	261	99	262	99	263	99	264	99
265	99	266	99	267	99	268	08	269	08	270	08*
271	08*	272	06	273	06	274	06	275	06	276	06
277	06	278	06	279	06	280	06	281	06	282	06
283	06	284	06	285	06	286	06	287	06	288	06
289	06	290	06	291	06	292	06	293	06	294	06
295	06	296	06	297	06	298	06	299	06	300	06
301	06	302	06	303	25	304	25	305	25	306	25
307	25	308	25	309	25	310	25	311	25	312	25
313	25	314	25	315	25*	316	23	317	23	318	02
319	02	320	02	321	02	322	02	323	02	324	02
325	02	326	02*	327	02*	328	98	329	98	330	98
331	98	332	98	333	98	334	98	335	98	336	98
337	98	338	98	339	98	340	98	341	98	342	98
343	98	344	98	345	98	346	98	347	98	348	98
349	98	350	98	351	98	352	98	353	98	354	98
355	98	356	98	357	98	358	98	359	98	360	98
361	98	362	29	363	29*	364	29*	365	27	366	27
367	27	368	27	369	27	370	27	371	27	372	27
373	27	374	27	375	27	376	27	377	27	378	27
379	27	380	27	381	27	382	27	383	27	384	27

385	27	386	27	387	23	388	23	389	23	390	23
391	23	392	21	393	23*	394	21	395	21	396	21
397	21	398	21	399	21	400	59	401	59	402	59
403	59	404	59	405	59	406	57	407	57	408	93
409	93	410	93	411	93	412	93	413	93	414	93
415	93*	416	55	417	55	418	55	419	53	420	53
421	53	422	53	423	53	424	53	425	93	426	91
427	91	428	91	429	99	430	99	431	99	432	99
433	99	434	99	435	99	436	99	437	99	438	99
439	99	440	17	441	17	442	17	443	17	444	17*
445	15	446	15	447	15	448	15	449	99	450	99
451	99	452	99	453	99	454	99	455	99	456	99
457	99	458	99	459	99	460	99	461	99	462	99
463	99	464	99	465	99	466	99	467	99	468	41
469	41	470	41	471	41	472	41	473	41	474	41
475	41	476	41*	477	39	478	33	479	33*	480	31
481	31	482	31	483	31	484	31	485	31	486	19
487	19	488	19	489	19	490	19	491	19	492	19
493	19	494	19	495	19	496	19	497	19*	498	17
499	17	500	17	501	29	502	27	503	33	504	33
505	45	506	45	507	45*	508	43	509	21	510	21
511	21	512	21	513	21	514	19	515	19	516	37
517	37	518	65	519	63	520	45	521	99	522	99
523	99	524	99	525	99	526	99	527	99	528	99
529	99	530	99	531	51	532	51	533	51*	534	49
535	49	536	49	537	49	538	49	539	49	540	63
541	63	542	63	543	61	544	61	545	99	546	99
547	99	548	99	549	99	550	99	551	99	552	99
553	99	554	99	555	99	556	99	557	99	558	99
559	99	560	99	561	99	562	99	563	99	564	99
565	99	566	99	567	99	568	99	569	99	570	99
571	99	572	99	573	99	574	37*	575	95	576	93

577	35*	578	33	579	33	580	35	581	99	582	99
583	99	584	99	585	99	586	49	587	91	589	99
590	99	591	99	592	99	593	99	594	99	595	99
596	72*	597	70	598	70	599	70	600	99	601	99
602	35	603	35	604	35	605	35	606	35	607	35
608	35	609	35	610	35	611	35*	612	35*	613	35*
614	35*	615	35*	616	35*	617	35*	618	35*	619	35*
620	33	621	33	622	33	623	33	624	33	625	33
626	33	627	84	628	84*	629	84*	630	84*	631	84*
632	82	633	82	634	82	635	82	636	82	637	82
638	82	639	82	640	82	641	82	642	82	643	82
644	82	645	82	646	68*	647	66	648	28	649	28
650	24	651	24	652	24	653	24*	654	14	655	14*
656	12	657	12	658	12	659	07	660	05	661	05
662	05	663	05	664	05	665	05	667	16	668	16
669	16	670	16	671	16	672	16	673	16*	674	14
675	14	676	03	677	03	678	03	679	03	680	44*
681	01*	700	18	701	18	702	18	703	18	704	18
705	18	706	18	707	18	708	18	709	18	710	18
711	18	712	18	713	18	714	18	715	18	716	18
717	18	718	18	719	18	720	18	721	18	722	18
723	18	724	28	725	18	726	18	727	10	728	14
764	24	765	24*	766	14	767	14	768	14	769	14
770	14*	771	14*	772	14*						

explain that you are looking for a house or condo or whatever type of property you are calling on. Here's an idea of how the conversation might go:

"Hi, Realtor Bill?"

"Yes, how can I be of excellent service?"

"I saw your listing at Megaplex Condos. I'm looking for a condo for my mother, and Megaplex seems like a ducky place."

"Oh, it's quite ducky. Care to make an offer right this very second?"

"Well, it's for my mom as I said, and she really doesn't need the place till fall. I plan to spend the summer looking around with a Realtor, but I'm only available one day a week because I'm so busy. You know how it is: work, the screamin' kids, my dog just ate a quilt and I had to take him to the vet—it was a family heirloom . . . ."

"Oh. Well, I can help you find a condo this summer. Thursdays are the best night for me."

"Oh great. Thursdays are good for me, too."

"You wanna see the Megaplex listing this Thursday?"

"Sure. Can you set up some showings for the following Thursday, too?"

"Yes, I'll pencil you in for Thursday nights, and we'll be sure to find your mom a ducky condo before the summer's out."

"Great! Ah, uh oh . . . ."

"What's the matter?"

"Well, I just remembered I'll be on vacation the Thursday after that."

"Okay, I'll keep that in mind while I'm setting up appointments for you. In fact, now that you remind me, I'm on vacation the week of the 22nd."

"Yeah? Where to?"

"Just up to Maine. Me, the wife and kids."

"Kids? Sounds like a carload."

"Yeah, the Taurus wagon will be filled to the roof."

"Wagon, eh? They're great if you have kids. When you leaving?"

"We're leaving the morning of the 22nd and I'll be back on the 30th. I can show you condos after that."

"Sounds good. It's nice up there. You staying in Ogunquit?"

"No, York Beach. We're renting a cottage on Long Sands."

"Oh! I did that last year. It was on one of those side streets. I can't remember the name."

"Ours is a detached condo in Pemigawasset Village."

"I don't think that's where we stayed, but it sounds nice. Anyway I'll see you next Thursday. What time?"

The conversation goes on and you, of course, call the Realtor back before Thursday and explain that you talked to your mother and she decided she doesn't want to live in a ducky condo after all.

During the week of July 22, you go to the Pemigawasset Village condominium with a buddy who can drive your car back after you repo the subject's wagon. Of course, you each have detailed directions and a full color road map (oh yeah, did I mention that Mapquest has actual road maps, too?) printed from your color printer after visiting www.mapquest.com. You should have no problem locating the vehicle and doing your job.

Case closed.

ENDNOTES

1   Often when you type in only a last name, you can pull up a lot of genealogical archives relative to that name. This fact might help you in other aspects of your PI business.

2   Bulletin Board Systems were mostly text-based pages on private computers or networks, not part of the Internet. To access a BBS, you had to manually dial a specific phone number with your computer's communications program. You also had to match the remote system's protocol (computer language), which involved a lot of tweaking. Each time you called a new BBS, it was very possible that you'd have to change the configuration or your own computer to "talk" with that BBS. In short, it was a mess.

CHAPTER 6: Computer Monitoring and Surveillance

"You had to live—did live, from habit that became instinct—in the assumption that every sound you made was overheard, and, except in darkness, every movement scrutinized."
—George Orwell, *1984*

Few people realize precisely how many corpuscles of personal data course through the vessels of their computer's motherboard as they thump across the keys and pulse the mouse onto dialog buttons and program icons. With the right equipment, you can compile and analyze every bit of data sent or received by any given user before it ever leaves his or her computer. This is the Computer Age science of Internet surveillance.

It doesn't matter what type of suspect you're investigating. Maybe he's a psychopath. He could be an embezzler, or maybe she's trying to hide her assets from her husband before their next divorce hearing. Or maybe he's a child sexual predator. If you've got probable cause and can secure a warrant, you can capture everything he types, looks at, reads, downloads, and e-mails on his personal computer, literally living inside your suspect's head for as long as the warrant is valid.

Cutting-edge computer monitoring and surveillance products are available to private detectives, law enforcement, even parents who want to see how their minor children spend their computer time. We'll look at a few of them in this chapter.

To use some of these products, you need to first understand a little bit about networks and each individual computer's place within a network. Perhaps the most important lesson you can learn right now is this: When you log onto the Internet, *your computer becomes part of a network.* It is crucial that you understand this.

NETWORKS AND IP ADDRESSES

Every computer logged onto the Internet is assigned an IP, or Internet Protocol, address. The IP address uniquely identifies your computer on the Internet so it can communicate with other computers sharing the network. It is often convenient for a detective to know the IP address of a subject he is investigating. For example, in order to use the KeyLogPro software described later, you will need your subject's IP address.

Some IP addresses are dynamic, some are static. "Dynamic" in cyberspeak means it changes on the fly, so to speak. If you use dial-up access to the Internet, you have a dynamic IP address. In other words, each time you log on, you'll most likely be assigned a different IP address. "Static" means the IP address remains constant, such as the static IP address of a cable modem (technically a cable modem's IP address can change, too, if the network goes down and then back up again). There are other types of Internet connections, but we don't have to go over them all. All you need to know is that some types of connections are more static than others. As a general rule, the more dedicated the connection is to the Internet, the more static it is. A library, college, or corporation would likely have a static Internet connection known as a T1 or T3, which are leased lines from the phone company, and the IP addresses will not change.

If you'd like to learn more about computer networks, you can take Cisco's on-line course at http://cisco.netacad.net. If you plan to specialize in investigating cybercrimes, the Cisco course is well worth the price.

Cable modems, which are becoming increasingly popular, are direct Internet connections. The cable modem is like a TV cable box and is external to the PC with its own power supply. The Internet Service Provider (ISP) assigns the IP address to the cable modem, not the computer, so the address of a cable modem computer will not change even if the user routinely turns off his computer between sessions.

It's possible that the cable modem could lose the IP address because it is stored in RAM (Random Access Memory), which needs power to maintain the information stored there. So what if the power goes out in your subject's neighborhood? All is not lost. The ISP has a record of the last IP address assigned to any given cable modem and will attempt to reassign the same IP address to the modem. Usually, the attempt is successful.

The foregoing is obviously good if your subject has a cable modem and you've managed to identify its IP address. If so, it would be possible to track your subject at that IP address for months or even years. On the other hand, some connections change their IP address often, making tracking more difficult. Let's look at DSL as an example.

DSL stands for Dedicated Subscriber Line. It is a telephone line reserved for exclusive use by your computer to connect to the Internet. Many people these days opt for DSL so they can surf the Internet without tying up their household's regular phone line.

The word "dedicated" is treacherous here. You might be tempted to think the IP address of a DSL never changes, and theoretically that's possible. If you have a DSL connection to the Internet, and you never shut off your computer or close your Internet connection, and your ISP never has a problem, glitch, or ripple, then your IP address could remain constant for months. In common practice, however, a DSL user's IP address changes just about as often as a standard dial-up user's does.

Whether your subject has a cable modem, DSL, or standard dial-up, you're going to have to get that damn IP address somehow—even if only once for a cable modem. If you only need the IP address once, then here's a trick you can use.

The AOL/IM IP Retrieval Trick

Contact your subject on AOL Instant Messenger (AOL/IM). If you haven't already established a dialog with him, you'll have to think up some ruse to contact him as a stranger. This will, of course, depend on the subject. If he is a child molester, he may be ready and willing to accept a chat invitation from just about anybody. He'll probably figure you're somebody he's previously tricked into contacting him! Other subjects may be very wary of talking to strangers, so you'll have to be clever. If you have your subject's high school yearbook (minimal gumshoe research involved here), you can pretend to be an old classmate that has "at last" found him, or whatever. Be imaginative, but be careful. Don't blow your cover.

The AOL/IM download site explains basic use of the AOL Instant Messenger software. If you are not already familiar with AOL/IM, you will need to go to www.aol.com, follow the links for Instant Messenger, and study up in order to fully understand the following procedure.

Once connected with your subject in a chat window, ask your AOL "buddy" for a direct connection. Why do you have to ask for a direct connection when you are already connected? Well, when you are chatting with someone in Instant Messenger, you are not really connected directly to their computer. Rather, AOL is acting as a middleman, so to speak. The word "messenger" is quite apt here—you are giving a message to AOL and they, in turn, are sending it along to the person on the other end of the conversation.

So you have to request a direct connection, and the connection has to be accepted. Imagine the liability AOL would have if they allowed direct computer connections all over the Internet? They'd be creating a hacker's dream world. Savvy AOL users know this, so as long as you're offering your "buddy" (subject) something pertinent to your discussion, he probably will not hesitate to accept a direct connection. For a child molester, you might want to say you have a picture of yourself undressing. For an "old classmate," maybe you have a photo you want to share. ("Hey! Remember so-and-so?

Check out this picture!") In either case, you better have some kind of picture ready. Alternately, you could offer an MP3 (sound file) of a song you'd like to share with your "long lost friend," or a sound-byte of yourself, or anything you suspect might entice your particular perp.

Once your buddy accepts the connection, get to a DOS prompt on your computer. [1] The quickest way to do this in Win 9x/2000/XP systems is to go to Start, Run, and type "command" without the quotes. In the command prompt window, type: netstat –n (a space is required before the hyphen). Netstat is a neat utility that comes with Windows and lists all open connections on your computer. The –n option forces the IP address to be displayed numerically (as opposed to an actual domain name, such as aol.com).

When you type in netstat –n, you will see something like this:

for, is your subject's IP address. In our example there is another high port number: 5190. But, having already seen that AOL itself was established in the IP range of 205.188.x.x, I could readily eliminate that as a connection to AOL as opposed to a direct connection to my subject's computer.

What do I mean by "not otherwise accounted for"? You need to use the process of elimination (read: detective work) to determine which IP address belongs to your subject. To start, ignore all addresses ending in port :80; those are all web page connections you have open. Similarly, ignore all addresses ending in port :21; those are FTP connections. To keep these to a minimum, close all your other connections except the AOL connection to your buddy. Even close the AOL advertisement box if for some reason you left it going at startup; it alone can be responsible for several open

```
C:\>netstat –n
Active Connections
Proto    Local Address          Foreign Address          State
TCP      63.114.221.173:1030    205.188.9.225:5190       ESTABLISHED
TCP      63.114.221.173:1030    205.188.165.121:80       TIME_WAIT
TCP      63.114.221.173:1030    127.0.0.1:4443           ESTABLISHED
C:\>
```

This sample netstat output is showing you the status of network connections that have recently been established on your computer. It shows the local address (the IP address assigned to your computer) followed by the port number (which appears after the colon) as well as the remote (labeled as "foreign") address and port number. Port numbers are handled internally by the respective computers, and you don't need to know precisely how they work for this example. You can see that netstat also shows you connections that have been established but have timed out due to inactivity (the TIME_WAIT connection).

Once netstat has run, look for the foreign IP address that uses a high number port, such as 4443 in our example. [2] The number to the left of the colon, that is not otherwise accounted

connections at once! In fact, familiarize yourself with which IP addresses belong to AOL because you will need to eliminate all of them in order to isolate the subject's address.

In the above example, I eliminated two connections as AOL IP addresses, one of which was a web page, probably their home page. This left only one connection, the direct connection I had with my subject (shown as 127.0.0.1 in the example).

One shortcut you can try is to do a netstat before you ask for the direct connection from your subject. Print that out and compare it to the netstat results after you make the connection. If this is all done in a short amount of time, the only difference will be the new direct connection, and the new IP address will be your subject's. If worse comes to worse, you can run all the listed IP addresses through VisualRoute (see Chapter 7).

Home Page Redirection Method

The AOL/IM retrieval technique is a good one if you only need your subject's IP address once or if you have a reason to regularly exchange pictures or files with him. But what if your subject has standard dial-up access, meaning his IP address changes constantly, and you have no way to con his address out of him?

A good trick is to create a short program that logs your subject's IP address every time he logs on to the Internet. Here is a sample program:

```
<?

$fp=fopen("track.txt","a");
$dd=date("m/d/y h:m a");
fputs($fp," connect from: {$dd} PST \n");
fputs($fp,"    HTTP_USER_AGENT:
{$_SERVER['HTTP_USER_AGENT']} \n");
fputs($fp,"    REMOTE_ADDR    :
{$_SERVER['REMOTE_ADDR']} \n");

fclose($fp);

?>
```

This php code opens a log file (track.txt) and writes specific information to it, most importantly the user's IP address. The output to the log file looks like this:

```
connect from: 12/16/02 04:12 am PST
    HTTP_USER_AGENT: Mozilla/4.0 (compatible;
MSIE 6.0; Windows NT 5.1)
    REMOTE_ADDR    : 64.80.226.186
```

The code might look like Greek to you, but you'll note it's quite short. This is to show you that a web programmer could set this up for you in a matter of minutes and should not charge you very much to do so.

The idea is to have your subject go to the page in which your IP logging program resides. The trick is to do this without him knowing about it.

Most people have a "home page" where their browser takes them each time they log onto the Internet. For me it's my jillett.com home page. But let's say your subject has Yahoo.com as his home page. As long as your subject sees Yahoo.com when he logs onto the Internet, he will not be suspicious of anything. The trick is to get the subject's browser to go to the page that has your IP address logger running on it and then redirect to Yahoo.com so fast that your subject will not notice that anything out of the ordinary has happened. Most people, even if they glimpse the process in action, are so mystified by the Internet that they wouldn't question it anyway.

There are two ways to make your IP logger page your subject's home page: you need physical access to his computer so you can start the browser and edit the default home page (see steps below), or you have to get your subject to unwittingly "choose" your IP logger page as his new home page. For the latter, you'll need to ask the web guru of a page that your subject frequents to insert a "make this your home page" script into the site.

Confused? Say your subject frequents www.illegalActivities.com. You contact the webmaster of that site and explain your investigation. If your subject is a real creep, the webmaster may be more than happy to help; otherwise, you may have to hire his or her services. One day, your subject goes to that site and sees a link: "Click here to make www.illegalActivities.com your home page and a chance to win $1,000!"

If your subject takes the bait, he will see a dialog box pop up on his screen saying something like, "Do your really want to change your home page to http://www.illegalActivities.com/l?" If he clicks YES, you're in.

In order for this to work, the web guru will have to add a special directory where your subject's IP address will be logged. In our example, the /l is that directory. It is meant to be discreet so your subject will not realize he is being sent anywhere but the home page. A comma, colon, or tilde would be even more discreet. To wit:

Do your really want to change your home page to http://www.illegalActivities.com/,/?

Do your really want to change your home page to http://www.illegalActivities.com/:/?

Do your really want to change your home page to http://www.illegalActivities.com/~/?

Any of these options would obscure the logging directory to a degree where most web surfers wouldn't even notice it or simply believe it to be computer garble. However, some operating systems won't allow these characters to be used as directory names, so the skinny "l" may have to suffice.

Dynamic DNS

Some individuals go out of their way to let you know their IP address. They may do this if they are using their computer as a server or otherwise want people to be able to dial into it. They may even do this so they can dial into their computer while they are away to retrieve important files and so forth.

Obviously this sort of user is very computer savvy, and it's unlikely you'll be able to trick him out of his IP address. In fact, any attempt to do so would probably alert him to the fact you are trying to gain access to his computer. In no time at all, you may find that *he* is investigating *you!*

But he has left himself open. In order for him or others to access his computer, there needs to be a record of his IP address at a dependable Internet site. Such sites do exist and are called Dynamic Domain Name Servers, or Dynamic DNS.

To use such a service, you first need to make up a domain name for yourself, such as mycomputer.com. You then need to tell the Dynamic DNS that this is your name. The Dynamic DNS will give you a small program that sends them your IP address, say, every five minutes. If your Internet service provider for some reason resets and gives you a new IP address, it will be recorded at the Dynamic DNS.

If you are traveling on business and need to get an important file from your computer, this is a good way to be sure you have access to it no matter what. Through the Dynamic DNS, you'd type in your domain name mycomputer.com and you will be taken to your computer no matter what the IP address is.

So what does all this mean to you as a detective? If you know your subject has this setup, or if you trick him into creating this setup, and you know his domain name, then you can get his IP address at anytime by accessing the Dynamic DNS.

With a basic understanding of networks and IP addresses, you will better understand some of the tools and techniques described in the rest of this book. I will reiterate here something I said earlier: The single most important thing to understand is that your computer is part of a network when you are logged onto the Internet. The same is true of any target computer on which you conduct surveillance activities. So your subject's computer is the beginning of the data stream you are hoping to intercept.

So does the subject *have* to be logged on to the Internet before you can begin intercepting that data stream? Not in the Computer Age! Today there are all sorts of computer surveillance tools—both hardware and software—available to the Computer Age detective that can reveal this information before your subject ever logs onto the Net or even if he never does. Let's look at some of them.

KEYSTROKE RECORDERS

The most basic computer monitoring device is a keystroke recorder. A keystroke recorder logs each keyboard key press in order and stores it somewhere for later review by the detective. It can be an external device or clandestine software running in the background of your subject's computer. By capturing every key your subject presses on his keyboard, it reveals to the detective an entire world of information useful for the investigation: user names, passwords, bank account numbers, and any suspect phrases such as "kilos" or "unmarked bills."

Because external hardware loggers require regular access to the target computer, they are best suited to parents monitoring children or bosses monitoring employees. Though hardware loggers are small and fairly easy to install, you wouldn't want to risk being caught by a suspected serial killer when you return to his apartment to retrieve the data.

With hardware loggers, keep in mind too that a savvy computer user would most likely notice something new attached to the back of his computer, even a small 2 inch extension cable. If he should happen to look back there during routine maintenance or if the machine starts acting funky, your proverbial jig will be up. Kids and employees, on the other hand, most likely won't be crawling behind the desk to make repairs (unless they are especially technically savvy, and some are—quite).

On the other hand, software-based keystroke loggers have several significant disadvantages:

- They are dependent on the host computer's operating system (OS), and you'd have to hope your target's computer will meet the hardware and OS requirements of the software.
- They do not record keystrokes before the OS is loaded, so any special codes your subject uses to access his OS will not be recorded.
- They do not record the keystrokes if an external boot diskette (a floppy disk instead of the computer's internal disk) is used to start the computer.
- They can corrupt the host computer's operating system, thus revealing their presence.
- They can be detected and disabled by suspicious users.
- The log file can be copied or modified because it is saved on the host computer's hard drive, thereby leaving defense attorneys a wide open door to have the "evidence" suppressed.
- They can be a security risk if the log file is not encrypted, especially if a third party happens upon the log file and becomes curious or suspicious about it.

So, when shopping for a keystroke recorder or choosing one for a specific gig, you will first want to consider the pros and cons of each kind (hardware vs. software) and decide where their

differences might affect a particular job or how you like to work in general. Now, let's have a look at some of these puppies.

KeyGhost

KeyGhost Ltd. has developed the KeyGhost, [3] a hardware key logger that records up to two million keystrokes on a flash memory chip. [4] It starts recording immediately and unobtrusively the moment the computer is turned on.

The KeyGhost is easy to use and does not need software to record or retrieve keystrokes. It can be attached externally to the keyboard cable or hardwired inside the keyboard for total stealth. It can be used in the following ways:

- As a tool for computer fraud investigations.
- As a monitoring device for detecting unauthorized access or unacceptable use of a computer.
- As a deterrent to prevent personal use of computer resources on company time. If employees know that their keyboard has a recording device, they will be less likely to use the company's computer for illegal, unauthorized, or frivolous purposes.
- As a tool to back up daily computer data.

As an example of a quality hardware keystroke recorder, KeyGhost offers several advantages:

- It does not require batteries.
- It cannot be disabled by software.
- It has nonvolatile flash memory.
- It operates completely independent of the computer's hardware and operating system.
- Stored keystrokes are protected with state-of-the-art 128-bit encryption.
- Once full, it drops out earlier keystrokes, keeping the log file as current as possible.
- It picks up every keystroke, even those typed in the critical period between computer power-up and the operating system being loaded.
- If hardwired, it cannot be easily found or removed.
- It is impossible to disable from a remote location.

- It is impossible for a computer to detect it.
- It is immune to magnetic fields, has no moving parts, and is shock resistant.
- The chance of failure is very low compared to conventional media like hard drives or CD-ROM discs because it uses flash memory to store data and has no moving parts.
- Users do not need to be computer experts to install it. The device installs between the keyboard plug and computer keyboard jack.
- Because it cannot be modified, the log is an authentic record of what was typed and therefore can be used as evidence in a court of law.

There are several versions of the KeyGhost, some of which are only available to law enforcement. KeyGhost Ltd., for instance, also makes an ordinary keyboard with a KeyGhost hidden inside. Because it looks and feels exactly like any ordinary keyboard, it can be utilized as an extra security control if you do not want a visible device attached to the back of the computer.

KeyGhost Ltd. offers a one-year warranty for all products and lifetime firmware upgrades. The price range at the time of this writing is $139 to $349, depending on the product.

KeyLogPro and Remote Spy

PAL Solutions Ltd., based in the United Kingdom (www.palsol.com), offers two products of interest to private detectives and law enforcement: KeyLogPro and Remote Spy. They are both software items, and no external hardware is needed to use them.

KeyLogPro is a basic keystroke logger with some advanced features that make it worth the price over freeware. [5] KeyLogPro records the task in which keystrokes are generated and time stamps the beginning of each new task. For example, if your subject sends an AOL instant message to somebody, KeyLogPro will let you know that the keystrokes were recorded during the instant messaging session. If your subject then checks his e-mail while waiting for his AOL accomplice to reply, KeyLogPro will note that your subject has changed tasks and will record what time this change occurred. When your subject returns to the AOL window, KeyLogPro

records that fact, time stamps it again, and continues to log keystrokes.

Here is a sample of what KeyLogPro captures, taken from an actual log file. For legal reasons, I have changed the names and some of the content.

User currently logged in: HP Authorized Customer
*** Task Name: d 1 s k r ee t - Direct Instant Message ***   Time: 21:44:11 Date: 08/26/02
W<Backspace><Backspace><Backspace>n
When?
Kewl.
HOld. Lemme check it.
*** Task Name: Yahoo! Mail – syko_nun_such_addy@yahoo.com - Microsoft Internet Explorer ***   Time: 21:45:51 Date: 08/26/02

*** Task Name: d 1 s k r ee t - Direct Instant Message ***   Time: 21:45:55 Date: 08/26/02
that's what I'm doing. I'm answering a yahoo e-mail right now.
HOLD!

*** Task Name: Yahoo! Mail - syko_nun_such_addy @yahoo.com - Microsoft Internet Explorer ***   Time: 21:46:12 Date: 08/26/02
<Num Del>Hi Mike,
I've been a little antsy about legalities lately.<Backspace>,
especaill<Backspace><Backspace><Backspace><Backspace>ially after 9/11 and all the w laws being r<Backspace>proposed.
You really need that job done?

Syko

*** Task Name: d 1 s k r ee t - Direct Instant Message ***   Time: 21:47:51 Date: 08/26/02
Make thoswe<Backspace><Backspace>e passports for me just in case.
The guy must have money.
Anything you think of about it is important so

please note it. I'll decide d<Backspace>what
to k<Backspace>do later.
In fact, save this log. Lot's g<Backspace>of
good info here. We might need it later.
No. If the PD knocks on your door, just keep
saying you're your brother and you have no ID
cuz the ;<Backspace>airport still hasn't
delivered your luggaged<Num Del>.
No. I'm tellin' ya there's nothin' they
cand<Backspace> do. You never been
photo'd or printed.
I gtg. Just sit tight.
No! Shit, man, just relax. Just tell them no. If
they don't have a warrant – and they won't
cuz I already set that up
wo<Backspace>ithe<Num Del> Baker – then
just tell them no. They can't do shit without it.
Now I really gtg.
OK.
K
Later.

If you, as detective, were analyzing this log file, there's quite a bit to be inferred from it, and it would likely help your case. But the only thing I'm trying to show here is exactly what KeyLogPro picks up for you. Note that it will show you the misintended keystrokes of the target along with his backspace strokes and deletes. This is important for prosecutors because it would be hard to get "cleaned up" evidence admitted into court. It could also help you better understand your subject. Maybe you'll note that he is a picky typer in that he'll backspace to correct would-be misspellings where others might not. This small fact might help you further along in your investigation. In a thorough investigation, *everything* counts.

As you can see from the transcript, the main limitation is that only one side of the AOL conversation is recorded. Same with the Yahoo e-mail. This is to be expected with a straight keystroke recorder because it only records keystrokes on the *subject's* computer. Of course, if you know who your subject's accomplices are, you could install KeyLogPro on their computers as well and piece conversations together later on.

PAL Solutions offers an adjunct to KeyLogPro that more than makes up for its

limitations. Remote Spy offers the ability to monitor your subject's keystrokes *in real time* from a remote computer, allowing you to see what he is typing as he types it. What's more, you do not need physical access to your subject's computer to implement this invaluable setup; everything can be done from a remote Internet connection. When your subject connects to the Internet to read, write, surf, or whatever, all activity is discreetly logged and sent to the investigator.

For this to work, however, you need to accomplish two things:

1. You have to get your subject to unwittingly download the logging software to his computer and start it.
2. You must either know your subject's IP address, or you must trick it out of him.

How you accomplish the above naturally depends on the situation. If you haven't established an open dialog with your suspect, it is going to be more difficult to trick him into doing things. However, if you've already used some ruse to chat with or exchange e-mails with him, things get much easier.

In either case, now that you have the Computer Age technology, you will need to rely on some old-school tricks to put it to its highest and best use. Here are some ideas to get you started.

Tricking Your Subject Into Downloading a Key Logger

If you have physical access to the target computer, then by all means find an appropriate moment to load the key logger onto it. Otherwise, you will have to resort to other methods. If you own a web site that your subject visits regularly, you can trick him into downloading the keystroke recorder. If you can't do it yourself, ask your web guru to create a link to the file. Call the link something else, like FreePornPictures or whatever floats your subject's boat. Your subject will see a dialog box asking whether he wishes to download the file and, thinking he's getting something he wants, will accept. Once he gets the file and attempts to

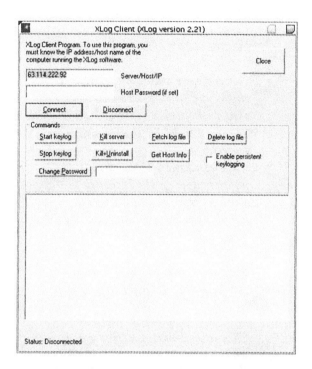

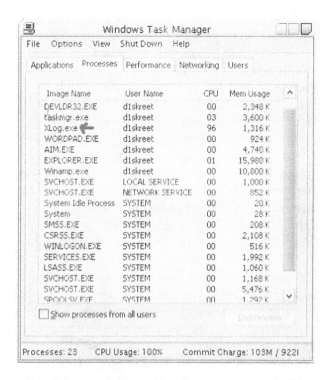

Screenshot 6.1. Xlog client window. Once you've tricked your subject into downloading and running the key logger, you use this window to fetch the log file from the remote computer and view it. From the client window, you can start and stop the key logging, delete the log file from the remote host, and uninstall the key logger from your subject's computer altogether.

Screenshot 6.2. Beware! A savvy subject may use ctrl-alt-del or some other task manager to see what's running on his computer. Best if you rename the Xlog.exe file to something more obscure before sending it, such as FAST_SYS.EXE. This will make it appear as an obscure operating system routine, which is not unusual to find when using such utilities.

open it, he won't be happy with it because nothing will happen. But if he's otherwise unsuspicious, you will have successfully planted the key logger onto his computer.

If you don't want your subject to be suspicious (or even disappointed) when he opens the file and nothing happens, you could try a more sophisticated ruse. For example, if you have an AOL Instant Messenger dialog going with the subject and he has come to trust you, you could say, "Hey, I just downloaded this Windows patch [6] and my mouse works better now." Before your subject even responds to your statement, use the AOL Instant Messenger menu to send him the Xlog.exe file. Of course, you will have already renamed this to WIN98mouse_errorFix_v11.exe.

Your subject will see a dialog box on his screen asking whether he wishes to accept the file from his "buddy." If he trusts you, he'll accept it. After it downloads, a new icon with a nice, long,

easy-to-find file name will appear on his desktop. You and he continue the chat:

YOU: Get the file?
HIM: Yea. What do I do?
YOU: There's an icon for it on your desktop
HIM: OK. I C it.
YOU: Just double click it and see if your mouse works any better.
HIM: I double clicked it.
YOU: Move your mouse really fast. Does it drag?
HIM: No, just moves fast.
YOU: Then it worked.

Or whatever. Maybe he'll say "things seem the same," but they won't be. You'll have a key logger running on his PC and you'll know everything he's typing on his computer, what programs he's running, and when he switches between them.

SPECTOR PRO

Beyond basic keystroke recorders, the world of Internet monitoring and surveillance offers more sophisticated utilities that, in addition to simply recording keystrokes, will also record both sides of "chat" conversations, sort keystrokes according to the program in which they were typed, and take periodic screenshots of the subject's monitor so you can see exactly what was happening on his screen. Was he pricing suites at a romantic getaway resort while chatting with a certain person? What might that say about a given situation? Spector Pro is such a utility.

SpectorSoft's Spector Pro Internet monitoring and surveillance software is chock-full of useful features. The client window is user-friendly, easy to navigate, and simple to understand. The help file is comprehensive, although the software is so easy to use I hardly needed to reference it. The software is stealthy, runs in the background, and cannot be detected by any ordinary means. Its biggest drawback is that you must have access to your subject's computer to install it.

The following introduction to Spector Pro is taken directly from the company's web site:

Spector 3.1 Professional Edition is a PC and Internet monitoring and surveillance tool designed for consumers and businesses. When you absolutely, positively need to know EXACTLY what your children, spouse or employees are doing on the Internet, Spector Pro will let you know in visual detail.

Spector is designed to operate under the following Windows operating systems: Windows 95, Windows 98, Windows Me, Windows NT 4.0 or higher, Windows 2000 and Windows XP.

We recommend that you have an Intel Pentium or Celeron processor, or an AMD Athlon or Duron or compatible processor running at a minimum of 166 MHz with a minimum of 64 megabytes of memory. If running Windows 2000 or Windows XP,

we recommend a minimum of 128 megabytes of memory.

Spector is appropriate for:

- *Parents concerned about what their children do on the Internet, who they chat with, and whether adults may be trying to solicit their children online.*
- *Spouses concerned about what their partner does on the Internet.*
- *Businesses trying to put a stop to inappropriate surfing on company time.*

Spector records PC and Internet activity by performing the following tasks:

1. *Taking automatic, periodic snapshots of whatever is on the computer screen.*
2. *Recording incoming and outgoing e-mails.*
3. *Recording chat conversations and instant messages.*
4. *Recording all keystrokes typed.*
5. *Recording all web sites visited.*
6. *E-mailing alert notifications when "keywords" are detected.*

Let's look at Spector Pro's features one at a time.

Periodic screenshots. You can set the rate at which low-resolution black-and-white screenshots of your subject's screen are recorded. For example, you can take a screenshot every five seconds or every two minutes. You, as a detective, would determine how important the screenshots are to you and configure this setting accordingly. When you are viewing the log file, you can play back the screenshots like a video, fast-forwarding and reversing through them as needed.

E-mail recording. Spector Pro neatly sorts e-mails into separate folders for each e-mail client used (AOL, Yahoo, etc.). All the e-mails are sorted again within each client folder, where you can view them in ascending or descending order based on sender, subject, date, or whatever. One

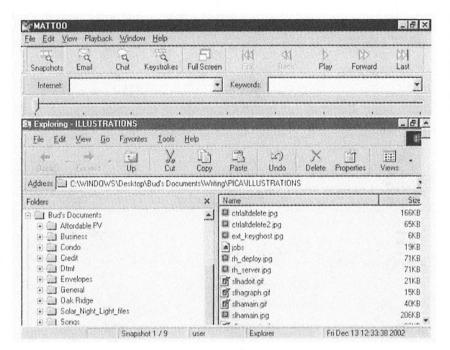

Screenshot 6.3. Spector Pro's screen snapshot window. I recorded myself working on this book. You can see what I was doing in Explorer in this snapshot. You can program Spector Pro to take a snapshot every few seconds, every few minutes, or anywhere in between.

of the major advantages of Spector's e-mail capturing feature is that it captures both incoming and outgoing e-mails, something other Internet monitors don't do.

Chat and instant messaging. As with e-mail, all chats are sorted according to client used (e.g., AOL chats will be stored separately from Yahoo! Messenger chats). Both sides of the conversation are recorded; again, something an ordinary key

logger simply won't do.

Keystroke recorder. Spector's main advantage over basic keystroke loggers is that it separates all keystrokes according to the program that was active when the keys were depressed. For example, if your subject types, "Cocaine AND Black Market" into an Internet Explorer search box, you will know this upon examining the log file. If he then switches to his AOL Instant

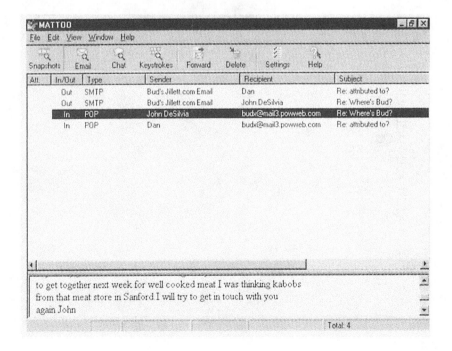

Screenshot 6.4. Spector Pro's e-mail window. All e-mails sent and received are logged. Click on any e-mail that interests you and the full text will appear in the bottom pane.

Screenshot 6.5. Spector Pro's chat window. In this screenshot you see only my one test conversation, but Spector Pro will record separate chat sessions over a long period of time. All chat sessions will be listed separately in the top pane. Click on the dates and names that interest you and the conversations appear in the bottom pane.

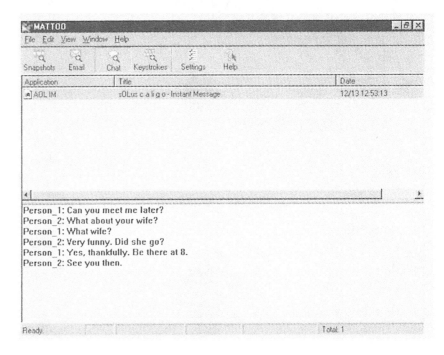

Messenger window and tells his buddy, "Hey, I just found some great links to black market cocaine!" you will know that the latter sentence was typed under the AOL/IM task. If he then composes a letter to his dear, sweet grandmother in Microsoft Word, those keystrokes will be recorded separately from the rest.

Visited web sites. Spector keeps a running list of all web sites your subject visits. Browsing this list will say a lot about your subject's web-surfing habits. Is he a scientist constantly in search of "how to" information? Does he buy nitrous oxide canisters from on-line head shops? Does he spend a lot of time at Victoria's Secret despite a noted lack of a female counterpart in his life?

Keyword alerts. If Spector Pro has one feature that makes it worth having over its discount counterparts, it's its Keyword Alert feature. The

Screenshot 6.6. Spector Pro's keystroke window. This is a very powerful tool. Every keystroke is recorded and sorted by process. This saves tons of time over a standard keystroke recorder, where you'd have to piece together which keys were pressed in which processes. The process events are dated, which is very useful to investigators and prosecutors.

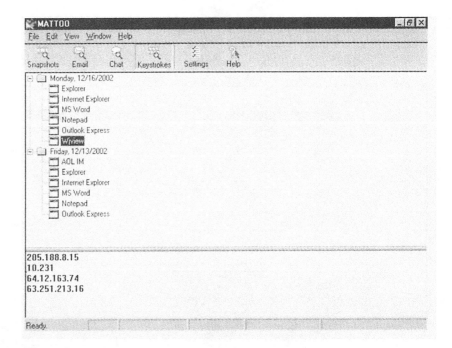

theory is simple: When your subject types a certain keyword or phrase, you are sent an e-mail alerting you to this fact. You can set more than one keyword or phrase, too. Sample keyword lists might look like this:

For a drug dealer suspect:
- Cocaine
- Meet me
- Page me
- Pager
- Cash

For a child molester suspect:
- What are you wearing
- How old are you
- Meet me
- Send me

If you are monitoring your teenager:
- Your address (to make sure they're not giving it out)
- Your phone number (to make sure they're not giving it out)
- Sex
- Virgin
- Pot
- Weed
- Booze
- Beer

A couple of pointers here. You'll notice under the molester's keyword list that I omitted the question marks in the first two entries. This is to increase the possibility of the keyword being triggered. In this case, if you were to set the key phrase for your child molester suspect as "What are you wearing?" and he types "What are you wearing, Jimmy?" an alert will not be sent because your subject used a comma instead of a question mark. Also notice I used the key phrase "send me." This will catch several possibilities: send me a picture of yourself; send me a private e-mail address; send me your home address.

You'll want to avoid keywords that will trigger too many unnecessary alerts. For example, you wouldn't set "hi" as a keyword (thinking it might be used as shorthand for "getting high" or whatever) because you'll be

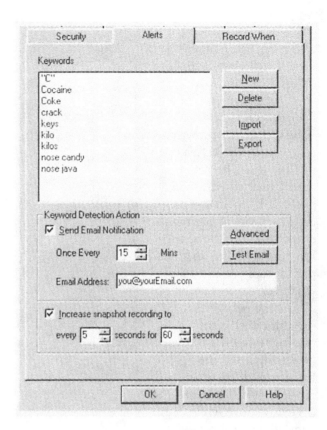

Screenshot 6.7. Spector Pro's keyword alert window. Want to be notified by e-mail when your subject types a certain keyword or phrase? You can configure Spector Pro to do exactly that.

alerted each time your subject begins an e-mail with the word "hi."

SPECTORSOFT'S eBLASTER

eBlaster is like Spector Pro, except it can be preconfigured and e-mailed to your subject. It's by no means foolproof. In order for eBlaster to be useful, you must have some way of getting your subject to open the executable (.exe) file when you e-mail it to him. There's no way around this. Unfortunately, some e-mail programs are set up to refuse executable files. Refusing executables is not usually the default configuration, and most people don't bother to invoke this protection because it limits what they can download on the Internet. Most people *do* take precautions as far as opening unfamiliar e-mail attachments for fear of catching a computer virus, but as we've discussed, you know there are ways to trick a subject into doing just that.

When you attach eBlaster to an e-mail, you do not need to name it eBlaster.exe and you shouldn't. You could name it PictureOfMe.exe or SongILike.exe or anything to get your subject to open it. If he does, he will report back to you that nothing happened. You could act stupid or you could send the file again, this time sending an actual photograph, sound file, or whatever.

As the pervert is drooling over your photograph, eBlaster will be setting up in the background. Next time he reboots, it will be watching his every move while running in stealth mode. eBlaster will send you the log file every so often, depending on how you preconfigured the settings. Because SpectorSoft's e-mail routine is proprietary, Windows knows nothing about it and your subject will not see any clues (in his taskbar or elsewhere) that a file is being e-mailed from his computer. Once you receive the log file in e-mail, you can view it in the same way as Spector Pro provides data as described in the preceding section.

Pretty neat, huh?

RED HAND

Red Hand is a software key logger similar to Spector Pro. A demo version is available at www.redhandsecurity.com. The demo is fully functional, except an annoying screen pops up each time the program loads or exits. The annoying screen goes away upon registration. Registration at the time of this writing is $59, almost one-third the cost of Spector Pro's advertised cost of $149.[7]

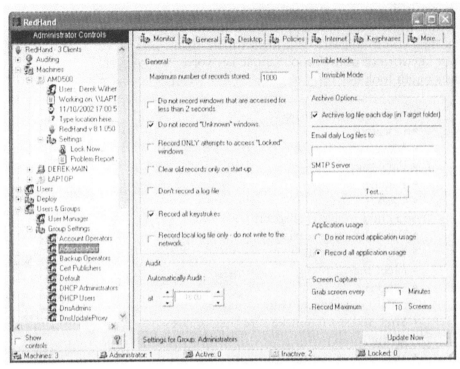

Screenshot 6.8. You can see that Red Hand is more than just a key logger—it's a complete and fully configurable computer surveillance package. Try it out yourself at www.redhandsecurity.com.

I test-drove the demo and was quite impressed. It's fully configurable, logs each process that records a keystroke, and logs programs as the subject opens, closes, and switches between them. (You can also view the entire key log as one file if you so choose; in other words, you are not forced to view keystrokes according to program.) Like Spector Pro, it has a screenshot recorder, but this feature did not work with my monitor.

Red Hand was working on some video compatibility problems at the time of this writing. The program was smart enough to catch the incompatibility and disable the feature rather than making a mess of my system. I'm willing to bet Red Hand will have solved this issue by the time you read this.

Overall, Spector Pro is a bit prettier but not by much. Red Hand has one big plus over Spector Pro, however—it will e-mail you the log file each day. I would make this a priority consideration if you do not have regular access to the computer you are monitoring.

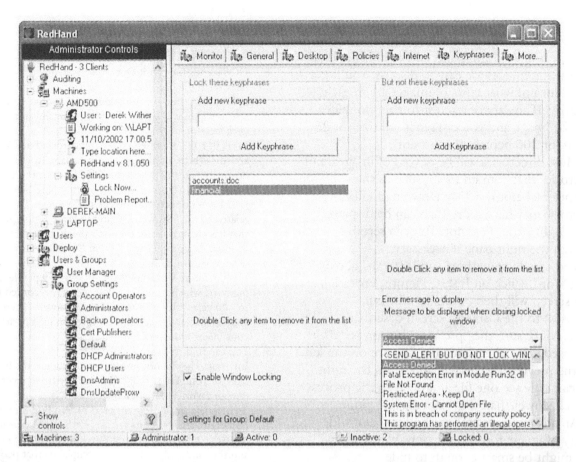

Screenshot 6.9. As with Spector Pro, you can set keywords and phrases. You can also assign certain events to certain keywords.

POOR MAN'S IMAGE-CAPTURING TECHNIQUES

Now that you've read the Spector Pro description above, you can see where image capturing can be useful when conducting a serious investigation. But what if you don't need to go hog wild? What if you're just generally curious about what images are stored on a given computer? Maybe you're not investigating a Mafia hit man, or maybe you just don't want to pony up the dough for new computer surveillance products. Perhaps you have a troubled teenager and feel his safety would be best maintained by doing some poking around in his computer. In such a case, having access to the graphic images he downloads would tell you volumes about his state of mind or recreational habits. If you find that he's been looking at

photos of methamphetamine labs that will fit into a basement crawlspace, you'll have a place to start.

To get an overview of what kinds of image files are stored on a given computer, you can use software like Olympus Camedia, which may already be loaded on your subject's system, especially if he has a digital camera. If it's not on your (teen's) system, it's easy enough to get. It's distributed free with Olympus digital cameras and is meant as support software for the camera.[8] Other digital cameras have similar software.

Camedia displays all available images in a given directory in the right pane of its main screen. The left pane allows you to move from directory to directory, which you can do by mouse clicks or by using the arrow keys. Your best bet is to expand all the directories, starting in the root C:\ directory and arrowing down through every directory and subdirectory. As you do so, all available jpg (pronounced "jay-peg" and often written as "jpeg") images in that directory will appear in the right pane. Although thumbnail size, the jpg images are easy to discern. You'll get a good idea of what types of images are in each directory. If any are of interest to you, double-click the image and you can see it full size (or 25, 33, 50, or 200 percent if you want).

Most directories will be devoid of images, but directories that contain them, such as the Internet cache or the "My Download Files" directory, may have more than can be displayed in the right pane. Fear not. You can scroll through the right pane if necessary.

You can do something similar to the above using Word. Click on Insert, Picture, From File. Your screen will then be similar (for our purposes) to the Camedia screen described above. Make sure the "preview" button is depressed. The directories and files are on the left and the preview images will appear on the right. You can only see one file at a time, so the process is much slower than the Camedia technique.

An advantage to this method is that a wide variety of image formats are viewable. A savvy teen might be smart enough to hide incriminating images by saving them as something more obscure than simple jpegs, which are viewable by many common programs. This method allows you to view TIF files or any number of image formats.

Windows Explorer in Win98 and later versions can also preview images. The methods you'd use are similar to those above. Your computer may have come with other image editing software that you can use as a poor man's image browser to get an idea of what seediness may be lurking on any given computer.

ENDNOTES

1 DOS stands for "Disk Operating System," a holdover term from the pre-Windows era. You are technically still in Windows, but you are taken to a DOS-like text screen where you type your own commands rather than click icons.

2 Ports 0–1023 are reserved for standardized networking activities (http, gopher, ping, time, date, ftp, telnet, hostname, etc.). Ports 1024–65535 are free to use. AOL assigns a port in that range. Anything below :1024 will not be your subject's IP address. The *s are related to the SSA web site and indicate a high group that has changed since the site's previous update.

3 Product descriptions taken from KeyGhost's web site: www.keyghost.com.

4 Flash memory is a nonvolatile, power-independent memory, which means the data will stay recorded for up to 100 years after power has been removed. Therefore you, as detective, need not retrieve it until a perfectly convenient moment.

5 You can find freeware keystroke recorders on the Internet. They're not pretty, but they'll get the basic data for you. Try typing "freeware keystroke recorder" in your favorite search engine.

6 A patch is a small program used to fix a bug found in a bigger program after its release. Let's say Microsoft releases a new version of its Windows operating system and they suddenly get a lot of complaints that people who've upgraded to it have problems getting their old Packard Bell Model 1010 monitor to display properly. Microsoft doesn't want these people to be too mad for too long, so they have their programmers figure out the compatibility problem and release a "patch" to fix it.

7 SpectorSoft seems to run perpetual sales on their products. I believe I've seen Spector Pro offered for $99.

8 Please note that Camedia and similar software are subject to licensing agreements, so be careful you are not breaking any laws in how you choose to obtain and use this software.

CHAPTER 7: Squeezing Clues from E-mail

"E-mail, baby, that's number one."
—Steve Ballmer, MicroSoft CEO

Whether it's to debunk spammers, quell harassers, or simply determine the true sender of an incriminating missive, a Computer Age detective must be adept at wringing an e-mail for every last clue. All of the old-school tactics apply, of course, such as scouring the text for word choices that lend clues to dialect and interpreting the overall tone of the letter to see if it rings true with its purported substance. Does the writer use regional terms like "you all"? How about clues that reveal the writer's age, such as "phat" (teens to twenties) or "picture show" instead of "movie" (60+)? Some baby boomers still use the word "album" when referring to CDs. Does the suicide note sound too contrived? Is the runaway daughter's "Don't worry, I'm okay" letter laden with the machinations of a sinister hand? These are all questions good detectives over the years have had to ask in order to thrive in their profession. Computer Age detectives need only learn a few more tricks to remain competitive.

In a way, an e-mailed letter may contain more clues and be easier to trace than its snailed counterpart. The principal reason for this is the sender's foolhardy assumption that he sits protected inside the anonymous glow of his computer monitor. Sure, he may have an inkling that his e-mail is not totally private, but he can't see how it could possibly be traced back to his keyboard. On the other hand, you as a detective interested in surviving in the Computer Age *must* know how to trace that e-mail back to the sender's keyboard.

E-MAIL HEADERS

A layman interested in tracing an e-mail might start with what he sees on his screen, otherwise known as a "header":

To: dHadly@Simonbar_Investigations_LLC.net
From:
YourDead@IKnowWhatYouDidTenSummersAgo.com
Subject: Think they could keep me in jail forever asshole?
Date: Thu, 02 May 2002 01:13:54 PDT

Anybody interested in tracing this e-mail and starting here would also be finishing here empty-handed shortly thereafter. Why? Because it's all bull, that's why. The "From" info, which is seemingly the most useful, is actually the most useless because it's the easiest thing to forge.

Any serious endeavor to trace an e-mail must be initiated by pulling the *full* header information. To do this in Outlook Express (e-mail programs other than Outlook will work similarly), right-click the message (not the message body), then select Properties, Details, Message Source. Highlight all the text (or right-click Select All). Right click, select Copy, and paste it into a Notepad file (which you'll later print and add to your case file with appropriate notes, I'm sure).

Okay, so now you've got something that resembles an ancient form of interplanetary Greek in a Notepad file. Good. Now what? Scanning through it, you may note that some of what I'd earlier classified as forgeable is resident amidst the mess before you (i.e. From, Subject, etc.). This is an important lesson. Even in the full header, information that supposedly identifies the true sender can be readily altered. In fact, the sender has control over other parts of the final e-mail header, as you'll soon see.

Let's look at an example of a full header:

```
Received: by roland (mbox simonbar)
(with Cubic Circle's cucipop (v1.31 1998/05/13) Wed May 1 00:08:20 2002)
X-From_: Simonbar@SimonbarsISP.net Wed May 01 00:08:14 2002
Received: from customer-12-345-678-90.dialup.simonbarsisp.net (HAL) [12.345.678.90]
    by roland.simonbarsisp.net with smtp (Exim 3.35 #1 (Debian))
    id 172IPO-0000Ox-00; Wed, 01 May 2002 00:08:02 -0400
Message-ID: <00d001c1f0c6$aeb3e2e0$7379fea9@flashcom.com>
From: "SIMONBAR" <simonbar@simonbarsisp.net>
To: <simonbar@simonbarsisp.net>
Subject: TEST
Date: Wed, 1 May 2002 00:14:25 -0400
MIME-Version: 1.0
Content-Type: multipart/alternative;
    boundary="——=_NextPart_000_00CD_01C1F0A5.26B746A0"
X-Priority: 3
X-MSMail-Priority: Normal
X-Mailer: Microsoft Outlook Express 5.50.4522.1200
X-MimeOLE: Produced By Microsoft MimeOLE V5.50.4522.1200
X-Scanner: exiscan *172IPO-0000Ox-00*fm5ca87OlbE* (Simonbars ISP -
http://www.simonbarsisp.net/)
```

The above full header is from an e-mail I sent to myself, with a few names changed to protect the innocent. I created it on my computer, whom I call "HAL." My username is Simonbar and my Internet Service Provider is simonbarsISP.net. If you scan the header now, you'll already begin to see where I might've caused it to look different had I taken certain steps before I sent the e-mail. For example, "HAL" on the fourth line down could just as easily have been "MADAMECURIE" or "TRACETHISANDDIE." What else could have been altered? Well, the subject "TEST," of course—no big revelation there. More significantly, the info after "From:" on the eighth line down could have read AgentX@X.X or just about anything else for that matter. There are more significant things that can be forged with more difficulty, but those will be better explained after a brief discussion of what can't be forged.

So, what's going on, exactly, with this header? The header compilation process begins when you first create your e-mail. As soon as you hit "compose" or "new mail," certain information is immediately gathered for entry into the header. This information consists of things you designated in your computer when you first installed your e-mail program and may have subsequently updated. Among them: your user name, your "real" name, your computer's name, and your e-mail address.

Username: The "simonbar" in simonbar@isp.net. This is the name you chose when you signed up with your ISP.

"Real" name: When you set up your e-mail program, you'll either be asked for this, or the install program will find and use the name you previously gave to the computer as your own (such as during setup of your operating system). I

say "real" name because many people either leave this blank, abbreviate it, or use a nickname or "handle." (A quick side note: Pay attention to what a person reveals about him or herself when choosing a username or alias. For example, NASCARfreak, ganjaman, and jerseygirl contain clues about each persons' habits, lifestyle, and location.)

Computer's name: You can give your computer a name if it is set up on a network or the network settings are otherwise enabled. As mentioned, I call my computer HAL. Even though it's not part of a specific workgroup, it's still on a network when I am logged on to the Internet. The computer name could be helpful to a prosecutor trying to prove an e-mail came from a certain computer. For example, what if the computer was named RicksCompaq? If the alleged perp in the case is named Rick and he owns a Compaq computer, these facts could be used as circumstantial evidence to support a case.

E-mail address: When you set up your account, the install program put this as your "reply to" address by default. You can, however, change it if you wish people to reply to you at a different address. A spammer (person who sends unsolicited e-mail) may include a phony e-mail on this line so you can't reply to him and tell him how much you hate unsolicited e-mail.

You would think that a person who hates unsolicited e-mail enough to alter his "reply to" address would be sensitive enough to not send unsolicited e-mails to others. Not the case. I have so much loathing for these cretins that I strongly encourage you to hone your e-mail tracing skills by tracing spam and forwarding the e-mail (with all header info) to the appropriate abuse department of the true sender's ISP (usually abuse@sendersISP.net/com/org). In fact, that's exactly how I learned how to trace e-mails. Once you get good at it, your complaint can be sent to the appropriate department within minutes after receiving the spam. It is rewarding when, every so often, you get an update from the abuse department that your spammer's account has been terminated.

But I digress. Spammers have that effect on me . . . .

After your e-mail program instantly compiles all of the above info for the full header, you then begin adding to the partial header that appears onscreen at the top of every e-mail message you initiate. You do this by typing in the recipient's name, e-mail address, and subject. All these things—along with whatever else your e-mail program likes to include, such as its name and version number—eventually wind up in the full header. After you type in your message and click send, your computer "stamps" certain header info at the top of the e-mail and sends it.

If you're like most Internet users and have no further control of any servers along the way (some folks do, as you'll see), your e-mail then goes to your ISP's mail server, which probably has a cute name of its own. Your ISP's mail server will add its two cents worth to the e-mail by including various information, which may even include the mail server's cute name. But the line you, as a detective, should be most interested in is the one that reads "Received:" Every server that deals with an e-mail stamps this line at the top to tell you when it received the e-mail and from where it was received.

A Received line cannot be altered. The logical assumption, then, is that an e-mail's true source can be determined by the information found in the very bottom Received line. (Remember, the e-mails are stamped at the very top so the first server that stamped it will have the last Received in the series.) This assumption would be incorrect. Even though they cannot be altered, Received lines can be *added* by a savvy spammer. To throw you off track, a knowledgeable spammer may pass his e-mails through a router that he has named gw.yahoo.com or something equally innocuous.

But just for the moment, let us suppose that the common misconception is true—since it usually is—and the bottommost line contains the information you seek. What information in it, exactly, is useful? Let's take the one from our previous example:

Received: from customer-12-345-678-90.dialup.simonbarsisp.net (HAL) [12.345.678.90]
    by roland.simonbarsisp.net with smtp (Exim 3.35 #1 (Debian))
    id 172lPO-0000Ox-00; Wed, 01 May 2002 00:08:02 -0400

If you're lucky you'll have an actual web site name such as simonbarisp.net, in which case you can save a step in the investigative process. [1] What would you do with this information? Well, if you were simply reporting an abusive spammer, you would forward the spammer's e-mail to simonbarsisp.net's abuse department. In most cases, you can report abuse to abuse@whoever.com, "whoever" being the name of the actual ISP in question. To be certain you're reporting abuse to the correct department, simply go to www.whoever.com and find out how best to contact their abuse department.

WHAT IS WHOIS?

What if you wanted to learn more about simonbarsisp.net? What if you wanted to write the owner? To do this, a detective would use a WhoIs server.

WhoIs is a domain name server (DNS) lookup utility. Once upon a time, a detective could go to www.internic.com and ask the WhoIs server who is jillett.com. The server would then spill its guts and tell you what you needed to know about jillett.com. If you've used this service before, you may have noticed that it's changed in recent years and no longer seems to give you any useful information.

Why? On December 1, 1999, Network Solutions began redirecting port 43 WhoIs service from rs.internic.net over to whois.nsiregistry.net. This techno mumbo-jumbo was the result of legal quarreling over Network Solutions' monopolistic position as DNS registrar. Registrar competition opened up, and a shared registry system was established. This means that the Internic WhoIs server began storing registrar information only. If you wanted further information on a particular registrant such as jillett.com, you had to get it directly from the entity that registered jillett.com.

If this all sounds confusing, that's because it was. Detectives were being bounced all over the Internet just to do a simple WhoIs query. Fortunately, programmers got on the ball immediately. They knew people had a need to seamlessly bypass all this legal flotsam and get the information that Internic's WhoIs server used to provide. Today there are some very good WhoIs servers that do all the digging for you. They return not only the registrar but also the actual contact info for a given domain just like Internic used to do. (See Table 7.1.)

You'll notice from Table 7.1 that the bottom four WhoIs servers deal directly with the registrar's name server and provide you the info you'd otherwise have to go digging for. Internic only provides you the registrar and refers you to the registrar's name server, which you probably won't be able to log into without a username and password. For you programmers in our midst, www.phpwhois.org maintains open php source code that does all this work. I'd recommend using the source code to maintain a WhoIs lookup on your own site. Even if you're not a programmer, reading through the source code explanations will enable you to see exactly what's involved these days in finding contact info for a given domain.

USING TRACEROUTE

How else could Received information be useful? Well, let's suppose the e-mail is from a runaway daughter to a sympathetic sibling. You go to www.simonbarsisp.net and learn they are a small ISP serving northern New Hampshire. You immediately know to call the investigator you dispatched to Las Vegas and redirect his ass to northern New Hampshire.

Not too shabby.

But what if you have only a string of cryptic numbers rather than an actual ISP? A firm understanding of exactly what those numbers are would be most helpful. So, what are they?

TABLE 7.1 WhoIs Providers	
WhoIs Provider	**Information Returned**
www.internic.com	Registrar and registrar's name server
www.phpwhois.org	Registrant contact info & Registrar
www.onewhois.com	Registrant contact info & Registrar
www.betterwhois.com	Registrant contact info & Registrar
www.accesswhois.com	Registrant contact info & Registrar

Every computer on a network needs a unique ID so it can be distinguished from every other computer on the network. When you log onto the Internet, your computer becomes part of a vast network and is assigned a unique ID, even if only temporarily. Networks do this so when someone sends you an e-mail, a chat invitation, or if the network otherwise needs to transact with your computer, it can do so without confusion.

A web site is really just a computer permanently set up on a network so people can access its information anytime. Every web site, therefore, has a unique identifier. In actuality, it's more accurate to say that every web *server* has a unique identifier. It's possible a web server may host several sites and break down its server space accordingly, assigning internal IDs to the individual sites. But to make things easier for now, just think of each web site as having its own identifier. The identifier is expressed as a group of four numbers, each from 0 to 255, separated by periods.

Now let's say you had a few favorite web sites and wanted to visit them often and talk with other people about them. It would certainly get cumbersome and confusing to ask your friends, "Hey, have you been to 127.0.0.1 [2] lately?" So the Internet allows a way to nickname all these sites. For example jillett.com points to 63.251.213.16. [3] Jillett.com is the domain name.

But in order for everybody else in the world to know that jillett.com points to 63.251.213.16, this information needs to be stored somewhere. It's stored on a domain name server, or DNS. Every ISP has access to a DNS that is constantly updated. As you may have already guessed, someone looking for jillett.com never needs to know that it is actually 63.251.213.16—their web browser and ISP do all the detective work for them. This brings us back to we detectives who wish to do the work ourselves—except in reverse—to learn the true sender of an e-mail.

In a world of greedy corporate conglomerates, an e-mail-tracing detective will seldom be lucky enough to find a small ISP as the source of an e-mail. More often you will find that an e-mail was sent via a big company such as mediaone.net or attbb.net. If this happens, you would say to yourself, "AT&T Broadband service? They're all over the place. This e-mail could've been sent from anywhere!"

You'd be right. So a detective would have to look at the next clue: that cryptic sequence of gobbledygook in the same Received line. It might look like this:

gob.l-d.gook.bos1.websrv.attbb.net [123.456.78.90]

Believe it or not, this garble is all useful. Somewhere in the world a server named gob.l-d.gook.bos1.websrv.attbb.net is sitting in a quiet room of a nondescript building of some industrial park or university. Unless the e-mail sender is a very advanced computer hacker, you can bet he or she lives in the area served by that server. This might be a big area, maybe consisting of several towns, but you will have at least narrowed things down that far.

But what is the area? To determine this, you could go to your favorite traceroute server on the Internet and punch in the server name or, easier, the sequence of numbers 123.456.78.90. Traceroute is a program that traces the likely route an e-mail might take as it works its way across the Internet. You can have traceroute running as a program on your computer or you can use your favorite search engine to find dozens of traceroute servers across the Internet. Geektools.com has a fairly comprehensive listing of traceroute sources.

Traceroute will spit out a series of servers between it and the server you typed in or between you and the server you typed in, depending on what you asked it to do. (Your options will vary depending on what Traceroute server you're using.) Either way doesn't matter. You're interested in the last few servers only because they are honing in on the source. These appear at the bottom of the list.

A nice feature of traceroute is that it returns the server name and its IP address. So if you only had an IP address (that series of four numbers separated by decimal points), this is a good way to get the server name. This is important because you are looking for clues as to the geographic location of the ultimate server, which can sometimes be derived from the server name. For example, tracing an e-mail back to me, you might see the letters "BOS" for "Boston" in the final server names. This is possible due to server naming conventions established by the networking industry, which were adopted to make network maintenance and troubleshooting easier for technicians.

When it comes to naming conventions, there are two schools of thought. Some network engineers don't use them at all. Rather, they obfuscate the name so a potential attacker cannot derive any information about the server from it. Most network engineers, however, realize that an obfuscated server name is only a minor speed bump to a hacker but a major inconvenience for network maintenance. Therefore they use naming conventions, but they are careful not to be too obvious with what the names tell about the server. For example, you'd never see bos1.creditCardNumbers.attbb.net.

Although naming conventions are by no means standardized throughout the industry, you are likely to encounter servers that specify their geographical locations with airport codes, city names, city abbreviations, two-letter U.S. state abbreviations, and international country codes. For example, ALTER.NET (a domain name used by UUNET, a part of MCI/WorldCom) names some of their router interfaces with three-letter airport codes as shown at the bottom of the page. [4]

By this time, you might be thinking that it would be nice if the exact geographic locations of every Internet server were available in a comprehensive database. You could then narrow down a sender's location to more than just a general area such as Boston. I once thought the same thing; even began compiling my own database as I solved cases. But I always kept an eye out for a software company that would do all this work for me. Finally, I found one.

VISUALWARE

Visualware is my all-time hero in the e-mail tracing software business. They have two products invaluable to the modern detective: e-mailTrackerPro and VisualRoute. Using them in combination will show you the geographic location of every server an e-mail passed through on its way to you.

Imagine an e-mail tracking program that not only interprets all the header information for you but also determines whether the bottommost Received line contains a registered domain or was added by the sender's personal router to throw off a recipient's investigation. That's what e-

---

193.ATM8-0-0.GW2.EWR1.ALTER.NET (EWR = Newark, NJ)
190.ATM8-0-0.GW3.BOS1.ALTER.NET (BOS = Boston, MA)
199.ATM6-0.XR1.ATL1.ALTER.NET (ATL = Atlanta, GA)

mailTrackerPro does for you. It completely analyzes the header info and flags anything that might be a forgery. Ultimately, it will tell you the e-mail's true origin. And E-mailTrackerPro has a hot button that invokes its sister component, VisualRoute.

VisualRoute has an actual, scalable map of the globe that shows you the actual path (rather than a probably one) an e-mail followed to its destination. Even if the sender used a service such as Hotmail or Yahoo!, they can still be pinpointed geographically. VisualRoute lists in a table every server the e-mail passed through along its way. It provides popup WhoIs information so you can direct inquiries or spam complaints to the appropriate party. Click on any server and a box will pop up showing you its coordinates.

These two Visualware packages are so user friendly, they are best demonstrated via pictures. Please see Screenshots 7.1 and 7.2 and their accompanying captions. A live demo of VisualRoute and fully functioning demos of both packages are available on-line at www.visualware.com. I highly recommend visiting this site and learning about all of their software.

In the future, expect to see more graphical traceroute software become available, including 3-D global router mapping. During my research I was able to find some other packages. WhereIsIP was not nearly as user-friendly as Visualware's products and did not seem to pinpoint the server hops very well. McAfee's VisualTrace, formerly Neoworx NeoTrace Pro, did not offer demo versions or even screenshots of the products on its web site. You can find information about GTrace at www.caida.org/tools/visualization/gtrace, which seems to be an ongoing project that looks promising. I did not download it because the files were compressed in the arcane .tar format, indicating to me that the software was not yet ready for prime time.

FINAL NOTES ON MANUAL E-MAIL TRACKING

I will leave you with some final thoughts on e-mail tracking and tracing. It is an important topic, among the most important in this book. Refer to the notes below in the future to refresh your mind as to this chapter's key points and to avoid the traps and pitfalls that spammers,

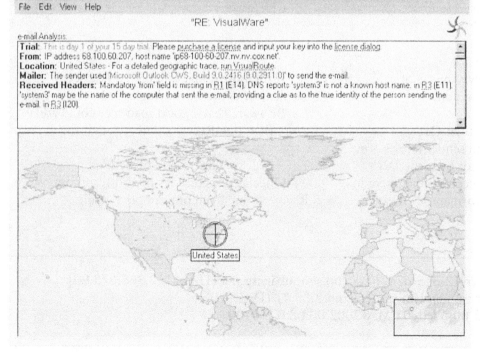

Screenshot 7.1. Copy the full header information of any e-mail you want to analyze and select File, Import Headers. E-mailTrackerPro will automatically begin analyzing the header information and a report will appear in the top pane.

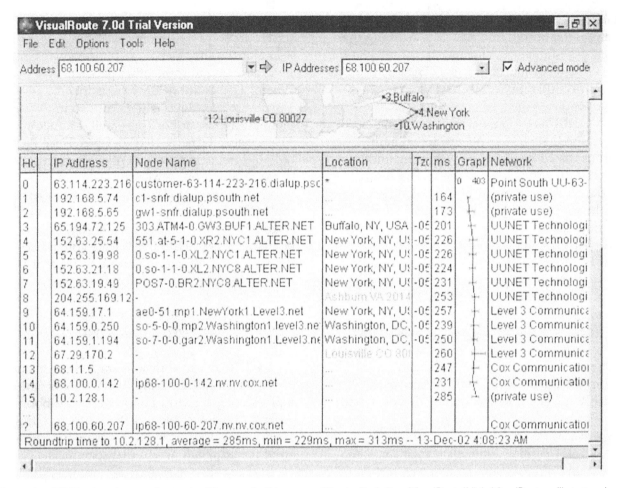

Screenshot 7.2. To view the complete path of the e-mail, click on e-mailTrackerPro's "run VisualRoute" link. VisualRoute will start and automatically begin its node-to-node analysis of the e-mail. You can see the major hops in the upper pane and view the complete analysis in the lower pane. Click on the individual fields to get more information such as the latitude and longitude of the city where the server is located and popup WhoIs information.

hackers, and computer-savvy subjects of your investigations might throw at you.

Don't Be Thrown Off

If you suspect the e-mail sender knows how to obscure his identity, do not trust the DNS name in the bottommost Received line; it could intentionally contain misinformation. Always trace the IP address.

If the bottommost Received line seems suspicious, use the next one up.

Be aware that a good spammer could add more than one Received line, though this is rare.

Time Zone of Sender

Once again, consider the bottommost Received line from our sample e-mail:

Received: from customer-12-345-678-90.dialup.simonbarsisp.net (HAL) [12.345.678.90]
    by roland.simonbarsisp.net with smtp (Exim 3.35 #1 (Debian))
    id 172lPO-0000Ox-00; Wed, 01 May 2002 00:08:02 -0400

Notice the day, date, and time stamp at the end of the last line. I sent this e-mail from the U.S. east coast, which is five hours earlier than Greenwich Mean Time (GMT), also known as Universal Time (UT). This is reflected in the time stamp. Each hour of adjustment from GMT indicates 15 degrees of longitude. A negative adjustment (–01:00) would be 15 degrees longitude west of Greenwich, England (this specific example would be very useful, as few places fall into this time zone), and a positive adjustment (+01:00) would be 15 degrees longitude east of Greenwich, England. In our example, the server decided to adjust for daylight savings time by adding an hour.

Learn your time zones and this will be a quick way to narrow down your subject's location, at least longitudinally. The standard time zone deviations from GMT for the United States are:

- Eastern–05:00 hrs.
- Central–06:00 hrs.
- Mountain–07:00 hrs.
- Pacific–08:00 hrs.

An e-mail originating in the Greenwich time zone would have a deviation of 00:00, and most of Europe and Asia would have positive (+xx:00) deviations.

Final Tips Courtesy of Visualware.com

• *Quick time zone check:* To quickly look up a time zone, go into Windows Control Panel and click the Time/Date icon.

• *X-Mailer:* This line in the full header field will usually tell you the e-mail sender's mailer software. Consider:

10: X-Mailer: QUALCOMM Windows Eudora Pro Version 4.1

This may or may not be immediately useful, but it can be very useful if there is a follow-up investigation by authorities.

• *X-Originating-IP:* If you are attempting to track down an e-mail received from a Hotmail e-mail account, look for the X-Originating-IP header field, which will tell you the IP address of the computer that sent the e-mail. Consider:

1: Received: from hotmail.com (f105.pav1.hotmail.com [64.4.31.105]) by s2.xyz.com (8.11.6) id f9BIvve34655; Thu, 11 Oct 2001 12:58:00 -0600 (MDT)
2: Received: from mail pickup service by hotmail.com with Microsoft SMTPSVC;
3: Thu, 11 Oct 2001 11:57:51 -0700
4: Received: from 202.156.2.147 by pv1fd.pav1.hotmail.msn.com with HTTP;
5: Thu, 11 Oct 2001 18:57:51 GMT
6: X-Originating-IP: [202.156.2.147]

Notice that we could have obtained the same IP address information by examining the Received header field. But it is nice to have this extra confirmation.

FINAL WARNINGS

Please pay attention to these warnings when attempting to track e-mail messages:

Host names vs. IP addresses: Always base your tracking decisions on the IP addresses that you find in the header information and not on host names (which are a lookup from the IP address anyway). Mapping an IP address into a host name and then back into an IP address may yield a different IP address.

False header information: Once again, be aware that spammers may try to insert fake Received header lines into the headers of the e-mail message to confuse you. Just follow the trail through the Received header fields from mail server to mail server, and use some common sense when the information makes no sense.

False IP address: The IP address where you finally end up is the IP address of the computer that sent the e-mail. But is that computer the real sender? Maybe it was a computer that was broken into so that a false e-mail could be sent. Or the sender could try to hide behind an "anonymizer" service, in which case you will get the IP address of the anonymizer company.

IP addresses change: Do not assume that the sender's computer has a fixed, constant IP address. This may be true in some cases, but most people who dial into the Internet almost always get a different IP address each and every time they connect. However, all is not lost. Many times you can report the IP address and full e-mail Internet headers (which many times contain time-of-day information) to the person's ISP, which can then track down to a unique end user (by examining login and logout logs) and take action.

Viruses: Do not assume the worst of the person sending the e-mail. They may have just been infected with a virus, which is using that person's computer to spread itself. Having said that, I must admit that there have been occasions where I was miffed at friends for leaving themselves open to computer virus infections, which then came uncomfortably close to infecting my computer. Nobody should wantonly forward e-mails of unknown origin or fail to maintain updated virus protection on their computer.

Open mail servers: Do not assume the worst of the company whose mail server was used to send the original e-mail. They may be involved in the spam, but they also may just have a misconfigured e-mail server, which is allowing a spammer to send the e-mail through their mail server.

ENDNOTES

[1] This assumes you trust the information—for example, if you know the e-mail was sent by an amateur or somebody who hasn't forged the header lines. When in doubt, use the IP address.

[2] A reserved IP address that points to "localhost," i.e., one's own computer.

[3] 63.251.213.16 is the lunar.powweb.com web server, which hosts many sites. PowWeb internally routes a visitor to jillett.com.

[4] Source: www.caida.org

CHAPTER 8: Computer Forensics

"When you go looking for something specific, your chances of finding it are very bad . . . . When you go looking for anything at all, your chances of finding it are very good."
—Daryl Zero

Anybody who goes to the movies or watches television can't help but realize that the Computer Age has given detectives a lot of new toys and gadgets to help solve crimes. In fact, if you are partial to some of the more educational programming TV has to offer, you will have seen that the Computer Age has dramatically enhanced—if not outright revolutionized—not only the way detectives process crime scenes for forensic evidence but how such evidence is subsequently analyzed, interpreted, and even stored.

In planning this chapter, I decided to limit its scope. Topics like computer-assisted geographic profiling or using the FBI's automated fingerprint identification system (AFIS) could fill entire volumes unto themselves. Cable TV shows like *Forensic Files, FBI Files,* and *The New Detectives* will give you an idea of how investigators use these modern tools to solve cases. I also drew the line here because the above topics, while extremely interesting, will not likely affect the private practices of most people reading this book. This chapter's focus, therefore, will be on a field of forensics that *is* likely to affect most of you: computer forensics.

What exactly is computer forensics? It is the science of locating hidden, deleted, or destroyed data in a computer that can be used as evidence in a court of law. Just as microscopic fibers and flakes of dander hold invaluable clues to a crime, so do the intangible bits of data stored on computer disks and memory chips.

It may seem an awesome prospect that a cryptic stream of bits might contain in it the incontrovertible sequence of ones and zeroes that will ultimately allow the state to lethally inject one of its citizens as punishment for a crime. But it wasn't too long ago when some of us were equally awed that a microscopic strand of polyester could send a man to the electric chair.

What evidence might a criminal leave on a computer? The same evidence he might leave on a piece of paper, just as countless criminals have done over the years, including:

- A second set of bookkeeping entries
- A threatening letter
- Plans to the inside of a bank
- Names and addresses of accomplices
- Correspondence with accomplices

Some criminals even keep journal entries of their crimes. This is not as uncommon as you may think. Guilt is a strong motivating force in our society. When a criminal feels he has no one to talk to about his acts, confessional writing is often the only method of releasing his pent-up angst. In pre-Computer Age times, a tension-relieving burst of chicken scratches on notepaper would invariably end up in the criminal's fireplace after the act of writing it made him feel better. Such written confessions were short-lived, and detectives certainly couldn't count on finding them.

But here is another instance where the Computer Age has the potential to make our lives easier—if the old-schoolers among us would only wake up and smell the electrons. Today's criminals are more likely to do their confessional writing on a computer. Rather than throw his cathartic creation into the fireplace, he simply deletes the file.

Another case of short-lived evidence that we detectives will seldom see? Nope. The criminal's unwavering faith in his delete key is his Achilles' heel. His belief that he has forever erased information from his computer gives him a false sense of security. More often than not, the information the criminal believes he's deleted is still buried in his computer system, intact and accessible.

Where can such information reside? The criminal's own hard disk for starters, a network server halfway around the globe, even 150 miles above the earth in a geosynchronous satellite. Some places where a Computer Age detective may find the goods on his subject include:

- Floppy drive
- Rewritable CD-ROM
- Tape drive
- Zip drive
- Removable hard drive
- Flash drive
- Flash RAM
- SmartMedia (digital cameras)
- CMOS data area (stored passwords, etc.)
- Network disk
- Local e-mail server
- Sender's ISP e-mail server
- Receiver's ISP e-mail server
- Receiver's computer, network drive, server, etc.

How does the science of computer forensics apply to you, the Computer Age private investigator? Using an embezzlement scheme as an example, the simplest application of computer forensics would go something like this.

Your subject leaves a telling file on his computer's hard drive. The file is in plain view. In fact it's a spreadsheet called cookedbooks.xls and it resides in a subdirectory labeled Hide_From_IRS. You copy the file to a floppy, present it as evidence in court, and you're a hero for a day.

This could actually happen. Incredibly, many people believe that the information on their computer will only be seen by them. Further, they think, "Hey, if I ever think the FBI is lurking outside my office, well, I'll just delete the files before they can get a warrant." Here I'll interject two quick things for any embezzlers who may be reading this. First, you won't see the FBI. They didn't get to be FBI agents by living a vivid existence. Second, you've probably already guessed that a deleted file—especially a freshly deleted file—is easily recovered.

Now I feel I must interject a not-so-quick detour. As I write, I realize that the computer literacy of those who will read this is going to cover an extremely wide range. I'm sure one reader (perhaps you) is already saying, "Damn this BS! I know a deleted file can easily be recovered. When is Bud going to get to the good stuff?" I'm equally sure another reader (perhaps you) is saying, "What the f!#* is a *subdirectory?*"

This wide-range-of-computer-literacy problem is a phenomenon particular to a few industries, ours being one. By comparison, the accounting industry does not have this problem. Once the first spreadsheet program, Visicalc, hit the market around 1980, an accountant either learned how to use a computer or he went back to college to learn another trade.

In 1980, the private investigation industry did not have the adapt-to-computers-or-die problem. Back then, it was too easy to ignore computers and go about our business without missing a beat. In fact, the syndrome did not rush upon us at all; rather, it waddled in like a baffled mother duck that should have six ducklings but only counts five.

In 1980, if a young upstart in a private detective firm finessed the requisition of an Apple II, the older investigators promptly relegated it to doorstop or paperweight status upon its arrival and went about their business the old-fashioned way. Many of those investigators are still cemented in their ways, and some of them still have Apple IIs propping open their office doors in case a customer accidentally wanders in. They think an iMac is a new type of fast-food burger.

But the once-upon-a-time upstart who convinced his boss to okay the purchase of the Apple II—the same upstart who lifted the computer from its relegated post and allowed the office door to fall closed after his last remaining officemate went home to his wife—the same upstart who then plugged that computer in, slid in a 5 1/4 inch floppy, and typed up his daily report—he's still around. He enjoys the lion's share of the investigative market.

Thus we have a wide range of computer literacy in our industry. So, those of you who already know that a deleted file is easily recovered from the recycle bin may wish to scan ahead to the more complex issues. If you have an Apple II holding down the dusty papers in your "In" box, keep reading.

EASY UNDELETES

Here's the case: Your client is part owner of a driving school. He's computer illiterate but his partner is not, so his partner does the books. His partner just bought a BMW while your client drives a Taurus. Each partner has a non-working wife, and each wife stays home to keep the house and care for two school-age children. They started the business using all their available capital and became 50-50 partners. They were both middle-class citizens when they began the business, and neither has ever worked a second job.

Your client has had vague suspicions about his partner for the past year or two, but since they are old friends, he brushed the suspicions aside, even blamed himself for being an untrusting friend. Then came the BMW.

And there was more. The Friday evening following the arrival of the new luxury car, your client returned to the office to pick up a bouquet he'd bought for his wife but had forgotten to take when he'd left for home. When he returned to the office, he saw his partner working on the computer, which was not unusual since he regularly did the bookkeeping on Fridays. But his partner seemed overly surprised to see him return. He'd seemed flustered and offered an unnecessary explanation for being in the office. "I'm just getting caught up with the books," he'd said. Seems like an innocent enough statement, but your client thought it was odd since after 20 years in business together, the partner had no need to explain anything. That oddity, the BMW, and a host of other subtle

clues that we humans usually consign to intuition led your client to call a detective agency the next day—yours.

During the initial interview, your client suddenly remembers something, as if recalling a previously forgotten detail from a strange dream. When he'd entered the office last evening, he remembered seeing in his peripheral vision a flutter of uncharacteristic finger fumbling, as if his partner suddenly needed to perform an unexpected task on the computer. Your client asks, "You think I surprised him?"

Of course, your years as an investigator have taught you to let the client solve as much of the case for you as possible. You ask a few more questions and learn that the two men left the office together a few minutes later. The partner was running late; he had told his wife and kids they'd leave Friday evening for a weekend trip. Your client says he had a preoccupied look on his face as he shut down the computer.

You, of course, should tell your client to take you to the office immediately so you can examine that computer. But you don't. Instead you look at the old Apple II propping open the door, turn back to your potential client with an apologetic expression, and embarrassingly confess that you are a computer illiterate.

Now, let's make sure that never happens again.

Here's the better scenario. Since you are not computer illiterate, you turn to him and say, "My fee is $150 an hour plus expenses. Sign this standard contract and we'll go to your office right now while your partner is gone for the weekend. I can then thoroughly examine that computer." He agrees and takes you to his office.

You astonish your client by knowing where the PC's power-on switch is. You nod knowledgeably at the barrage of messages scrolling up the monitor during the power-on self-test (POST), even though it's as Greek to you as it is to him. He looks upon you as a god. The Windows desktop appears.

Then, a little message box pops up asking you for your password. Panic. You say, "Er, does your partner have any grandchildren?"

Your client says, "One."

"Name?"

Your client tells you the grandchild's name and you type it in. Password accepted. [1]

You double-click the Recycle Bin icon and a list of files pops up. You click the "date deleted" field header and sort the files by date, most recent to oldest. You see that a file named BooksAdjust.xls was deleted from the accounting subdirectory last night. You note the time the file was deleted, right-click the file name, and click restore.

Using Windows Explorer or My Computer, you copy the restored file to a floppy disk that you brought with you because you're such a genius. You reset the system clock to yesterday's date at the time the file was deleted and delete the file again so the partner will find things as he'd left them if he ever were to look. You reset the system clock to the correct time, start Excel, and read the BooksAdjust.xls file from the floppy drive.

You scan the spreadsheet, find an interesting number, and ask your client, "Did you receive a dividend check for $5,000 last month?"

"Yes," says your client.

"So did your partner," you say.

"No kidding," says client. "It's what we always do."

You say, "Did you receive a second check for "$3,500?"

"What?"

"Your partner did."

Your client begins to shake.

"Did you spend $8,500 in payroll to driving instructors last month?"

"Well," says client. "We have three instructors and each one makes $20,000 per year, so that's $60,000 divided by 12, so we should have spent $5,000."

"Says here you spent $8,500."

And so on. You bag the partner embezzling $3,500 per month by offsetting it with an inflated payroll line item, hence the BMW. It's an age-old scheme. Not a difficult assignment, but one you couldn't have accepted without understanding how to use a personal computer.

The foregoing case was contrived and stripped down to make a point. Sure you'll solve an occasional case by browsing the good ol' recycle bin or even by looking through recently viewed documents, but you'll need a grander bag of cybertricks to thrive as a private investigator in the Computer Age.

HARD-CORE COMPUTER FORENSICS

What are the hard-core aspects of computer forensics? This could range from undeleting a file that has been "permanently" deleted from the recycle bin all the way to a bit-by-bit data parsing of a reformatted hard disk.

There is a pretty decent book that overviews many advanced data recovery techniques. It's a quick and dirty manual, but it's accurate and inexpensive so I see no point in rehashing it here. It's entitled *Disk Detective* [2] by Norbert Zaenglein. Topics range from undeleting files to recovering information from reformatted disks. *Disk Detective* was published in 1998, making it practically ancient by Computer Age standards. But I still highly recommend it. It will help you understand the structure of data on a computer disk, which is invaluable information.

Computer Forensics Software

If the Computer Age has opened up an entire new field called computer forensics, then of course it answered its own call with software that does the investigative work for you.

While researching this chapter, I looked for demo versions of computer forensic software that would find hidden and deleted files on my own computer. There were a few companies that seemed as if they had good products, but their demos were either web or CD-ROM based and did not operate on my actual hard drive or floppy drives. My goal was to find software that would locate and undelete files that I knew to exist on my hard drive from a previous format—that is, a file that survived repartitioning, reformatting, and reloading a new operating system onto my hard drive.

My plan was to set up one of my old computers, put some "important files" on it, then repartition, reformat, and reload Windows onto the drive to see which computer forensics packages would be able to find the files that were supposed to no longer exist. Circumstances conspired, and I never had to set up a computer for this purpose. Somehow, one of my computers became infected with the Monkey_B virus. I reformatted the drive and, while doing so, added several disk partitions because I had a copy of Linux I wanted to set up as a second operating system.

Once the drive was repartitioned and reformatted and reloaded with Windows and Linux, I struggled with it for weeks. It just wouldn't work right. I kept getting messages that there was a problem with the boot sector of the hard drive. Scandisk wouldn't work right, and when it worked at all, it kept marking sections of my hard drive "bad" even though I strongly suspected they weren't. The computer crashed all the time. I finally got fed up. I changed the drive back to a single DOS partition, reformatted, cleared the master boot record in case part of the virus was still in there, and reloaded my system *again*.

Shortly after that I decided to try out computer forensic demos on that same computer to see if any of them could find even one of my old files. I was very skeptical that anything could be found after two disparate partitioning schemes, a boot sector virus, a foreign operating system, and two reformats.

The first software I tried that met my criteria was called FileRecovery for Windows by LC Technologies International (LCTI). The demo version is fully functional except that recovered file size is limited to 10 kilobytes. To remove this limitation, you must register the software. You can demo it yourself at www.lc-tech.com.

FileRecovery is one utility in LCTI's Forensic Utility Suite, which includes:

- FileRecovery for Windows
- PhotoRecovery for Digital Media
- RecoverNT

FileRecovery is essentially a very advanced undelete utility that can undelete files that have been removed from the recycle bin, among other things. PhotoRecovery can recover lost images from Smart Media, CompactFlash, Memory Sticks, SD Cards CD, MiniDisk, or almost any other type of media used by digital cameras. RecoverNT is the most powerful tool. If you accidentally reformat your hard drive, you can recover most of your files with it. Because all of the tools in the Forensic Utility Suite are noninvasive, recovered files must be saved to another drive.

Using FileRecovery and its sister utilities, you can make a thorough analysis of your subject's computer environment by retrieving all possible evidence that may exist on digital media, whether it's a floppy disk, smart card, computer system, or network attached storage. LCTI's utilities allow you to perform these analyses according to U.S. Department of Justice guidelines. These include:

- Protecting the computer system from alteration, damage, data corruption, or virus introduction during the forensic examination.
- Finding and recording all files on the system. This includes currently active files, deleted yet remaining files, hidden files, password-protected files, and encrypted files.
- Recovering deleted files.
- Revealing the contents of hidden files as well as temporary or swap files used by both the application programs and the operating system.
- Analyzing all potentially relevant data found in special areas of a disk. This includes what is called "unallocated disk space" as well as "slack space" in a file. [3]

The ability of LCTI's utilities to view data stored in unallocated and slack space is of particular interest. Slack space is space on a hard drive that has been allocated to a newer file but not entirely used up by it. Let's say your perpetrator is part of a terrorist network. He had a file named AlqedaCellsUS.txt that listed all the al-Qaeda terrorist cell locations across the United States. When the U.S. government turned up the heat after September 11, 2001, your perpetrator decided to overwrite that file in case the government seized his computer. He deleted all the info in the file except for one letter, [4] saved it, then renamed it to nothing.txt to be sure the valuable information was gone forever.

Unbeknownst to your perpetrator, virtually all of the information he thought he'd destroyed still resides on his hard drive. Where is it? Well, for a small text file most of it is still in his slack space, which is preserved as long as he keeps nothing.txt on his hard drive. In a way, he's helped you by locking the allocation unit so you can eventually find the incriminating evidence.

You see, to run efficiently, a computer operating system allocates disk space in controlled portions. Windows 95, for example, allocates one kilobyte at a time. This is equal to a text file of about 1,000 characters long. If your perp overwrote this space with one character, all of the other characters are still there. They can't be viewed by regular software, such as word processors, because such software does not look at the slack space. Specialized computer forensics software, however, does look at this space.

What about larger files? If your perp overwrote a larger file with one character, there would still be about one kilobyte's worth of that file saved in slack space. The rest of the file would be returned to unallocated disk space, which is also viewable by computer forensics software. The thing to keep in mind about file remnants in unallocated disk space is that they disappear in whole or in part once the space gets allocated to another file. This may or may not ever happen, depending on how your subject uses the computer and how old the deleted file is. As a general rule, the more your subject stores on his computer and the older the deleted file is, the more likely it has been truly overwritten by new files. However, if your perp uses his computer mostly for e-mail and surfing the Internet, deleted files may remain recoverable by computer forensics software for a long time.

So what of my experience with FileRecovery for Windows? It was a successful one. FileRecovery did indeed find files that had been deleted and then reformatted over twice! One such file was more than three years old.

So what else can the Forensic Utility Suite do? According to promotional literature and confirmed by my testing, it:

- Recovers deleted files from such media as hard drives, floppy drives, digital camera programs, and other types of removable media.
- Recovers files that have been deleted, whether by DOS command line, program file menu, or desktop navigator such as Windows Explorer—even after being removed from the Recycle Bin.
- Scans the drive and brings up a list of recoverable files.
- Operates in a nondestructive read-only manner and does not write or make changes to the drive it is recovering from.
- Runs under the Windows 95/98/Me/ NT 2000/XP operating systems.
- Supports all partitions using FAT 12, FAT 16, FAT 32, and all versions of NTFS file systems.
- Scans all volumes in a local machine and builds a directory tree of all deleted files.
- Searches deleted files matching file name criteria.
- Accesses network and other installed peripherals such as Zip, SyQuest, and external hard drives.

Please note that FileRecovery is *not* able to find data on a physically damaged drive. Nor does it work on NTFS drives that are compressed or encrypted.

THE FUTURE OF COMPUTER FORENSICS

Many decades ago, before fingerprint identification technology had undergone its many revolutions, criminals never wore gloves. They committed their dastardly deeds believing that all they needed to do was avoid being seen. Eventually, there were a few newspaper reports about how certain people were convicted with the help of fingerprint evidence. Criminals, upon hearing of these accounts, dismissed them as scientific trickery, mere aberrations in justice that the courts would never uphold. Criminals

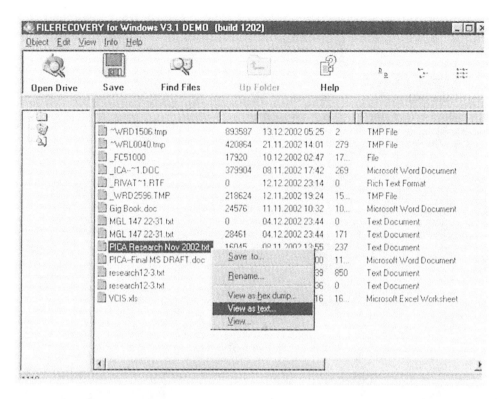

Screenshot 8.1. The demo version of FileRecovery for Windows is fully functional except that it will only recover files up to 10 kilobytes.

continued to commit their iniquitous improprieties gloveless and, in increasing numbers, were caught and convicted by their own fingerprints.

This is where we are now with computer forensics. There have been scattered news reports of criminals, usually pedophiles and child pornographers, being convicted with the help of computer forensic evidence. Most criminals currently disregard such reports, believing the information on their computer is safe and can be readily deleted if the authorities should begin to suspect them.

A few criminals, however, are getting wise and donning Computer Age gloves. Software programs that guarantee clean deletes and reformats are already available. Soon, giving a suspect any advance warning, even accidentally, could spell disaster for a case. Drive by his house once too often or interview a sympathetic neighbor and it might alert the suspect to permanently delete mountains of potential evidence.

So our industry can expect a cat-and-mouse game for a while. Some new technology will come along that enables us to defeat clean-delete software and the game will start all over again. But keep one thing in mind: Even in the Computer Age, people still go to prison every day based on *fingerprint* information. They believe they'd never be considered a suspect, or gloves come off during an attack, or they think they can wipe away all fingerprints after the fact. For whatever reason, they still get caught by the fingerprint, just as they will for years to come by computer forensic evidence.

ENDNOTES

1 This is an ideal situation for example purposes. Passwords are rarely *this* easy, though many people do choose remarkably obvious passwords for fear of forgetting it themselves. These obvious candidates are always worth trying: names of kids, grandkids, spouse, pets, birthdays, 1234, and even the word "password." Sometimes the password is the same as the username, for convenience. In practice, you will likely have to resort to the services of an on-call computer hacker subcontractor.

2   Zaenglein, Norbert. *Disk Detective*. Boulder, Colorado:
     Paladin Press, 1998.
3   Functional descriptions from www.lc-tech.com.
4   If the perp tried to save a blank text file, Notepad
     would have alerted him to the fact that you can't do
     this. He then would have typed a single letter or even a
     space to make it "legal" to save.·

CHAPTER 9: Lie Detection

"You are infinitely more intelligent in your nature than you ever will be in your conscious thoughts."
—Alan Watts, Zen philosopher

Anyone scanning this book's table of contents would readily expect one thing from a chapter titled "Lie Detection"—to learn about the polygraph machine and, given this book's title, how it has changed with the Computer Age. Here's a little tidbit: The first polygraph machine wasn't even a polygraph at all. In fact, it was an analog machine as opposed to a digital one, and it only measured one thing. Thus the invention was actually called a Unigraph. But we'll get to all that. First I'd like to discuss some old-school fundamentals of lie detection. This is important because you'll later see that the polygraph does not, in fact, detect lies. Nothing does. Except for maybe we humans . . . if we learn some basic information and allow ourselves to trust our instincts.

UNCOVERING DECEPTIVE BEHAVIOR

It's important for a detective to know when he's being lied to. Often we rely on information gained through personal interviews. Just as often, we don't.

Why? Obviously, if we feel the interviewee is spewing a colossal load of bovine excrement from his pie hole, there's no sense in relying on that information.

Who lies to us? Even if you're a rookie with only a handful of cases, you already know that the lying begins with the client. Even the parent of a runaway teen might tell you, "We were good parents," or "There were no problems," or the teen "had no reason to run away." Right. I'm sure your daughter ran away because her home life was pure bliss.

How do you know if someone is lying? For some of us, myself included, it's more often than not a feeling that you get. For intuitive people, that's usually enough.

What about detectives who don't wish to rely on their feelings? Or what do you put in a client report if you only *think* a particular interviewee was lying to you? Some of us have no problem stating, "I felt your daughter's best friend was lying when she said she had no idea of your daughter's whereabouts." Other detectives prefer to give their clients detailed reasons as to why they believe a potential witness was lying to them.

What do these detectives look for? Probably the same things that an intuitive person subconsciously picks up on, except a detective on the lookout for concrete evidence explicitly looks for certain things. Most of these things have to do with the behavior of the interviewee.

Did they pause before every question? Or just certain ones? Did they smirk, shrug their shoulders, cover their mouths, fidget, break eye contact, look toward the door, or try to misdirect you by offering you a drink or requesting one? Any one of these behaviors could be meaningless, but too many such behaviors or a certain repeated behavior could indicate that a person is being less than truthful with you. The list of behaviors is much longer than this, of course (see Tables 9.1 through 9.3), although I'm not suggesting anybody should memorize dozens of typical signs of deception. Rather, be open to all behaviors that are potential signs of deception because they can't all possibly be listed.

Here's one I've never seen on a list but I know someone who exhibits it. A certain person I know, upon becoming entangled in a web of lies, will exaggerate her mild diabetic condition, claiming she suddenly needs a granola bar, to wiggle out of her web. Another example: during a post-trial interview, O.J. Simpson repeatedly coughed or cleared his throat before all the tough questions.

What about a person who uses incorrect grammar when they otherwise are eloquent speakers? I learned this trick from one of the greatest liars of all time, Mr. William Jefferson Clinton. Don't get me wrong. The man is such a good liar I actually respect him. In fact, using Mr. Clinton's techniques, I've learned to dodge some of those annoying questions you get at family parties.

Mr. Clinton's most famous example was his direct response to the media as to whether he had ever had relations with a White House intern. Remember his response?

"I did not have sexual relations with that woman." Then he added, "Ms. Lewinsky."

Curious, isn't it? The media never commented on this odd phrasing. When I saw it on TV, I knew it was a lie. Frankly, I didn't care. The man is entitled to his privacy. But let's look at that sentence again. Why did the President of the United States phrase it in such a strange manner?

Well, consider the punctuation: there wasn't any. It was a spoken statement with a carefully planned pause. When it was reported in the papers, it was paraphrased because nobody knew how to punctuate the sentence. This was not an accident, my friends. This was a deliberate escape attempt.

How did Mr. Clinton punctuate that sentence in his head? There are three possibilities:

- "I did not have sexual relations with that woman, Ms. Lewinsky."
- "I did not have sexual relations with that woman. Ms. Lewinsky."
- "I did not have sexual relations with that woman. Ms. Lewinsky . . ."

For a seasoned or perhaps borderline pathological liar, these actually are all outs, deliberate or subconscious escape hatches that allow the liar to believe that he hasn't lied at all. Let's look at each one.

As read, #1 is Mr. Clinton telling Ms. Lewinsky that he did not have sex with some unnamed woman (probably his wife).

As read, #2 is Mr. Clinton stating that he did not have sex with some unnamed woman and then, for no apparent reason, speaking the sentence fragment, "Ms. Lewinsky."

As read, #3 is Mr. Clinton stating that he did not have sex with some unnamed woman and then beginning a sentence about Ms. Lewinsky that he decides not to finish.

Bunk? Remember his video interview for the grand jury? [1] Remember his quibbling over the definition of the word "is"? Do you really believe this is a person who does not use grammar to justify his lies?

Why do liars do this? They do it because on some level they believe if their phrasing is inaccurate, then it's not *really* a lie. In essence the liar is lying to himself and doing it so well that he doesn't even realize his own self-deception. Keep an eye out for this sort of person. They can tell you quite a bit provided you don't believe a word they say.

Misdirection is another popular liar's trick. Generally, liars use misdirection to keep things as vague and irrelevant as possible. That way they cannot be nailed down anywhere.

Recall the infamous murdering mother and son, Sante and Kenny Kimes. While awaiting trial, a TV interviewer asked them how they felt about being known in headlines as the mother-son grifter team. They both spoke at once, laughing it off, and in no time at all they were saying, and I paraphrase, "Grifters? Drifters? Whatever! We're not drifters. We've lived in the same place for 20 years. We have roots . . . blah blah blah." The interviewer didn't go back to the question and the mother-son grifter team never had to answer it. They're professional cons. Not wanting to answer the embarrassing question of whether they were grifters, they misdirected the interviewer by discussing how they were certainly not drifters. Well, a grifter is one who gains by swindling or cheating, and a drifter is something else entirely. The interviewer was unwise to choose such an archaic word, and the Kimes capitalized on this by shooting down the attempted nametag entirely. As a result, they were never branded by the media with a colorful moniker as were "The Boston Strangler" and the "Unabomber."

So how do you dodge an annoying question at a family party using the same techniques the pros use? Here are some examples:

> DISTANT COUSIN: "So, you coming to my wedding in June?"
> YOU: "Hey! That's right, congratulations! I heard you were getting married. Who's the lucky guy?"

> ANY RELATIVE: "So what do you do again?"
> YOU: "Oh, the same, the same. You and the Mrs. still got that candle making business going?"

> YOUR AUNT: "You gonna be at Phil's on the Fourth of July?"
> YOU: "Oh, it's Phil's turn this year, is it? You know me, I like the Fourth of July."

There's a great scene in *2001: A Space Odyssey* where Dr. Haywood Floyd is being subtly grilled by a Russian scientist as to whether he knows anything about a potential epidemic at Clavius. If you watch this scene and carefully note Dr. Floyd's responses, you'll see that he manages to avoid the truth without lying. Dr. Floyd bumps into a Russian scientist and some companions on a space station. He knows Elena, who introduces him to Dr. Smyslov and the two others. They engage in small talk until Smyslov learns that Floyd is on his way to Clavius. Here's the dialog:

FLOYD: I'm just on my way up to Clavius.
SMYSLOV: Oh are you? Well, Dr. Floyd, I hope you don't think I'm being too inquisitive. But perhaps you can clear up the great big mystery about what has been going on up there?

FLOYD: I'm afraid I don't know what you mean.
SMYSLOV: Well it's just that for the past two weeks some extremely odd things have been happening at Clavius.
FLOYD: Oh really?
SMYSLOV: Yes, oh yes, yes. Well for one thing, whenever you phone the base all you can get is a recording which repeats that the phone lines are temporarily out of order.
FLOYD: Well, they're probably having trouble with their equipment or something like that.
SMYSLOV: Yes, yes. That's what we thought was the explanation at first, but it's been going on for the past 10 days.
FLOYD: You mean you haven't been able to contact anyone for the past 10 days?
SMYSLOV: That's right
FLOYD: Oh I see.
ELENA: And there's another thing, Haywood. Two days ago one of our rocket buses was denied permission for emergency landing at Clavius.
FLOYD: Oh? That does sound odd.
SMYSLOV: Yes, yes. I'm afraid there's going to be a bit of a row about it. Denying the men permission to land is a direct violation of the IAS convention.
FLOYD: Yes, of course, of course. Well did the crew get back all right?
SMYSLOV: Yes, yes. Fortunately they did.
FLOYD: Oh, I'm glad about that.
SMYSLOV: Dr. Floyd, at the risk of pressing you on a point you seem reticent to discuss, may I ask you a straightforward question?
FLOYD: Oh, well certainly.
SMYSLOV: Quite frankly, we've had some very reliable intelligence reports that quite a serious epidemic has broken out into Clavius. Something apparently of an unknown origin. Is this in fact what has happened?
FLOYD: Well, sorry, Dr. Smyslov, but I'm really not at liberty to discuss this.
SMYSLOV: I understand. But this epidemic could quite easily spread to our base. We should be given all the facts, Dr. Floyd.
FLOYD: Yes, I know. As I said I'm not at liberty to discuss it.

Elena finally breaks the tension by resuming

the small talk. After a minute Floyd makes an excuse to leave, and after he does, the Russians begin talking about him in Russian, seeming very displeased with the outcome of the preceding conversation. Only when Dr. Floyd was asked a direct question did he ever give a direct answer.

The above snippet is included here to show you how subjects might avoid telling you the truth, even when they have a strong desire to not lie to you. Why is this important? An interviewee demonstrating this behavior is likely one of two things: 1) a potential ally who needs reassurance before trusting you with the truth, or 2) a potential conspirator who sees that he must play the middle in order to "get through" the investigation.

These sorts of subtle guilt and lie indicators will never appear in a list. There are some behaviors, however, that are common enough to list, if for no other reason than to get you thinking in this vein. See Table 9.2 for a list of behaviors and their possible meanings. Considering the complexities of the human condition, there could be innumerable reasons why a person may act a given way. Be aware that this is a list of *potential* indicators only—a person could display some of these behaviors and not necessarily be lying. You must look at the whole picture and use your intuition.

It's also important to be aware that telltale lying behaviors are based in the human "fight or flight" response and are not actually indicators of lying but of stress. When a person is confronted by a stressful situation (such as lying), his body reacts involuntarily while trying to decide whether to flee the confrontation or stay and fight. [2] These responses can be measured by a polygraph, as we'll see later, or read by a trained observer.

The detective's job is to determine if the stress indicates deception or not. Is the interviewee generally stressed by the interview process, or do the stress indicators occur most frequently after certain direct questions? In order to know this, the detective must know enough about the interview process to control the situation. You do not need a doctorate in

psychology, but you should be aware of the basic psychological processes that drive a properly conducted interview. Lee Lapin does a good job demonstrating these processes in his video *Expert Body Language,* available through Paladin Press. Much of the following section is derived from Mr. Lapin's excellent video.

CONTROLLING AN INTERVIEW

Most people, even innocent ones, are nervous about being interviewed. Your job as detective is to determine at the beginning of the session what an interviewee's normal level of nervousness is. You want to use this time to note the subject's normal posture, gesturing habits, and talkativeness. Carefully note the subject's eye and pupil state and whether their lips are moist or dry. See Tables 9.1 through 9.3 to understand why.

In noting the above, you are establishing a baseline by which to measure the verbal and nonverbal observations you will make later in the interview. You establish this baseline by making small talk and maintaining a noninvasive posture and distance. At the beginning of the interview you should be situated at least 4 feet away from your subject and in the same visual plane, not seated or standing over him or her.

A quick understanding of proxemics will help you understand the logic behind this. Proxemics is the study of a person's personal space. Most psychologists agree that humans have four proxemic zones, delineated by distance: intimate, personal, social, and public.

The distance delineations vary by culture. Generally speaking, however, an American's intimate zone ranges from direct contact to 18 inches from his body, the personal zone is from 18 inches to 4 feet, the social zone from 4 to 7 feet, and the public zone from 7 to 12 feet.

You, as detective and interviewer, are concerned primarily with the social and personal zones. Specifically, you begin the interview in the social zone and when you need to turn up the pressure, you move into the person's personal zone.

After the beginning (or "control") phase of

TABLE 9.1	
Alphabetical Stress Indicators	
STRESS INDICATOR	**EXPLANATION**
A change in dialog rhythm	If he normally pauses before answering and doesn't or vice versa. Pausing *too* long before an explanation or blurting one out. Whichever is opposite of his usual rhythm may be a lie.
Blushing	Interviewer is honing in on a sensitive topic.
Breaking eye contact	Closing or covering of eyes. Looking away or down. Anything that breaks eye contact. The person is afraid you'll see the lie in his eyes. Looking at a watch, clock, window, door, or ceiling indicates an additional desire to escape the interview.
Breaking rhythm	Doing anything to distract the interviewer from the interview process. Could range anywhere from asking for a drink to sexual advances.
Changing speed of talking	Talking faster: liar wants to get it over with. Talking slower: contriving lies as he speaks.
Constricting pupils	May be caused by stress of lying.
Cracking voice	May be caused by stress of lying.
Crossing of arms, squirming, tightening body	At the very least indicates someone who is not being "open" with you.
Dry lips	May be caused by stress of lying.
Eyebrow movement	Especially raising, if otherwise steady eyebrow.
Eyes	Pupils constrict (dilate in some people), or irises change color. All stress reactions.
Eyes look up to the right	Person is accessing the right, creative half of the brain, possibly creating a lie. Be aware that the rare person who writes with a straight (un-hooked, uncurled) left hand accesses the left hemisphere of the brain for creativity.
Feet	In "ready to run" position. Pointing toward a window or door. Stepping away. Toe on floor ready to get up from seat.
Flipping/flicking of hand	Doesn't want to talk about that subject.
Hands touching the face, especially over the mouth	Subconscious reaction to lying.

STRESS INDICATOR	EXPLANATION
Increased blood pressure/pulse rate	Sometimes can be witnessed by watching the carotid artery, which runs along the windpipe.
Inappropriate overtures of friendship	He acts like he knows you better than he does. He hopes if you feel you know him well, then you will trusthim.
Larynx bouncing, moving up and down	Stress reaction. Watch Adam's Apple.
Leaning toward window, gate, or other egress	Desires to escape the interview.
Lips keep moving	Subtle lip movements after the subject has finished answering, especially if appearing to articulate words, may indicate he has more to say.
Looking down; failure to make eye contact	Deep down, he is ashamed of his lies and cannot face you.
Looking toward the exit	Be it a door, driveway, or any way "out" of your questioning indicates a person who is not being truthful.
Mispronunciation, poor grammar, mumbling	Especially if this is not usual for the person. See text.
Monopolizing the conversation	A technique to keep you from inquiring further and discovering the lie.
Nervous laughter	An attempt to make light of a situation he knows to be a dark lie.
Nodding "yes"	Nodding yes when indicating a "no" would be suspect.
Nose rubbing, touching, wiping	Often thought of as a "dead giveaway" to a lie, but don't give it too much extra weight.
Perspiration on forehead, face, chest, neck, armpits	Possible stress reaction
Providing plausible scenarios rather than probable ones	A person who too often provides plausible excuses rather than probable ones is likely lying.
Rambling	Giving more than one excuse for being late is a dead giveaway. He knows his first excuse is a lie. He feels it's therefore not good enough and gives another (or more).
Requesting a drink	May indicate dry mouth, a desire to break the interviewer's rhythm, or an attempt to get time to think of a good lie.
Rubbing ear	Stress reaction.

STRESS INDICATOR	EXPLANATION
Saying "just trust me" when there is no good reason for their discretion	Ask the person to at least tell you the reason for his discretion. If he doesn't have a good one, he may be obscuring a lie.
Shaking head "no"	Subconscious movement because the liar doesn't believe himself.
Shifting in seat	Uncomfortable with the question.
Sudden bout of ignorance	A generally informed person conveniently forgetting a crucial fact is very suspect.
"Thinker" pose	Listening with chin in hand. Acting attentive but might be thinking of an alternate answer or way out of the situation.
White of eyes visible below iris	Indicates involuntary widening of eyes, a stress reaction.
You feel he is lying	Your intuition may be your best indicator because it is subconsciously tuned to all of the above behaviors and thousands more that can never be listed.

the interview, it's time to get to the tough questions and see how he holds up under scrutiny. Move a bit closer to your subject, lean forward, and sit taller. Toward the end of the interview, you might even stand if the matter you are investigating is a serious one. If the subject seems too relaxed during this portion of the interview, turn up the pressure by moving deeper into his personal zone and, if necessary, breaching his intimate zone with hand gestures if he's a particularly tough case or demonstrating unusual resistance to a particularly tough question.

How do you know when to turn up the pressure? A subject is too relaxed if he's reclining in his chair, has his hands behind his head, or forms a pyramid with his fingers. These are all signals that he feels in control of the interview or is getting away with deception. Use what you know about proxemics to keep control of the session.

Once you are in control of the interview, begin asking your subject direct questions about the investigation. Compare your current observations of his behavior to your baselines. Is the subject talking faster? Using more hand gestures? Showing more white under his irises? All of these are indicators of stress and thus possible deception.

One final note: Stress indicators should be given more weight when observed in a normally calm subject (as determined by your baseline) and less weight when observed in a normally effusive, nervous, or hyperactive subject.

Indicators of guilt involve more than stress alone. In addition to a stress reaction, a guilty person will do or say certain telltale things. I've included these in Table 9.2. For study purposes, I have also arranged these guilt and stress indicators by body part in Table 9.3.

A Note on Intuition

Many detectives balk at using intuition to detect lies and clues. I would only suggest "don't balk it till you try it."

You see, people discount intuition as unscientific or insubstantial. After all, a juror certainly wouldn't convict a man based solely on intuition. Doing so would be a crime. A jury demands hard physical evidence if they are going to take a person's freedom away, and I would want nothing less from a jury if I ever find myself in front of one.

But there is nothing wrong with letting your intuition guide you through a case. Maybe your instinct will not be right 100 percent of the time, which is why we shouldn't use it in the jury box. But even for a person who doesn't trust his feelings, I'd bet his intuition is right 75 percent of the time. I'd bet it's right 90 percent of the time for most of us. After all, how many times have we gone against our gut instinct, only to say later, "I should've listened to my gut," or "I should've gone with my first answer" on a test?

If you know your instinct is right more often

TABLE 9.2 Alphabetical Guilt Indicators	
GUILT INDICATOR	**EXPLANATION**
Appealing to divinity	Says "I swear," "God help me," or "As God as my witness."
Appealing to honor	Says, "To be perfectly honest," "Honestly," "Truthfully," "Trust me."
Appealing to respect	Says, "No, sir," "No, ma'am," when not called for.
Belittling the situation	Says that the missing person/money will turn up. Says, "What's the big deal?" Or, "It's only a few dollars [that's missing]."
Lips keep moving after subject stops talking	Subtle lip movements after the subject has finished answering, especially if appearing to articulate words, may indicate he has more to say.
Non-answers to direct questions of involvement	Do I strike you as someone who would do that? I have never done such a thing. It wouldn't be me to do that. I couldn't possibly be involved. Why would you accuse me? What makes you say that?
Non-straightforward "no"	Shaking head side to side. Hesitating before answering. Pleading or apologetic no. Too casual. Too sincere. Too friendly. Breathless or exasperated no. Saying no, then appearing thoughtful. Eyes directed elsewhere when saying no. An innocent person says no in a straightforward manner without breaking eye contact.

GUILT INDICATOR	EXPLANATION
Says guilty party should be helped rather than punished	When asked what should be done when the guilty part is caught, a guilty person will say, "help them," or "give them counseling." An innocent person would say, "punish them."
Shifts blame	Maybe so-and-so did it. Jane was the last one to see him. John closed up the store. Maybe it was the cleaning staff or security?
Turns in profile	May be ready or willing to confess.

TABLE 9.3
Guilt and Stress Indicators by Body Part

INDICATOR	EXPLANATION
BODY	
Crossing of arms, squirming, tightening body	At the very least indicates someone who is not being "open" with you.
Leaning toward window, gate, or other egress	Desires to escape the interview.
Perspiration on forehead, face, chest, neck, armpits	Possible stress reaction.
Shifting in seat	Uncomfortable with the question.
EYES	
Breaking eye contact	Closing or covering of eyes. Looking away or down. Anything that breaks eye contact. The person is afraid you'll see the lie in his eyes. Looking at a watch, clock, window, door, or ceiling indicates an additional desire to escape the interview.
Constricting pupils	May be caused by stress of lying.
Eyes look up to the right	Person is accessing the right, creative half of the brain, possibly creating a lie. Be aware that the rare person who writes with a straight (un-hooked, uncurled) left hand accesses the left hemisphere of the brain for creativity.
Eyes	Pupils constrict (dilate in some people), or irises change color. All stress reactions.
White of eyes visible below iris	Indicates involuntary widening of eyes, a stress reaction.

INDICATOR	EXPLANATION
FACE	
Blushing	Interviewer is honing in on a sensitive topic.
Dry lips	May be caused by stress of lying.
Eyebrow movement	Especially raising, if otherwise steady eyebrow.
Hands touching the face, especially over the mouth	Subconscious reaction to lying.
Lips keep moving	Subtle lip movements after the subject has finished answering, especially if appearing to articulate words, may indicate he has more to say.
Nose rubbing, touching, wiping	Often thought of as a "dead giveaway" to a lie, but don't give it too much extra weight.
HANDS AND FEET	
Feet	In "ready to run" position. Pointing toward a window or door. Stepping away. Toe on floor ready to get up from seat.
Flipping/flicking of hand	Doesn't want to talk about that subject.
HEAD	
"Thinker" pose	Listening with chin in hand. Acting attentive, but might be thinking of an alternate answer or way out of the situation.
Looking down; failure to make eye contact	Deep down, he is ashamed of his lies and cannot face you.
Looking toward the exit	Be it a door, driveway, or any way "out" of your questioning indicates a person who is not being truthful.
Nodding "yes"	Nodding yes when indicating a "no" would be suspect.
Rubbing ear	Stress reaction.
Shaking head "no"	Subconscious movement because the liar doesn't believe himself.
Turns in profile	May be ready or willing to confess.
NECK	
Increased blood pressure/pulse rate	Sometimes can be witnessed by watching the carotid artery, which runs along the windpipe.
Larynx bouncing, moving up and down	Possible stress reaction. Watch Adam's Apple.
VOICE/GENERAL	
A change in dialog rhythm	If he normally pauses before answering and doesn't or vice versa. Pausing *too* long before

INDICATOR	EXPLANATION
	an explanation or blurting one out. Whichever is opposite of his usual rhythm may be a lie.
Appealing to divinity	Says "I swear," "God help me," or "As God as my witness."
Appealing to honor	Says, "To be perfectly honest," "Honestly," "Truthfully," "Trust me."
Appealing to respect	Says, "No, sir," "No, ma'am," when not called for.
Belittling the situation	Says that the missing person/money will turn up. Says, "What's the big deal?" Or, "It's only a few dollars [that's missing]."
Changing speed of talking	Talking faster: liar wants to get it over with. Talking slower: contriving lies as he speaks.
Cracking voice	May be caused by stress of lying.
Mispronunciation, poor grammar, mumbling	Especially if this is not usual for the person. See text.
Monopolizing the conversation	A technique to keep you from inquiring further and discovering the lie.
Nervous laughter	An attempt to make light of a situation he knows to be a dark lie.
Non-answers to direct questions of involvement	Do I strike you as someone who would do that? I have never done such a thing. It wouldn't be me to do that. I couldn't possibly be involved. Why would you accuse me? What makes you say that?
Non-straightforward "no"	Shaking head side to side. Hesitating before answering. Pleading or apologetic no. Too casual. Too sincere. Too friendly. Breathless or exasperated no. Saying no, then appearing thoughtful. Eyes directed elsewhere when saying no. An innocent person says no in a straightforward manner without breaking eye contact.
Providing plausible scenarios rather than probable ones	A person who too often provides plausible excuses rather than probable ones is likely lying.
Rambling	Giving more than one excuse for being late is a dead giveaway. He knows his first excuse is a

INDICATOR	EXPLANATION
	lie. He feels it's therefore not good enough and gives another (or more).
Requesting a drink	May indicate dry mouth, a desire to break the interviewer's rhythm, or an attempt to get time to think of a good lie.
Saying "just trust me" when there is no good reason for their discretion	Ask the person to at least tell you the reason for his discretion. If he doesn't have a good one, he may be obscuring a lie.
Says guilty party should be helped rather than punished	When asked what should be done when the guilty part is caught, a guilty person will say, "help them," or "give them counseling." An innocent person would say, "punish them."
Shifts blame	Maybe so-and-so did it. Jane was the last one to see him. John closed up the store. Maybe it was the cleaning staff or security?
Sudden bout of ignorance	A generally informed person conveniently forgetting a crucial fact is very suspect.
Breaking rhythm	Doing anything to distract the interviewer from the interview process. Could range anywhere from asking for a drink to sexual advances.
Inappropriate overtures of friendship	He acts like he knows you better than he does. He hopes if you feel you know him well, then you will trust him.
You feel he is lying	Your intuition may be your best indicator because it is subconsciously tuned to all of the above behaviors and thousands more that can never be listed.

than not, there's nothing wrong with playing the numbers to advance a case. It's certainly better than flipping a coin if you have no other clues.

FORENSIC PSYCHOPHYSIOLOGY

For who's sick psycho fizzy what-o-gee? Forensic psychophysiology is the investigative study of interactions between mental and physiological processes for use in legal proceedings. Esoterically, the term is applied to polygraph examiners and their craft, a.k.a. lie detection. The reason for the new term has to do with the fact that polygraph examiners and defense attorneys like to point out that there is no such thing as a "lie detector."

It's true—the polygraph machine cannot detect a lie. No machine can. It can only detect changes in a person's physiology. Depending on when these changes occur, the polygraph examiner can infer the likelihood of a person's truthfulness. For example, polygraph electrodes placed on the fingers are used to measure perspiration. If a person's fingertips get sweaty after responding to a certain question about a murder investigation, the polygraph examiner may infer that the sweat is caused by the stress of lying. However, if perspiration is the only physiological response to the question, the examiner may discount it as mere test anxiety. [3]

The pre-Computer Age polygraph was an analog, as opposed to digital, device. In fact, the first "lie detector" to enjoy widespread forensic use was called the Unigraph because it had only one indicator needle that graphed a person's cardiovascular activity. Later machines graphed heart rate, blood pressure, respiratory rate, and perspiration levels. The measuring processes were simple yet intriguing:

- *Heart rate/blood pressure:* The examiner placed one of those black tubes around the examinee's arm just as a nurse might do in a doctor's office. The blood pressure band was connected pneumatically to a needle that fluctuated in tandem with his blood pressure and moved a pen across scrolling paper to graph the response.
- *Respiratory rate:* This was also done pneumatically by placing tubes around the examinee's chest. As the chest moved in and out, the needle moved a pen up and down across the paper.
- *Perspiration:* Perspiration was measured by placing electrodes called fingerplates, or galvanometers, on two of the examinee's fingertips. Technically, this measured something called galvanic skin resistance, or GSR. Skin hydrated with perspiration will conduct more electricity than dry skin.

The Computer Age polygraph still uses the same pneumatic devices and electrodes, except transducers convert the pneumatic responses to electronic signals, which are fed into—what else?—a computer. The needles and graph paper have been subsumed by the ubiquitous computer monitor. (The Computer Age polygraph examiner is still a sterile-looking geek in a white lab coat, though.) The computer uses complex software algorithms to ensure it's really detecting what it thinks it's detecting and to help the polygraph examiner derive inferences from the data.

The Computer Age brought with it standardized laboratory testing to improve the interpretation of test results. This laboratory testing has shown that a polygraph examination is actually slightly biased against truthful people, which is good to know. [4] Turns out, a truthful person is more likely to register a false positive than a liar is to register a false negative. Personally I think this is of little significance, though defense attorneys love to point it out.

With the Computer Age also came refined procedures for prepping an examinee. It's not like you see in the movies where the cops throw a suspect on the poly and grill him. In fact, there is no grilling involved, as this is deemed to severely skew the already tenuous results. Rather, about an hour of prep work is done, where a certified polygraph examiner psychologically profiles the examinee. The examiner tries to learn what types of questions make the person anxious. Using this information, the examiner tailors his questions to keep the subject as relaxed as possible, thereby keeping the test results as unbiased as possible.

The actual polygraph examination consists of a mere 10 questions or so, only about four of which have anything to do with the actual investigation. The remaining questions are control questions. Responses to control questions are later compared with responses to critical questions. This is the essence of the test. Some of the questions, especially the critical ones, may be asked more than once to be certain a positive reading is consistently positive or a negative reading is consistently negative.

Despite all the Computer Age improvements to the polygraph and the examination process, the test is still seldom admissible in court. This is appropriate since even polygraph proponents estimate its accuracy to be 90 percent. Even by those generous standards, if justice relied on the results of a polygraph, 10 percent of prison inmates would be innocent. This is not something we, as a free society, want to have happen.

THE FUTURE OF LIE DETECTION

After the advent of any new technology, history has shown that creative, driven people will invariably improve upon it. Such is the case with polygraphs. Some polygraph examinations already involve electrodes placed on the arms and legs to detect and measure how a person shifts in his seat during the test. Look for future polygraphs to point lasers at the eyes to detect pupil constriction/dilation, blink rate, and direction of eye movement. Is the person looking down? Up and to the right? This information will be sent to a computer, where it will be compared with other physiological data and run through complex algorithms. Would an increased blink rate, pupil constriction, squirm in the seat, and sweaty-finger-tipped skipped heartbeat indicate a lie? Eventually a computer will decide all of this.

And why take this data from the extremities? Why not go directly to the source: the brain? Someday examinees will wear nothing but a helmet. Brain signals will be sent by infrared to a computer. Maybe the computer will be called JURY and the examinee will sit right in an electric chair. If the computer decides he's lying, he can be executed on the spot, saving the state a lot of time and money. [5]

Don't believe the helmet on the head theory? Too late. It's already being done. The process is known as "brain fingerprinting."

Scientists have found a way to detect brain activity with sensors placed about the head. The current test is a simple one, but I guarantee you that in the future it will be used as a full-blown lie detector. For now it remains a very controversial procedure, with only minor laboratory evidence that it's more accurate than not. The examinee is shown a picture of, say, the victim of a murder investigation. The test supposedly measures whether the examinee recognizes the picture. If the brain fingerprinter says he does but the examinee says he doesn't, then the examiner slides an executioner's axe out from underneath an adjacent hay pile and chops off the examinee's head. Well, not yet.

Also on the horizon, researchers have discovered that standard Magnetic Resonance Imagery (MRI) scans can detect activity of the brain's memory centers. When these centers are monitored during questioning, they become hyperactive when test subjects lie. Researchers believe that this is because the subject has to access memory in order to keep track of his lies. This system of lie detection shows more promise than brain fingerprinting.

Keep an eye out for brain fingerprinting and MRI lie detection. They're sure to be the next controversial lie detectors, and they are right around the corner.

ENDNOTES

[1] Why did Clinton give his testimony by video instead of in person, like most grand juries? Because it's easier to lie when you don't have to face the people you're lying to.

[2] Quoted from the video *Expert Body Language* with Lee Lapin, Paladin Press, 1992.

[3] Although proponents of the polygraph are adamant that anxiety will not bias a properly administered polygraph examination.

[4] Proponents of polygraphs adamantly deny this, but my research shows the evidence to be undeniable.

[5] I'm not suggesting any of this is good or will actually happen. I merely offer it as a potential ultimate outcome to our current direction in the hope that we, as a society, will consider our own future very carefully.

CHAPTER 10: Graphology

"A scraggly, skeletal, fleshless list of abstractions."
—Alan Watts

Graphology is the study of handwriting. A graphologist is a person who analyzes handwriting and infers from it psychological attributes of its writer. Every good detective should at least be familiar with graphology, if not become a graphologist on some level himself.

Is graphology an exact science? No. Is it a useful science? Most definitely. A person whose handwriting exhibits attributes of, say, criminal intellect, is not necessarily a criminal. But it's sure useful to know whether a particular subject under investigation has greater criminal potential than, say, a person whose handwriting shows conformity and a desire to feel safe.

These psychological profiles and countless more can be inferred from a person's handwriting. Ever browse the employment classifieds and see ads where potential employers request a "handwritten letter of interest"? Ever notice that such potential employers are often security and detective agencies? If you didn't already, now you know why they ask for a *handwritten* letter.

Analyzing handwriting to pick employees is one thing, but if I needed a solid analysis for an actual case, I would not rely on my own unpolished abilities. If fact, I would hire the person who literally "wrote the book" on the topic: Shiela Lowe. Author of the excellent book *The Complete Idiot's Guide to Handwriting Analysis* (Alpha Books, 1999), Ms. Lowe operates a full-time handwriting consulting business from her home office in Southern California. If your detective firm ever needs a graphologist, I recommend you contact Sheila Lowe & Associates (www.writinganalysis.com).

GRAPHOLOGY IN THE COMPUTER AGE

If your case files contain handwriting samples just begging for analysis but you don't want to hire a professional or invest the time to become a polished graphologist yourself, then you'll be pleased to learn that the Computer Age has given you another option: handwriting analysis software. There are two major packages available at the moment. One is Shiela Lowe's Handwriting Analyzer; the other is Handwriting Analyst by Career Solutions (www.garthmichaels.com).

Zen philosopher Alan Watts once referred to a description of a man's day as "a scraggly, skeletal, fleshless list of abstractions." Mr. Watts believed, as I and many others believe, that reality can never by described by scrawny words. You can never get at it, Mr. Watts would say. A handwritten list of what you did yesterday is certainly a list of abstractions because the words on the paper have nothing to do with the reality of what actually happened. Graphologists believe the pen strokes that make up the list speak far more about a person's reality than the list itself. This is the essence of graphology.

Much of the following text is taken directly from Chapter 26 of Ms. Lowe's aforementioned book, which describes her software and the events leading up to its development and implementation. I would like to thank Ms. Lowe for allowing me to use her copy.

There are certain nuances in a human pen stroke that a computer will simply never be able to "see," so handwriting analysis software will never put graphologists out of business. But if you can train yourself to identify and classify these nuances, then you can feed them into a computer. The graphologist (you) can then use the computer as a tool, which is all a computer ever really is. No matter what amazing feats a computer can accomplish, it is only doing what humans could do on their own, except that it can do it mind-bogglingly fast.

Since about 1978, when personal computers first appeared on the scene, Ms. Lowe had many offers from software companies to help them develop a handwriting analyzer. But the representatives of these companies could never convince her that a computer could accurately quantify the myriad handwriting characteristics that a graphologist had to consider.

Computer technology, of course, improved at an exponential rate over the years, and one day Ms. Lowe received a call from a representative of RI Software who had an

unwavering confidence in his firm's ability to create a handwriting analyzer worthy of the name. Ms. Lowe argued, "There are just too many variables for a computer to be able to give an accurate analysis, and I wouldn't want to be associated with something that comes out looking like a canned report."

But the RI rep was undaunted. "I don't care how many variables there are," he told Ms. Lowe firmly. "If they can be defined, we can computerize them." RI Software was so confident in its conviction that Ms. Lowe was offered full control over what went into the software and given carte blanche to include in the software spec anything she deemed important. The rep also noted that a workable handwriting analysis software would help validate graphology as a science, pointing out to Sheila that solid scientific principles are those that can be dependably and consistently replicated. A handwriting analyzer that consistently outputted

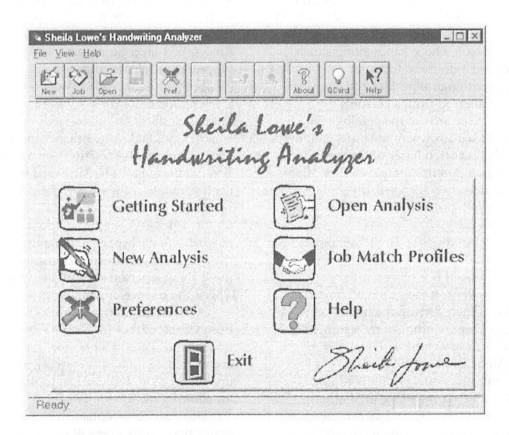

Sheila Lowe's Handwriting Analyzer in action. Screenshots 10.1 through 10.4 show the look and feel of Ms. Lowe's excellent software and give you an idea of how to use it.

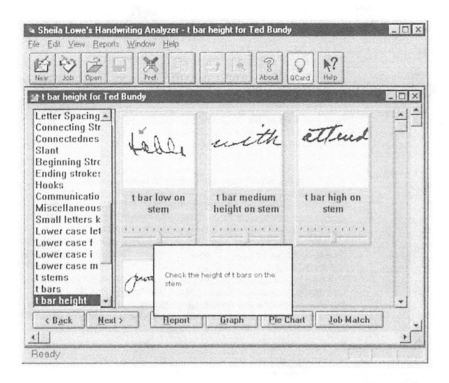

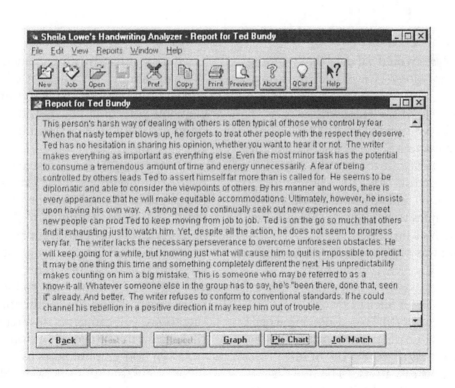

Screenshots 10.2 and 10.3.

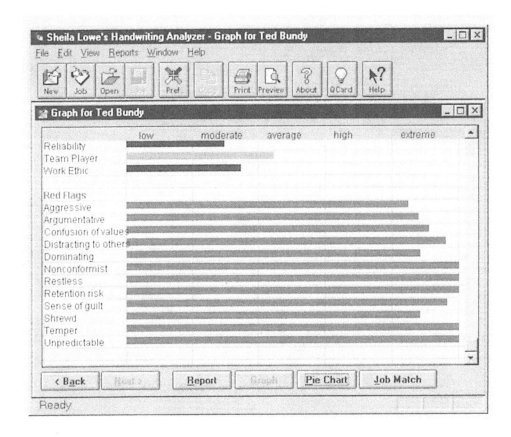

Screenshot 10.4.

predictable analyses would validate the founding principles of graphology. How could Ms. Lowe say no to that?

For version one of the Handwriting Analyzer, Ms. Lowe decided on 4,000 handwriting characteristic variables. She assigned each one a personality attribute and a value (score). She then wrote 200 pages of text for reports and scanned and edited more than 400 handwriting samples to help guide the end user through the analysis process.

RI Software was responsible for designing the "look" and the extremely complicated programming to make the whole thing work properly. They called it Sheila Lowe's Handwriting Analyzer (SLHA). Knowing what I know about Sheila Lowe, the software would not bear her name unless it was worthy of it.

The software is easy to use. The user compares aspects of a handwriting sample under analysis to on-screen illustrations. Once you enter the Analyzer, you'll find a list of 48

categories of handwriting elements, including "Organization," "Writing Style," "Rhythm," and so on. Of course, to better understand these elements you should have studied some books on graphology, such as Ms. Lowe's *Complete Idiot's Guide*.

Each category shows a series of pictures of handwriting on the screen. Let's say you selected the category "Slant." Seven types of slant are illustrated, from "Upright" to "Variable." All you do is click your mouse on the picture where the slant looks most like the handwriting sample you are analyzing (descriptions on the illustrations and "Qcards" tell you what to look for). After you've matched up the handwriting in at least 10 categories, you can generate a report simply by clicking on the "Report" button.

Even non-graphologists using the software report accuracy ratings between 89 and 99 percent. That's because the scores assigned to each of the 4,000+ variables are carefully weighted, with the most important handwriting

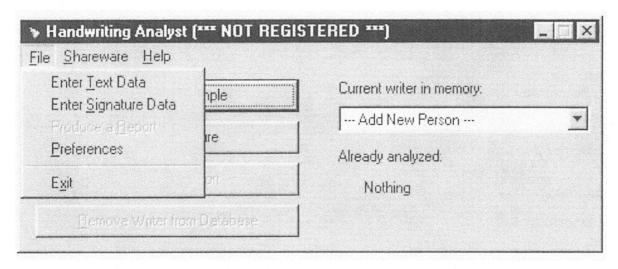

Screenshot 10.5. Career Solutions' Handwriting Analyst offers a multiple-choice format that is extremely easy to use.

characteristics having greater weight than the lesser ones. The program also performs a series of checks, balances, and algorithms before generating the final report.

Chapter 26 of Ms. Lowe's book contains a more detailed explanation of the software. However, you are welcome to download a free demo of the Handwriting Analyzer from her web site at www.writinganalysis.com. The demo version will not allow you to save or print reports, but it will give you a good idea of how the software works.

Career Solutions' Handwriting Analyst is the second major graphology software currently available to the private investigator. The program breaks the complexities of handwriting into about 60 multiple-choice questions. Illustrations of each choice are provided on-screen. You can answer the questions quickly and accurately using a short sample of a person's writing and/or a signature. Handwriting Analyst reports uncover highly accurate descriptions of physical and material drives, emotional characteristics, intellectual style, personality traits, social behavior, and vocational implications. The brief report provides a thumbnail sketch of the writer's personality; the detailed report offers more elaboration and explanation of each trait. Two writers can be compared to each other, or differences between a writer's public personality (signature) and private personality (text) can be identified. Signature Analyst is a program within Handwriting Analyst, which, by itself, is capable of analyzing signatures only. Price for Handwriting Analyst 5.0 at the time of this writing is $39.95.

SECTION THREE

TIPS, TRICKS, AND TALES

CHAPTER 11: The Very Personal Computer

"I give the fight up: let there be an end, a privacy, an obscure nook for me. I want to be forgotten even by God."
—Robert Browning

This chapter will show how and where people unwittingly leave bits of personal data on their computer. The detective in you will readily see how an uninformed person may allow this personal data to pile into a mountain of evidence on his PC.

Ever wonder why it's called a PC, or *personal computer*? It should be called a very, very personal computer because even if you're not data logging your subject (see Chapter 6), his computer is still gathering and storing a wealth of personal information. It began when he first bought it and set up the software and operating system. If nothing else, he was probably asked a few basic questions, such as his name and company name. Now, somewhere in the dark recesses of his computer's hard drive, these two bits of information have been permanently stored.

Even a non-PI stranger sitting down at this computer would not need long to find out who it belonged to. Start any major piece of software and a screen pops up revealing the owner's name and company name. The same thing is true if you click Help, then click About in any major software application. Among other things, it will say, "This product is licensed to . . . " and the owner's name and company name are again revealed. With all you've read in this book so far, you're probably left with a lurking suspicion that computers store other data about their owners. They do. This chapter discusses some of those data bits, how they are collected, and where they are stored.

JUNK E-MAIL

Junk e-mail may be generated by information stored in "cookies" on your subject's computer, or he may have unwittingly asked for it when he visited a certain web site. A cookie is a very small file that a remote computer puts on a visitor's computer when he visits a web site. Not only can a particular cookie reveal personal information about your subject and his habits, an externally generated piece of junk mail also has tales to tell. Consider the following situation.

A man lives with his girlfriend, whom he's planning to propose marriage to. They share a computer and on-line service provider. The man begins shopping on-line for engagement rings while his girlfriend is at work. He checks out the web sites of various jewelers within driving distance to get an idea of what he'll be able to afford for his love. While visiting a certain site, a screen pops up telling him to take a survey for a chance at winning a one-karat diamond. The man takes and submits the survey and continues shopping.

The next day, the man's girlfriend checks the e-mail. She notices the inbox contains an e-mail with the subject "Thanks for Taking our Survey." Curious, she reads it. It's not long before she adds things up and realizes her beau is shopping for an engagement ring. The man's surprise is totally destroyed.

The foregoing is an example of a simple pitfall that some people might have seen coming and avoided. But even a savvy person's privacy can be compromised during one unguarded moment of haste. The next example demonstrates a more insidious trap.

Let's again use the two people from the above scenario. Suppose the man and woman have separate e-mail accounts on Yahoo or wherever. The man may even be somewhat computer savvy but takes the survey anyway, figuring that if it generates any junk e-mail, his girlfriend has no access to his account (see caveat below under "Web Accessible E-mail Accounts"). So the man shops for the diamond while his girl is at work. What he doesn't know is that a bulk advertising service is tracking his buying habits and has set a cookie on his computer, which indicates he may be in the market for a diamond. Note that the cookie has been attached to their shared computer, not his personal e-mail account. People confuse this point and therefore think they are safe. Who would've thought that? Few people, that's who.

The next day the woman goes on-line to do some research and is greeted by an inordinate number of Internet ads and pop-up boxes trying to sell her a diamond. She'd seen a similar pattern once after she bought a sewing machine on-line—for the next several months she had been greeted by all sorts of ads from arts and crafts suppliers. She doesn't know how or why the computer knows what it does, but she realizes her boyfriend is probably shopping for a diamond, or at least some serious jewelry. Again, the man's surprise is compromised, if not ruined.

If you personally want to be safe from the above scenarios, delete any cookies from doubleclick.com and similar data miners. These outfits track your web surfing habits. They then use this information to sort you into various mailing lists so advertisers can send you junk e-mail or know whether it's worth their money to show you a particular pop-up ad when you visit a certain web site.

Now, from a PI's perspective, if you want to know your subject's buying habits, check *his* cookie directory. If you see a lot of ads for dating services on his computer, you know he or someone else that uses that computer has visited or signed up with an on-line dating service. If you see a lot of X-rated solicitations, then you can draw different conclusions about your subject.

AUTOCOMPLETE

Maybe the man in the above examples is very computer savvy and deletes his cookies.

Maybe he's extra careful to delete them because after he went shopping for a diamond, he entered the name of his favorite porn star into a search engine. Her name is Crystal Ball, and he learned she's in a new movie. She plays an international spy who has various encounters with "the other side" while searching for goods on the enemy during the Cold War. The name of the movie is *Improper Gander*. The man searches for the movie, finds it, and orders it. But he's not worried. He's erased all cookies generated that night.

The next day his girlfriend decides they need some new dishes and goes searching on the web. She begins typing "dishes" into a search engine, but before she finishes, the word "diamonds" pops up. Internet Explorer is using AutoComplete to save her time. AutoComplete is an option most computer users unwittingly turn on. It "reads" the first few letters you type into a dialog box and offers a list of words it predicts you intend to spell based on other words you have (or someone else has) typed in the past. You then arrow down or click on the word, saving on typing time.

So, now that AutoComplete has done her this "favor," she gets excited because she instantly realizes that her boyfriend must have recently typed the word "diamond" into a search box.

Well, if they're to be married they'll need some imported wine, plus crystal glasses in which to serve it. But wouldn't you know? AutoComplete displays "Crystal Ball" before she can finish typing. She's not yet heard of Crystal Ball, so she only notes it. Fifteen minutes later, though, when searching for imported wines, AutoComplete displays "Improper Gander" before she finishes typing. Curious, she presses enter to see what will pop up. Not only does she immediately learn who Crystal Ball is, she follows the viewed links right to the order page her boyfriend arrived at last night.

Maybe she'll refuse his marriage proposal, maybe she won't. It depends on how much such things matter to her. One thing's for certain, however: In trying to do the computer user a favor, AutoComplete seriously compromised the man's privacy.

As a detective, you probably can see how AutoComplete can assist an investigation. If you want to know if your subject is into sniping, type "sni" into an Internet Explorer search box. If the rest of the word pops up, you'll have your answer.

The AutoComplete function also works in Internet Explorer's address block. Type in the first few letters of a web site address you've visited before and the computer will take a guess at where you want to go and fill in the rest of the address for you. A detective can learn a lot about a subject by visiting the sites he's visited before. The most recent web addresses are stored as "history," accessed by clicking the down arrow to the right of the main address block.

WEB-ACCESSIBLE E-MAIL ACCOUNTS

Web-accessible e-mail accounts such as Yahoo have a hidden danger for those who access their e-mail via a shared computer, like the man and girlfriend in the earlier examples. Some people set up such accounts specifically so they can access their e-mail in libraries, classrooms, and Internet cafes wherever they go. This method is called "web-based access" because you don't download your e-mail to your local computer but rather read it on the remote web site's server. Using web-based (also called "web-side") e-mail is also a great way to keep viruses and junk mail off your computer—simply delete any unfamiliar e-mails before they are ever downloaded to your computer.

Though companies like Yahoo and Hotmail don't want you to know it, most ISPs offer their users web-based e-mail access. For example, if your ISP is www.myDomain.com, it will usually have a web-based e-mail server at mail.myDomain.com, pop3.myDomain.com, or webmail.myDomain.com.

Whether it's Yahoo or your local ISP's web-based access, the login usually consists of typing in your username and password. This is where the trouble begins. Let's say you're sitting in your local library and decide to check your web-based e-mail. If you forget to log out, or if the system is configured to AutoComplete forms, or if the web-based system stores your login information in a cookie, the next person who sits at that computer will be able to access your e-mail account. Good system administrators will configure all computers on the network so that the foregoing situation can't happen, but do you want to put your privacy in the hands of system administrators?

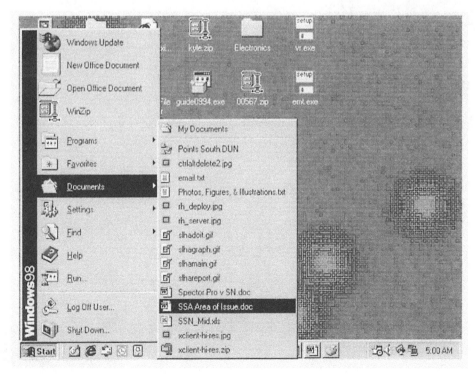

Screenshot 11.1. A quick way to see what your subject's been up to.

Though I've used Yahoo as an example, their current security procedures are actually pretty good. I ran some tests before this book went to press and, provided you remember to log out, Yahoo does a good job at requiring a password. Watch out for smaller providers, however, and just remember that failing to log out of any system is always a danger.

RECENT DOCUMENTS

If your subject has a standard PC with Windows operating system that you can access, you can find out what he's been up to recently by going to the Start menu and placing the mouse pointer over Documents. A list of the most recently opened documents will appear. See Screenshot 11.1.

You can peruse the files by clicking on them, but be sure not to save any changes you may accidentally make. Saving a file causes the time stamp to change, and a savvy computer user will become suspicious upon seeing that the file was stamped after he last remembered accessing the file or when he wasn't there.

CHAPTER 12: Better Business Bureau

"Seest thou a man diligent in his business? He shall stand before kings."
—Proverbs

Most people have heard of the Better Business Bureau, but few people understand exactly what it is. Occasionally I'll hear a client, friend, or family member talk about how upset they are about a particular business transaction. Maybe they feel the auto mechanic acted unethically, so they declare, "I'm going to call the Better Business Bureau on them!"

I've heard that sentence many times, spoken with the conviction that says the speaker knows that the Better Business Bureau is a government regulatory agency, one that will promptly admonish the auto mechanic and make him think twice before ever putting the wrong lug nut on a tire ever again. Some people even think the BBB can "have that place closed down!"

The Better Business Bureau is not a government agency and will likely never admonish anybody. It is a private, nonprofit organization that acts, in essence, as a watchdog over businesses and sole proprietors that do business with the general public. It has no authority to close down a business.

The BBB encourages businesses to join its service. This means the company or proprietor pays dues and becomes a member business of the BBB. In doing so, it enjoys the privilege of being able to tell its customers that it cooperates with the BBB; it may even have a plaque on its wall to that effect. Cooperating with the BBB means that if the BBB should ever inform the business that it has received a complaint against it, then the business is morally and ethically (though not legally) bound to resolve the complaint to the best of its abilities. The BBB oversees the complaint resolution process, and if

it's satisfied that the business has done everything it could do to appease the customer, it will remain as a "business in good standing" with the BBB.

Including a Better Business Bureau (BBB) Reliability Report in your background check on a businessperson or company will at the very least show your due diligence and at best generate clues to aid further investigation of the subject, should your client so desire. Moreover, it's easy to do—thanks once again to the Computer Age.

Let's say I was finishing up a background check on my publisher, Paladin Press. Of course everything came out squeaky clean, as would be expected for a business entity that has managed to stay in business for more than 30 years. To make my report complete, I go to www.bbb.org, click their "Check Out a Company" link, and type in Paladin Press. After a few seconds, the following information appears on my screen:

BBB Reliability Report

Paladin Press
2523 Broadway
Boulder, CO 80304

General Information
Original Business Start Date: January 1970
Principal: Mr. Peder C. Lund, President
Phone Number: (303) 443–7250
Type-of-Business Classification: PUBLISHERS

The information in this report has either been provided by the company or has been compiled by the Bureau from other sources.

Customer Experience

Based on BBB files, this company has a satisfactory record with the Bureau. Any complaints processed by the Bureau in its three-year reporting period have been resolved. The number and type of complaints are not unusual for a company in this industry.

To have a "Satisfactory Record" with the Bureau, a company must be in business for at least 12 months, properly and promptly address matters referred to it by the Bureau, and be free from an unusual volume or pattern of complaints and law enforcement action involving its marketplace conduct. In addition, the Bureau must have a clear understanding of the company's business and no concerns about its industry.

When evaluating complaint information, please consider the company's size and volume of business. The number of complaints filed against the company may not be as important as the type of complaints and how the company handled them.

Closed Complaints

Number of complaints processed by the BBB in last 36 months: 3

Number of complaints processed by the BBB in last 12 months: 3

Complaints Concerned

Delivery Issues: 2
Outcome of all complaints:
Resolved: 2
Product Quality Issues: 1
Outcome of the complaint:
Resolved: 1

Additional Information

Additional Doing-Business-As Names:
    CEP Inc.
    Paladin Enterprises Inc.
Additional Addresses:
    P.O. Box 1307, Boulder, CO 80306-1307

Company Management

Additional company management personnel include:
    Mr. Dana Roberts, Chief Financial Officer
    Ms. Cindy North, Accounting Manager
    Ms. Beverly Baker, Customer Service Manager
    Ms. Christina Miller, Marketing Director
    Ms. Paula Harden, Customer Service Manager

Report as of 12/04/2002
Copyright 2002, Denver/Boulder Better Business Bureau

As a matter of policy, the Better Business Bureau does not endorse any product, service, or company. BBB reports generally cover a three-year reporting period, and are provided solely to assist you in exercising your own best judgment. Information contained herein is believed reliable but not guaranteed as to accuracy. Reports are subject to change at any time.

The Better Business Bureau reports on members and non-members. Membership in the BBB is voluntary, and members must meet and maintain BBB standards. If a company is a member of this BBB, it is stated in this report.

This is an excellent report for any company and an exceptional one for a company that does the volume of business a mid-sized book publisher does. But what if my background check had turned up problems and my client wanted further investigation? You can see by this report that a number of leads have been generated, including the names of five key personnel, two other DBAs, and a post office box to check into.

BBB Reliability Reports are an excellent way to round out any background check. Thanks to the Computer Age, your agency can access these reports in a matter of minutes at no cost.

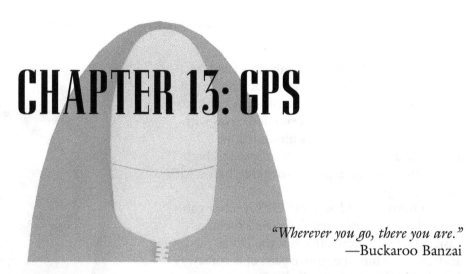

CHAPTER 13: GPS

"Wherever you go, there you are."
—Buckaroo Banzai

The Global Positioning System (GPS) is a satellite-based navigation system made up of a network of 24 satellites placed into orbit by the U.S. Department of Defense. GPS was originally intended for military applications, but in the 1980s the government made the system available for civilian use. GPS works in any weather conditions, anywhere in the world, 24 hours a day. There are no subscription fees or setup charges to use GPS. [1]

GPS satellites circle the earth twice a day in a very precise orbit and transmit signal information to GPS receivers on the ground. The receivers take this information and use triangulation to calculate the user's exact location. Essentially, the GPS receiver compares the time a signal was transmitted by a satellite with the time it was received. The time difference tells the receiver how far away the satellite is. With similar distance measurements from a few more satellites, the receiver can determine the user's position and display it on the unit's electronic map.

A GPS receiver must be locked on to the signal of at least three satellites to calculate a two-dimensional position (latitude and longitude) and track movement. With four or more satellites in view, the receiver can determine the user's three-dimensional position (latitude, longitude, and altitude). Once the user's position has been determined, the GPS unit can calculate such other information as speed, bearing, route, trip distance, distance to destination, sunrise and sunset time, and more.

The 24 satellites that make up the GPS space segment are orbiting about 12,000 miles above the earth. They are constantly moving, traveling

at speeds of roughly 7,000 miles an hour and making two complete orbits in less than 24 hours.

GPS satellites are powered by solar energy. They have backup batteries onboard to keep them running in the event of a solar eclipse, when there's no solar power. Small rocket boosters on each satellite keep them flying in the correct path.

GPS satellites transmit two low-power radio signals, designated L1 and L2. Civilian GPS uses the L1 frequency of 1575.42 MHz in the UHF band. The signals travel by line of sight, meaning they will pass through clouds, glass, and plastic but will not go through most solid objects such as buildings and mountains.

Here are some other interesting facts about the GPS satellites (also called NAVSTAR, the official U.S. Department of Defense name for GPS):

- The first GPS satellite was launched in 1978.
- A full constellation of 24 satellites was achieved in 1994.
- Each satellite is built to last about 10 years. Replacements are constantly being built and launched into orbit.
- A GPS satellite weighs approximately 2,000 pounds and is about 17 feet across with the solar panels extended.
- Transmitter power is only 50 watts or less.

GPS FOR THE DETECTIVE

So, how can GPS help you with an investigation? Suppose you have a rural area gig and need to cut through a mile of woods, exit at a specific point where high-voltage power lines cut a swath just beyond the subject's farm, and conduct a surveillance from the back border of the subject's property? In the old days you'd use a compass and a map, but even detectives with military training became confounded by magnetic deviation, inaccurate maps, and high iron content in the bedrock wreaking havoc with field readings.

An inexpensive handheld GPS receiver can make the Computer Age detective's life much easier. The GPS network maps the entire earth's surface to within one square yard of accuracy. A handheld GPS receiver will allow you to receive transmitted signals from the overhead satellites that can tell you exactly where you are and exactly where you want to go.

Want one? The best bang for the buck is Garmin's eTrex 12-Channel Handheld GPS Receiver. I had one shipped to my door for a total cost of $104 from Amazon.com during a free shipping promotion.

What will it do for you? Let's look again at the above rural surveillance example. I had a similar circumstance where I had to traverse over a mile of dense woods and then cross a river in winter to exit at some power lines cutting through my target property. Why? Well, as I said, there was snow on the ground so I could not risk footprints on or near the target property. What if his neighbor saw my footprints entering *his* property and then followed them to the target's property? He would call the target and ask if he'd been out walking between the properties for any reason. Things would fall apart from there. Another reason is that I couldn't risk being seen entering and exiting the surveillance post, especially since it was a long-term gig.

I stood with my GPS receiver at a reasonably accessible entry point through the woods and saved my current location in the receiver's memory as "Entry." The receiver allows you to label coordinates with recognizable names so you can later "track back" or "go to" the same point. I then drove by the subject's property and marked the point right in front of his property where I had clear line of site to the back power lines. Returning to the entrance point, two miles away by car, I parked at a local establishment and

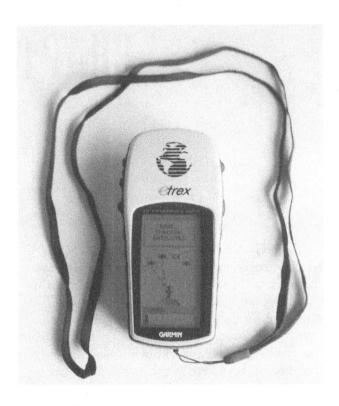

A Garmin GPS receiver. No bells and whistles, but it gets the job done in an affordable package. In my opinion, it's the best bang for your buck as far as GPS receivers go.

programmed my GPS to "go to" the target's property. Obviously I was not going to go all the way to the point I marked, but because I had clear line of site to the rear of the property, I knew I would have to exit somewhere along those power lines. The rest of the gig was routine. So there you have one of the simplest ways to use a GPS receiver.

The foregoing is a skeletal example of how you might use a GPS receiver in your investigations. You must remember all the old-school ruses and call upon your acting abilities if necessary to remain clandestine. For example, if you are a stranger in a rural area who, for no apparent reason, parks at a local establishment, whips out a GPS receiver, and troops off into the woods, people *will* talk. To avoid compromising your investigation, you may have to dress like a hiker, act a little stupid, and have some eggs and sausage links with the locals first. Ask if there are any good hiking trails around. Have a tourist-looking camera strapped around your neck. Ask where you might see an alligator or a moose, depending on your location.

You can easily imagine where the GPS receiver could be helpful in other situations. It can help you return or find a more direct route to a point where you had followed someone. It can allow you to trail someone through a national park without fear of getting lost. It can enable you to find equipment such as infrared video recorders you may have previously placed at strategic points. You can safely trail someone by boat, provided you prepare properly. You can instantly see your trip's time, distance from home, path traveled, hour of sunset, and a host of other bits of information that could prove useful in particular situations. Where's the nearest cell tower that gives you a clear, nonroaming signal? You'll relay important information back to your partner or office that much quicker because you saved the cell tower's location in your GPS and can go right to it.

ENDNOTE

[1]   General information about GPS courtesy of the Garmin web site: www.garmin.com.

CHAPTER 14: Lip Reading

"Although you took very thorough precautions in the pod against my hearing you, I could see your lips move."
—HAL in *2001: A Space Odyssey*

It's intriguing how many young detectives these days are surprised to learn that lip reading is a powerful weapon to have in your investigation arsenal. How many times has an investigation been stymied because a judge insisted on more probable cause before issuing an electronic surveillance warrant? Or what about we detectives who now reside in the private sector and can't get warrants? How many times have you seen your subject engaged in an impromptu conversation on his front steps, only to be much chagrinned that he is just out of earshot and you don't have time to set up your equipment? A lip reader needs no equipment, except maybe binoculars if the subject is far away.

Given the fact that the FBI maintains lip readers on its payroll, I'm willing to bet that legislators will never require detectives and law enforcement officers to obtain a warrant for lip reading detail. Imagine that: A completely legal means of being a virtual fly on the wall without a warrant. Powerful indeed.

And the Computer Age makes this skill even more powerful. Before I get to the reasons behind this, let me share with you an example where lip reading aided a police detective. I've omitted names and changed some details because, as you'll see, this case is not yet settled. However, this is a true story based on a real-life case.

A young couple, Romeo and Juliet, were out cruising around one Friday evening with some friends. At some point, another driver cut in front of Romeo's car. This angered Romeo and he pursued the vehicle, which had sped away in the dark. After passing other cars to catch up with the vehicle and following it down a side street, Romeo came up behind it at a light, blowing his horn and flashing his headlights.

As Romeo got out of his car, the other driver rolled down his window to find out what the problem was. Little did Romeo know, he had lost the original vehicle—this was simply another car of the same make and color. Romeo reached in and stabbed the innocent man with a knife.

The man later died and Romeo was charged with murder. Hailing from a somewhat affluent family, Romeo was able to remain free during a long trial, which eventually found him guilty. He remained free pending sentencing.

Romeo and Juliet committed suicide just before sentencing. Romeo's car was left on a bridge with a suicide note, and some clothes were found in the river below. Their bodies were never found.

So the young couple committed a romantic double suicide to escape the evil overlords of justice. End of story, right? Maybe not.

The prosecution team went back to a courthouse surveillance tape made just after Romeo's conviction. There was no audio on the tape, but the video clearly showed he and Juliet holding a private yet heated discussion. What were they saying? It would certainly be helpful to the prosecution team to know. But with no audio, how could they?

They hired a lip reader. She carefully studied the tape and was able to piece together the conversation. It went something like this:

Romeo: I can't believe they found me guilty.
Juliet: This is horrible.

Romeo: I'm going to prison for a long, long time.
Juliet: No! Let's just do what we planned. Like we said we would.

What was the plan? Based upon other information it had, the prosecution highly doubted it included a double suicide. The lovebirds almost certainly conjured up something more interesting than that and had planned all along to escape justice. The point is that armed with lip-read information, the prosecution knew they had fugitives on their hands and authorities knew to continue searching for them.

LIP READING PRIMER

If you have no plans to incorporate lip reading into your arsenal, I'd strongly suggest rethinking that sentiment. These days, anything that can give your agency an edge could make the difference between success and bankruptcy. Before I get to how the Computer Age has affected lip reading, here's a quick lip reading primer given in the hopes that you will consider adding this useful weapon to your detective toolkit.

First of all, you've probably lip-read before. Have you ever been at a party or sporting event where there was lots of background noise? Maybe you were standing in a small group of people and the conversation diverged into two or more conversations. This has happened to many of us before, where we suddenly find we somehow are being considered party to *both* conversations. Out of politeness, we try to keep up. But who's saying what? If you'd tried to close your eyes, you would have found it impossible to distinguish the words. Your only hope in such a situation is to keep your eyes open and play table tennis—glancing back and forth between the loquacious parties, looking at their lips to figure out which one is talking and what they are saying. This is basic lip reading.

Of course closing your eyes in such a situation would be considered rude, but you could try a similar experiment in a loud bar or nightclub. Look toward a distant corner of the room. Without focusing on anybody, it all sounds like a big jumble of noise. Now, look at someone's lips. Within 10 seconds or so, you will

be able to distinguish their voice from the rest. If the person is making a comment about you or someone in your party, you'd know it instantly. Another example of lip reading.

Watch football on TV? They don't broadcast the audio from the sidelines, but if you've ever looked at the coach's lips after the officials made a bad call, I'm sure you've *seen* a few choice words. How 'bout when they have the camera on the running back who just made the touchdown. What are his lips saying? "Hi mom," of course.

At the Boston Garden before it became the Fleet Center, I once saw bass player Geddy Lee of the rock band Rush miss a string of notes of his solo during the instrumental tune "YYZ." He turned his head and yelled something that could not be heard above the music. I had no problem reading his lips, nor did anybody else within 100 feet of the stage I would imagine. Hopefully his mother was not in the crowd to read his lips.

More advanced lip reading operates along the same lines as incidental lip reading, except you bring with you a broader knowledge base. You take the time beforehand to learn some basic mouth shapes, and you use this information to help determine what a person is saying. In fact, it's more correct these days to refer to the process as "speech reading" because you take clues from more than just the lips. Posture, emphasis, body language, gestures, and educated guesses based on the subject at hand all come into play when speech reading.

The setting is also an important indicator. For example, you see a group of people coming out of a movie theater. You're in your vehicle and you can't hear them. They are all animated, their gums flapping away. What do you suppose they're discussing? More likely than not, they are discussing the movie. If that presumption doesn't seem to gel with what your lip reading abilities are picking up, perhaps they are discussing where to have dinner? See if that assumption better helps you follow the conversation.

Next time you see a football player on TV mouth the words "hi mom," see if you can't use subject-context to figure out what he says after that. Hi dad? I love you? Wish you were here? Probably. A recitation of the

Pythagorean theorem? Probably not. That's using subject-context.

My favorite way of practicing lip reading takes absolutely no time at all. I simply mute the TV when commercials come on. Being familiar with the actual dialog of the commercial (from all the times my significant other refused to give me the remote) helps me to practice lip reading. I sometimes do this with TV shows I've seen before or movies I know by heart. Once you get good at it, you can mute the TV during shows that are new to you. Listen to the first half of a sentence (thereby acquiring context) and mute the second half. How much can you pick up?

Remember the above example of real-life detective lip reading? If you've captured someone on silent surveillance video, then in essence you are deaf. Their lips are moving and you can't hear anything. This is precisely the situation faced by a deaf person, except that you have the advantage of rewinding the video as many times as you need to.

Suppose you have silent video of two burglars who broke into a house. Before they leave, one says something to the other. You suspect what was said might be a clue as to where you can find them and the $10,000 diamond necklace they stole. Time is of the essence. So what exactly do you look for on their iniquitous lips?

Put simply, certain sounds require the speaker to make certain shapes with his mouth and lips. B, M, and P are evidenced by the lips completely closing together for a split second. M cannot be followed by another consonant, so if you detect another consonant you know the closed lips must've been a B or P. Once you become adept at it, this all happens in a split second. The consonant L would be evidenced by seeing the tongue still curled upward after the closed lips. So now you've got BL or PL. The brain instantly and instinctively knows a vowel sound is coming next, unless the person is speaking an obscure Martian dialect or something. What is it? Well, without getting into the nitty-gritty of things, let's just say that an *oo* sound would look very

different than an *ee* sound—*oo* curls the lips outward; *ee* flattens them into a half smile.

What if you detect a definite emphasis but no lip movement? How the hell do you decode that? Elementary, my dear waffle: process of elimination. You definitely know it's not B, P, or M, and there's a whole bunch of other sounds you can eliminate. A very guttural emphasis with no lip or tongue movement would most likely indicate a hard C, K, or G. An R would not be as guttural and it would draw in the lower jaw first.

J, CH, and SH all share a distinct look. Try it right now (*jeez*, *cheese*, and *she's*) and you'll see what I mean.

What if you figured out that the crook on the surveillance tape said "blue man" and you happen to know that this is the nickname of a popular local pawnbroker? Your ability to lip read probably just solved this case for you.

Delving into lip reading beyond this brief primer is beyond the scope of this book. I hope I've inspired you to further your education. There are books and videos available on the subject. There's plenty of information on the Internet as well. Just type "lip reading" or "speech reading" into any search engine and you'll be on your way.

LIP READING IN THE COMPUTER AGE

What if you're just too damn busy to learn anything else? In that case, it's the Computer Age to the rescue once again.

Scientist and software engineers are working closely with the deaf community to develop gesture-recognition software, which will encompass more than just lip reading. For about a decade now, the computer world has been able to capture motion information from people and animals wired up with sensors. Hollywood uses this technique to make realistic computerized extras for movies. Today, this and similar technologies are being combined to create computerized lip readers, among other things.

Lip reading technology is being combined with speech-recognition technology to make more reliable voice interfaces with computers. Background noise is a big problem with voice recognition, so scientists are adding lip reading technology as a way to cross-check what the computer thinks it hears. Did it hear an M or N? If the lips closed, then it heard an M. Gesture-recognition technology has already increased voice-recognition reliability from 60 to 80 percent accuracy. Once the bugs and cobwebs are worked out, I expect accuracy of greater than 95 percent to be the norm. It's only a matter of time before you'll be able to feed a silent video clip of moving lips into a computer, which will then help you analyze what is being said, if not completely decode it for you.

To keep abreast of this technology, do Internet searches and read books about computerized gesture recognition. The study of "haptics" (relating to the sense of touch and kinetics) is also closely related to this field, so you may wish to keep abreast of that topic as well.

CHAPTER 15: Heir Finding

"Like a young eagle, who has lent his plume; To fledge the shaft by which he meets his doom; See their own feathers pluck'd to wing the dart; Which rank corruption destines for their heart."
—Thomas Moore

Because my heir finding experience in Massachusetts is itself a case worth investigating, I've decided to write this chapter as a personal account. You will simultaneously see the evolution of the case, my career, and the Computer Age's effect on the heir finding aspect of our industry.

Early in my investigative career, I was an heir finder. For those who don't know, an heir finder finds the appropriate owners or heirs of misplaced money (money held by state and federal governments, probate courts, etc.) and asks them for a finder's fee.

Initially, my partner and I focused solely on funds already transferred to the state treasurer's office under the abandoned property laws. These laws are a story unto themselves. A few decades ago, a bank account used to be considered abandoned after 20 years of inactivity (no deposits, withdrawals, or inquiry from the account holder). This was reasonable.

Today these accounts are considered abandoned after only five years of inactivity—as few as two to three years in some states! Have some stock you've been hanging onto? Ask your broker to sell it and you may be surprised to learn that it has been turned over to the state for "safekeeping." A few states ignore the "safekeeping" façade altogether and take possession of the property by "escheat," which means you can't get it back. That's right, escheat: pay attention to the last five letters of that word.

Fortunately, most states will return this "abandoned" property to the rightful owner or heir upon receiving proper proof of entitlement. I tell you from experience that the process is a lengthy, bureaucratic one; so much so that people who are owed less than a few hundred dollars typically give up on chasing it. Most states have laws limiting heir finders to a 10 percent fee. Because of this, many detective agencies won't even look at a case involving less than $2,000. It's simply not worth the trouble. You can see why most of this money remains unclaimed.

How do states use the unclaimed property fund? Massachusetts apparently believes it's a big cookie jar full of loose change. About $90 million is unaccounted for and, according to court records, seems to be lining the pockets of some previous state employees and their old classmates. Convenient cookie jar . . . unless an astute bank teller happens to catch you with your hand in it, as happened in the Massachusetts case. (More on that later.)

When my partner and I first began the business, there apparently were no other heir finders in Massachusetts tracing accounts from the abandoned property division of the state treasurer's office. At first this surprised us. Billions of dollars were available and we expected serious competition. Little did we know, we had it—but not from other heir finders.

We were suspicious from the get-go. Our business proceeded smoothly at first—so smoothly that we could not fathom why we had no apparent competition. But after we tried to file our first few claims, reasons began to surface. Outright hostility by the state was the first one. State employees were totally uncooperative. We heard comments like, "I don't have to talk to you," "Why should I tell you?" and "We won't recognize your power-of-attorney." The employees were typically unavailable, seldom returned phone calls, and answered written correspondence only in the most politically correct fashion. We learned quickly that if we left them any wiggle room, they would use it to refuse or delay the claim.

Now we knew why there were no other heir finding businesses: they all got fed up. After a few months, we too were fed up. We threw all our files in a box and moved on to other endeavors.

During the sixth month of our (then inactive) heir finding business, something astounding happened: we got paid. Several of our clients had apparently pestered the state enough to actually get their money. They wrote us letters saying that they knew the delays were caused by the state and felt the state did it on purpose to discourage people. In short, they honored our contracts and paid us. Encouraged, we unboxed all the files and were back in the heir finding business. The state was not happy.

When my partner and I began the heir finding, there was no 10 percent finder's fee limit. Our first few heir finding checks were healthy ones, and this encouraged us and made it financially feasible for us to continue our efforts (we charged between 20 and 33 percent for a finder's fee). But wouldn't you know? After the state saw us get back in the game, there suddenly appeared on the law books a provision that now limited us to a 10 percent cut!

I went to the statehouse to research the legislative procedure that enacted the new law. Flipping through obscure journals, I couldn't believe what I was seeing. I checked it with a state librarian, who shall at her request remain anonymous.

"Yes," she said. "That law was enacted as part of HR-1." She was clearly hesitant to elaborate.

"But that's the annual budget," I said.

"Yes," she said, then leaned forward. "It looks like they sneaked it in," she whispered, "but you didn't hear that from me."

I checked this out with my district representative's office. My sister had worked there and they remembered the name—even

remembered my dog. The man who remembered my dog was comfortable enough with me to tell me his thoughts on the matter. He said it was somewhat odd that the state house budget had been sent to the attorney general's office for approval. "I've never seen a budget like that before," he said, and he'd been working for the state for 20 years.

My partner and I were dumbfounded. We were just two little guys chasing $2,000 to $4,000 cases. There were billions of unclaimed dollars at stake. We were the only ones doing it. Even if we worked the next 30 years, we'd never put a dent in it! What was the state trying to hide?

We got a small clue when the 10 percent limit forced us to chase higher amounts. We found a woman entitled to more than $50,000 from her dead husband's old bank account. She was living on welfare! She didn't believe our story and called the state. Now you must understand, the new law required us to tell her where the money was before she agreed to pay us a fee. Unfortunately, most people just went and got the money themselves without paying us. And that's what this lady did.

It turns out the state was painting us as opportunists and encouraging people to, well, stiff us. This is the same state that let this woman live on welfare for 20 years even though they had more than $50K of her dough—and she was still living at the same address they had on file! For some reason, their in-house heir finders couldn't find her . . . until after we notified her, that is.

A few months later the state treasurer was on radio talking about the abandoned property fund. He actually cited the above case as an example of how their in-house heir finders help the poor, unfortunate citizens of Massachusetts. I was driving in my truck at the time, and I do believe a brown, mushy substance with an odor vaguely reminiscent of bovine excrement began to ooze from my speaker grates.

The state treasurer did not mention my agency during that interview. Here's a few more things state treasurers fail to mention in their required annual newspaper listings of abandoned property:

- The names in the listing are for that year only.
- The listing does not include accounts under a certain dollar amount.
- The listing omits certain abandoned property sources.

The font size used in the listing is not readable to many of the people (elderly, disabled) who are owed money.

In various captions, the listing implies or outright states that:

- The above names represent all of the accounts in the state's possession (when in fact the listing is merely a fraction of what they have).
- You do not have to pay anyone a fee to claim your money. (Geez, where'd they come up with that one?)

We experienced a few more incidents like the one described above. We'd find someone owed big money. They'd act very surprised. A week later, they'd tell us, "Oh yeah, a guy from the state called me on that a week before you guys did." Funny; the client hadn't mentioned that tidbit of information during our initial conversation.

We tried other states, but they all had their scam. New York, for example, will tell you the name of the person to whom money is owed but will not tell you the value of the property. Since the files are riddled with "accounts" valued in the $0.02 to $.99 range, an heir finder is left with no financially feasible way to proceed. Convenient.

Texas charges more than $1,000 for its list and requires heir finders to be licensed private detectives. Licensed private detective? To look up names in a phone book? Better have a license to carry a pistol, too. Those phone books get rough.

California is pretty reasonable, except that all their good accounts have already been settled by a single heir finder who was paid his cut directly by the state. Hmmmm.

Years after I'd given up on the heir finding game, Massachusetts newspapers broke the story:

A state insider working on abandoned property accounts was feeding all the good cases to a sham heir finding agency set up by one of his buddies. This is bad enough in itself, but it doesn't stop there. His buddy did not have the same difficulty my heir finding agency had in filing claims. In fact, he did not even need a claimant! Remember how they refused to acknowledge my power-of-attorney? Not a problem . . . *if you went to high school with the man overseeing the funds!* Not even a problem if the power-of-attorney is a known forgery and purports to be executed by a long-defunct company owed $6.5 million. It's only a problem for outsiders with real powers-of-attorney trying to help real people get their hard-earned money back.

Thus present and former state employees, their attorneys, and companions managed to funnel millions of dollars from the state treasurer's office into their personal bank accounts. No wonder the state didn't want any private detective agencies poking around.

Here are some brief media excerpts pertinent to facts mentioned above (my italics added to certain passages for emphasis). From a press release from the attorney general's office:

"The charges for which Robbins was sentenced today involved an illegal kickback scheme and several thefts involving or relating to heir finder claims. The Robbins Associates kickback scheme involved codefendant John Trischitta and Robbins. The two men utilized an heir finder company doing business as Robbins Associates in an arrangement *where in return for Robbins receiving inside information and preferential treatment from Trischitta, Robbins paid Trischitta 1/3 of all of the profits from the claims he submitted* to the UPCF. Robbins received 2/3 of those profits, and submitted in excess of 150 claims in a little over a half of a year."

One hundred and fifty claims? That's more than I did in my five years. Here's another excerpt from a *Boston Globe* article entitled "For Malden High Graduates, Differing Paths May Have Led to Dangerous Crossroads" by David Armstrong, Ellen O'Brien, Stephen Kurkjian, and Peter J. Howe, 02/28/99 (pertinent text italicized):

"Initially, according to sources, Trischitta, 47, gave Robbins, 51, *exclusive access* to the list of those owed the most from the unclaimed money fund . . . Then, last fall, state prosecutors allege Robbins offered a $50,000 bribe to Trischitta to issue $6.5 million in checks from the Unpaid Check Fund to a defunct government development corporation that Robbins fraudulently claimed to represent. Once the money was safely deposited in Robbins's BankBoston checking account, Trischitta was to receive one-third of the proceeds, prosecutors charge."

"Exclusive access" means that these crooks had to find a way to exclude legitimate heir finding agencies such as mine. With no legal means to do this, intimidation became the tactic.

At least seven people were charged in this conspiracy and at least six were awarded prison time for their service to the Commonwealth of Massachusetts.

HEIR FINDING IN THE COMPUTER AGE

When my partner and I first started heir finding, we had no computer. Few people did back then. Well, okay, we had a Commodore 64 that we toyed around with, but it couldn't help us in our business. We tested the waters by sticking with only those cases that could be researched in our local telephone directory. We had a pretty decent "hit" ratio and realized we could solve a good number of cases simply by flipping through phone books.

But how do you get phone books for the entire state? Turns out you can if you're a business. So we did. We had a whole living room filled with directories from every calling area in every county. And thus we proceeded flipping through easily torn pages, squinting at the small text, underlining names, and making calls.

Our need to research probate law (in order to determine which heir stood next in line and how

to administer estates) often took us to the local library. One day, something new appeared at the library: a computer. We were only mildly curious at first. Initially we used it to look up research material and initiate interlibrary loans. During one research trip, my partner went to look something up but the computer was already in use. My partner became very excited and took me to see the man using the computer. He pointed subtly, but I'd already seen it—he was using the computer to look up phone numbers! We fetched the librarian, who told us about a new CD-ROM database that allowed you to look up names, phone numbers, and addresses. Unlike a phone book, you could type in a phone number and the associated name and address would pop up. You could type in an address and get a phone number. And you could do all this on a nationwide basis. Since New England had the highest transient population in the country, we saw the potential of being able to search for people out of state. To go nationwide, the old-fashioned way would've required more than a living room full of phone books. In short, we saw dollar signs.

For a few weeks we made regular trips to the library to solve cases using the CD-ROM, but we eventually invested in a computer and CD-ROM of our own. We found the company that made the software, Pro-CD in Massachusetts, and gladly forked over $300 to purchase the disks. Next trash day we clearly heard the pickup men grumbling over whether they had to take all the f***ing phone books from the sidewalk. They did. The little office of our detective agency suddenly seemed a lot bigger.

For the next several years we paid the annual $79 to update our CDs. But today even that seems like ancient history. I haven't used my Pro-CD SelectPhone software in ages. In fact, I still haven't loaded it onto the hard drive of my new PC. Haven't had the need. Why?

For $17 a month I get unlimited Internet access to the same information. If I need to look up a phone number, I go to whitepages.com. For the same $17 I can communicate with my clients via e-mail, and I get access to a wealth of other on-line search services.

Fact is, I no longer trace accounts held by state treasuries. With the advent of the Internet, state treasuries have been forced to go on-line to keep up with the times. It wasn't long before taxpayers pushed them to get their abandoned accounts on-line for easier searching. Today there are also third-party clearinghouses on the Internet that, for a small fee, allow you to search all participating states at once. Very convenient, and well worth the small fee if you believe you or your immediate ancestors have lost money somewhere. One such site is www.foundmoney.com.

An interesting side note, which demonstrates yet another way the Computer Age has affected our industry. Before there were Internet sites for abandoned property and before I quit the heir finding business altogether, I spent a few years trying my business on the honor system. My partner and I had gone our separate ways, and I didn't have the time to do heir finding by myself. One day I had an idea. Why not find 50 potential claimants per day—even ones owed just a few dollars—and send them a brochure on how to collect their money? The brochure listed the original account holder's name and address and the name of the institution that held the funds. If my "client" recognized the property and felt he or she deserved to claim it, the brochure told them how to do that. My cover letter was short and to the point. I asked them to remember me if they ever got any money from the state, and I included a return envelope.

Several months later, the envelopes began coming back to me: $10 here, $20 there, an occasional big hit in the $1,000 range. It all added up, and computers made it possible. By merging my database with a form letter, I was able to print out customized brochures for each person to better help them collect their inheritance. If you add it all up, the computer helped me to:

- Database relevant cases from microfiche files.
- Look up cases in CD-ROM phone books.
- Use the Internet to determine a stock's current value (to determine if a case was worth chasing and, if so, to tell the potential

client how much they'd been left).
- Create a professional-looking cover letter.
- Create a brochure that had individualized information filled in via associated fields in the database.
- Print out professional-looking envelopes with correct address and barcode.
- Account for funds as cases were solved.
- Note which cases were solved so I wouldn't go back to them.

The honor system had been very successful for two reasons. One, I didn't fret over the people who didn't pay me. Two, I exploited the personal computer at just the right time—when the information was difficult to access and before it became readily available via the Internet, therefore serving a need. Even though it's been years since I've done honor system heir finding, a check straggles in every once in a while. I even got one this year. My last? Maybe, maybe not.

Take the Computer Age out of this chapter and you'd have different stories entirely. In the first story, I would've been so busy flipping through phone books I never would've become suspicious of the state. With my honor-system program, how long would it have taken me to look up 50 cases without nationwide telephone data on a CD-ROM? How long would it have taken to write individualized letters to each of those 50 people and type up address labels for the envelopes? Without a computer, it wouldn't have happened.

THE FUTURE OF HEIR FINDING

Today, politicians have gotten smart. Incumbent state treasurers across the country have learned that it pays to return the money to the citizens. A couple states even have kiosks set up in malls where you can find out via computer whether you have any money owed to you. Of course, the state treasurer's picture is plastered all over the kiosk. For big cases involving thousands of dollars, state treasurers make a publicity stunt out of it, showing up at your door with cameras like Ed McMahon from Publisher's Clearinghouse.

Despite the availability of on-line clearinghouses and the occasional politically motivated kiosk, there's still billions of dollars out there waiting to be returned. Some states have records going back more than 100 years, and the heirs, even if they are once-removed third cousins or great-grandnephews, are still entitled to it. These are the people who will never see their names in the paper and won't even turn up as matches at a kiosk or on-line database. These people need, well, a private detective. So there's still plenty of work out there for you.

The honor system method described above is still quite viable. You'll be surprised at how many people will send you a check years down the road just because you were nice enough to tip them off and send them an instruction pamphlet on how to retrieve their money.

CONCLUSION

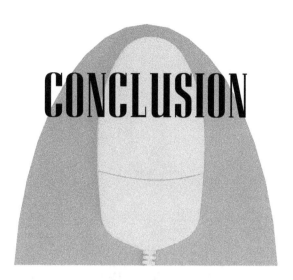

As stated in this book's introduction, the tools of man define the "Age" in which he lives. Clearly, we are in the Computer Age. The Computer Age had a rapid and profound effect on many industries, and the players in those industries were of two sorts: the quick and the dead.

Today, even a novice detective can spot the clues. Be it freeing valuable office space from hundreds of phone books, getting instant on-line directions to a suspect's hideout, or unraveling a complicated financial money trail without ever leaving your desk, the Computer Age has left its footprint on our industry. Yet many of us were caught off guard, realizing almost too late that we were enveloped in unwarranted complacency. We needed either to learn to use computers effectively *and daily* or go the way of the gumshoe private dick with his fedora, snubby revolver, and collection of underworld contacts. We've each had our individual wake-up calls that private investigation no longer fits this Sam Spade stereotype. If you haven't, then maybe this book was your wake-up call.

A PI who can't compute is a caveman. If he's retiring in a few years and has a good client base, he'll make it to retirement. But a new detective or one who is years away from retirement has little choice but to accept change. Otherwise his faster-moving colleagues will outmaneuver him. If he insists on pounding pavement between public information sources, then he will be outpaced by those competitors who can peruse this information on-line. "Outpaced" here is a grand understatement. The data will be whizzing through overhead phone lines and fiber optic cables at light speed as he hoofs through city streets, ending up on his competitors' desks before he even steps off the sidewalk a block from his office.

I believe this book has introduced you to the changes in our industry and how to best deal with them. Not only have we seen how new tools and technology can help us work faster and more efficiently in solving typical, old-fashioned cases (e.g. missing persons, domestic surveillance), we've also seen where existing fields have changed (e.g., heir finding) or entire new ones have sprung up (e.g., computer monitoring and surveillance, data mining, computer security).

Finally, we've seen where the effect of the Computer Age on our industry is not just something that requires a one-time adjustment. We must keep a vigilant eye toward the horizon. To remain competitive, we must watch for new tools yet to come, new fields yet to open.

I've said that the Computer Age has left its footprint on our industry. The modern PI should pour plaster in this footprint and mount the casting on his desk. Let it forever remind him that man's modern tools will continue to find new homes with successful PIs. To keep his own home in this industry, the modern private investigator must fully embrace the Computer Age.

BIBLIOGRAPHY

Bugman, Shifty. *The Basement Bugger's Bible* (Paladin Press, Boulder, CO), 1999.

Charrett, Sheldon. *Electronic Circuits and Secrets of an Old-Fashioned Spy* (Paladin Press, Boulder, CO), 1999.

Chesbro, Michael. *Complete Guide to E-Security* (Paladin Press, Boulder, CO), 2002.

Culligan, Joseph J. *Requirements to Become a P.I. in the 50 States and Elsewhere* (Hallmark Press, Inc., North Miami, FL), 1992.

Lapin, Lee. *Expert Body Language: The Science of People Reading* (Intelligence Here, Mt. Shasta, CA), 1992.

Lowe, Sheila R. *The Complete Idiot's Guide to Handwriting Analysis* (Alpha Books, New York, NY), 1999.

Schlein, Alan M. *Find it Online* (Facts on Demand Press, Tempe, AZ), 2000.

Scott, Robert. *Investigator's Little Black Book 2* (Crime Time Publishing Co., Beverly Hills, CA), 1998.

Scott, Robert. *Sexual Predator* (Crime Time Publishing Co., Beverly Hills, CA), 1999.

Time Finance Adjusters. *TFA 2001–2002 Guide* (Time Finance Adjusters, Daytona Beach, FL), 2001.

Zaenglein, Norbert. *Disk Detective* (Paladin Press: Boulder, CO), 1998.

_____. *Secret Software* (Paladin Press, Boulder, CO), 2000.

APPENDIX 1: Sources

This appendix is just a very short list of resources I've found to be reliable. The companies were in business and their associated URLs (web addresses) were current at the time of this writing.

All Electronics
www.allelectronics.com
(pinhole cameras; surplus dealer so they
occasionally have other goodies)

DigiKey
www.digiKey.com
(RF transmitters, RF transmitter modules,
pinhole cameras)

JDR Microdevices
www.jdr.com
(RF transmitters, RF transmitter modules, pinhole cameras, occasionally DTMF decoder kits)

Ramsey Electronics
www.ramseyelectronics.com
www.ramseykits.com
(miniature, long-range, crystal-controlled video
transmitters)

X10
www.x10.com
(wireless camera systems)

APPENDIX F: SPECS

APPENDIX 2: Geographical and Chronological Distribution of Social Security Numbers

As you'll recall from Table 5.3, the Social Security Administration issues SSNs in groupings enumerated by the middle digits. You'll also recall that the SSA issues these groups in a very specific pattern. By knowing this pattern and keeping track of when the highest group changes in a given area, one can compile a listing of which year the SSA issued a given group in a given area. Banks and credit reporting agencies have done this over the years, as has the SSA. This appendix is such a listing. It is the most complete one I have at the time of this writing. It is valid for all states for the years 1951 through 1978.

STATE	Area	1951	1952	1953	1954	1955	1956	1957	1958	1959	1960	1961	1962	1963	1964	1965	1966	1967	1968	1969	1970	1971	1972	1973	1974	1975	1976	1977	78
NH	001	26	26	28	28	28	30	32	32	32	32	34	36	36	38	40	42	42	44	46	46	48	48	54	56	56	58	60	60
NH	002	26	26	26	28	28	30	30	30	32	32	34	34	38	38	40	40	42	44	44	46	46	48	52	54	56	58	60	60
NH	003	24	26	26	26	28	28	30	30	32	32	32	34	38	38	38	40	42	42	44	46	46	48	52	54	56	58	58	58
ME	004	32	34	36	36	38	40	40	40	42	42	44	46	50	50	50	52	54	56	56	58	60	62	66	68	70	72	72	74
ME	005	32	34	34	36	38	40	40	40	42	42	44	44	48	50	50	52	54	54	56	58	60	62	64	66	68	70	72	72
ME	006	32	34	34	34	36	38	40	40	40	42	44	44	48	48	50	52	54	54	56	58	60	62	64	66	68	70	72	72
ME	007	32	32	34	34	36	38	38	40	40	42	42	44	46	48	50	50	52	54	56	58	58	60	64	66	68	70	70	72
VT	008	24	24	26	26	28	28	28	30	30	32	32	34	36	36	38	40	40	42	42	44	46	46	54	54	58	60	60	60
VT	009	22	24	24	24	26	28	28	28	30	30	32	32	34	36	38	38	40	40	42	44	46	52	54	56	58	58	58	58
MA	010	28	28	28	30	30	30	32	32	32	34	34	36	38	38	40	42	42	44	46	46	48	48	50	52	54	54	58	58
MA	011	26	28	28	30	30	30	32	32	32	34	34	36	38	38	40	42	42	44	46	46	48	48	50	52	54	54	58	58
MA	012	26	28	28	28	28	30	32	32	32	34	34	36	38	38	40	42	42	44	46	46	48	48	50	52	54	54	58	58
MA	013	28	28	28	28	30	30	32	32	32	34	34	36	38	38	40	42	42	44	44	46	48	48	50	52	54	54	58	58
MA	014	26	28	28	28	30	30	32	32	32	34	34	36	38	38	40	42	44	46	46	46	48	48	50	52	54	54	56	58
MA	015	26	28	28	28	30	30	30	32	32	34	34	34	38	38	40	42	42	44	46	46	48	48	50	52	54	54	56	58
MA	016	28	28	28	28	30	30	30	32	32	32	34	34	38	38	40	42	42	44	46	46	48	48	50	52	54	54	56	58
MA	017	26	28	28	28	30	30	30	32	32	32	34	36	38	38	40	40	42	44	44	46	48	48	50	52	54	54	56	58
MA	018	26	28	28	28	30	30	30	32	32	32	35	34	36	38	40	40	42	44	44	46	48	48	50	52	54	54	56	58
MA	019	26	28	28	28	30	30	30	32	32	32	34	34	38	38	40	40	42	44	44	46	48	48	50	52	54	54	56	58
MA	020	26	28	28	28	30	30	30	32	32	32	34	34	36	38	40	40	42	44	44	46	48	48	50	52	52	54	56	58
MA	021	26	28	28	28	30	30	30	32	32	32	34	34	36	38	40	40	42	44	44	46	48	48	50	52	52	54	56	58
MA	022	26	26	28	28	30	30	30	30	32	32	34	34	38	38	40	40	42	44	44	46	48	48	50	52	52	54	56	58
MA	023	26	26	28	28	28	30	30	30	32	32	34	34	36	38	40	40	42	42	44	46	48	48	50	52	52	54	56	58
MA	024	26	26	28	28	28	30	30	30	32	32	34	34	36	38	38	40	42	42	44	46	48	48	50	52	52	54	56	58
MA	025	26	26	28	28	28	30	30	30	32	32	34	34	36	38	38	40	42	42	44	46	48	48	50	52	52	54	56	58
MA	026	26	26	28	28	28	30	30	30	32	32	34	34	36	38	38	40	42	42	44	46	46	48	50	52	52	54	56	58
MA	027	26	26	28	28	28	30	30	30	32	32	32	34	36	38	38	40	42	42	44	46	46	48	50	52	52	54	56	58
MA	028	26	26	28	28	28	30	30	30	32	32	32	34	36	38	38	40	40	42	44	46	46	48	50	52	52	54	56	58
MA	029	26	26	28	28	28	30	30	30	32	32	32	34	36	38	38	40	42	42	44	46	48	48	50	50	52	54	56	56
MA	030	26	26	28	28	28	30	30	30	32	32	34	36	38	38	40	42	42	44	46	46	48	50	50	52	54	54	56	56
MA	031	26	26	28	28	28	30	30	30	32	32	34	34	36	38	38	40	42	42	44	44	46	48	50	50	52	54	56	56
MA	032	26	26	28	28	28	28	30	30	30	32	32	34	36	38	38	40	42	42	44	44	46	48	50	50	52	54	56	56
MA	033	26	26	28	28	28	28	30	30	30	32	32	34	36	38	38	40	42	42	44	44	46	48	50	50	52	54	56	56
MA	034	26	26	28	28	28	28	30	30	30	32	32	34	36	36	38	40	42	42	44	46	46	50	50	52	52	54	56	56
RI	035	22	24	24	26	26	26	26	26	28	28	28	30	32	32	32	34	36	36	38	38	38	40	42	44	46	46	48	48
RI	036	22	24	24	24	24	26	26	26	26	28	28	30	32	32	32	34	34	36	36	38	38	40	42	44	44	46	48	48

138

STATE	Area	1951	1952	1953	1954	1955	1956	1957	1958	1959	1960	1961	1962	1963	1964	1965	1966	1967	1968	1969	1970	1971	1972	1973	1974	1975	1976	1977	78
RI	037	22	22	24	24	24	26	26	26	26	28	28	28	30	32	32	34	34	36	36	38	38	40	42	44	44	46	46	46
RI	038	22	22	24	24	24	24	26	26	28	28	28	28	30	30	32	32	34	34	36	36	38	38	42	42	44	46	46	46
RI	039	22	22	24	24	24	24	24	26	26	26	26	28	30	30	32	32	34	34	36	36	38	38	42	42	44	46	46	46
CT	040	28	28	30	30	30	32	32	34	34	34	36	38	42	42	44	46	48	48	50	52	54	56	60	62	64	68	68	68
CT	041	26	28	30	30	30	32	32	34	34	36	38	40	40	42	44	46	48	48	50	52	54	56	60	62	64	66	68	68
CT	042	26	28	30	30	30	32	32	34	34	34	36	36	40	42	44	46	46	48	50	52	54	54	60	62	64	66	68	68
CT	043	26	28	30	30	30	30	32	34	34	34	36	36	40	42	42	44	46	48	50	52	54	54	60	62	64	66	68	68
CT	044	26	28	28	30	30	30	32	32	34	34	34	36	40	42	44	44	46	48	50	52	54	54	60	62	64	66	66	68
CT	045	26	28	28	30	30	30	32	32	34	34	36	36	40	42	44	44	46	48	50	52	52	54	60	62	64	66	66	68
CT	046	26	28	28	30	30	30	32	32	32	34	34	36	40	40	42	44	46	48	50	52	52	54	58	60	64	66	66	68
CT	047	26	26	28	30	30	30	30	32	32	34	34	36	38	40	42	44	46	48	48	50	52	54	58	60	64	66	66	66
CT	048	26	26	28	30	30	30	30	32	32	34	34	36	38	40	42	44	46	48	50	50	52	54	58	60	62	66	66	66
CT	049	26	26	28	28	28	30	30	32	32	34	34	36	38	40	42	44	46	46	48	50	52	54	58	60	62	66	66	66
NY	050	28	28	30	30	30	32	32	34	34	34	36	36	38	40	42	42	44	46	46	48	50	50	54	54	56	60	60	62
NY	051	28	28	30	30	30	32	32	34	34	34	36	36	40	40	42	42	44	46	46	48	50	50	54	54	56	60	60	62
NY	052	28	28	30	30	30	32	32	34	34	34	36	36	40	40	42	42	44	46	46	48	50	50	54	54	56	60	60	62
NY	053	28	28	30	30	30	32	32	34	34	34	36	36	40	40	42	42	44	46	46	48	50	50	54	54	56	60	60	62
NY	054	28	28	30	30	30	32	32	34	34	34	36	36	40	40	42	42	44	46	46	48	50	50	54	54	56	60	60	62
NY	055	28	28	30	30	30	32	32	34	34	34	36	36	40	40	42	42	44	46	46	48	50	50	54	54	56	58	60	62
NY	056	28	28	30	30	30	32	32	34	34	34	36	36	40	40	42	42	44	46	46	48	50	50	54	54	56	58	60	62
NY	057	28	28	30	30	30	32	32	34	34	34	36	36	40	40	42	42	44	46	46	48	50	50	54	54	56	58	60	62
NY	058	28	28	30	30	30	32	32	34	34	34	36	36	40	40	42	42	44	44	46	48	50	50	54	54	56	58	60	62
NY	059	28	28	30	30	30	32	32	32	34	34	36	36	40	40	42	42	44	46	46	48	50	50	54	54	56	58	60	62
NY	060	28	28	30	30	30	32	32	34	34	34	36	36	40	40	42	42	44	46	46	48	50	50	54	54	56	58	60	62
NY	061	28	28	30	30	30	32	32	34	34	34	36	36	40	40	42	42	44	46	46	48	50	50	54	54	56	58	60	62
NY	062	28	28	30	30	30	32	32	34	34	34	36	36	40	40	42	42	44	46	46	48	50	50	54	54	56	58	60	62
NY	063	28	28	30	30	30	32	32	34	34	34	36	36	40	40	42	42	44	46	46	48	50	50	54	54	56	58	60	62
NY	064	28	28	30	30	30	32	32	34	34	34	36	36	40	40	42	42	44	46	46	48	50	50	52	54	56	58	60	62
NY	065	28	28	30	30	30	32	32	34	34	34	36	36	40	40	42	42	44	44	46	48	50	50	52	54	56	58	60	62
NY	066	28	28	30	30	30	32	32	34	34	34	36	36	40	40	40	42	44	44	46	48	50	50	52	54	56	58	60	62
NY	067	28	28	30	30	30	32	32	32	34	34	36	36	40	40	40	42	44	44	46	48	50	50	52	54	56	58	60	62
NY	068	28	28	30	30	30	32	32	34	34	34	36	36	40	40	40	42	44	44	46	48	50	50	52	54	56	58	60	62
NY	069	28	28	28	30	30	32	32	32	34	34	36	36	40	40	40	42	44	44	46	48	50	50	52	54	56	58	60	62
NY	070	28	28	30	30	30	32	32	32	34	34	36	36	40	40	40	42	44	46	46	48	50	50	52	54	56	58	60	62
NY	071	28	28	30	30	30	32	32	32	34	34	36	36	40	40	40	42	44	44	46	48	50	50	52	54	56	58	60	62
NY	072	28	28	28	30	30	32	32	32	34	34	36	36	40	40	40	42	44	46	46	48	50	50	52	54	56	58	60	62
NY	073	28	28	28	30	30	32	32	32	34	34	36	36	40	40	40	42	44	46	46	48	50	50	52	54	56	58	60	62
NY	074	28	28	28	30	30	32	32	34	34	34	36	36	40	40	40	42	44	46	46	48	50	50	52	54	56	58	60	62

STATE	Area	1951	1952	1953	1954	1955	1956	1957	1958	1959	1960	1961	1962	1963	1964	1965	1966	1967	1968	1969	1970	1971	1972	1973	1974	1975	1976	1977	78
NY	075	28	28	28	30	30	32	32	32	34	34	36	36	40	40	40	42	44	44	46	48	50	50	52	54	56	58	60	62
NY	076	28	28	28	30	30	32	32	32	34	34	36	36	38	40	40	42	44	46	46	48	50	52	52	54	56	58	60	62
NY	077	26	28	28	30	30	32	32	32	34	34	34	36	38	40	40	42	44	44	46	48	50	52	52	54	56	58	60	62
NY	078	26	28	28	30	30	32	32	32	34	34	34	36	38	40	40	42	44	44	46	48	50	52	52	54	56	58	60	62
NY	079	28	28	28	30	30	32	32	32	34	34	34	36	38	40	40	42	44	44	46	48	50	52	52	54	56	58	60	62
NY	080	26	28	28	30	30	32	32	32	34	34	34	36	38	40	40	42	44	44	46	48	50	52	52	54	56	58	60	62
NY	081	28	28	28	30	30	32	32	32	34	34	34	36	38	40	40	42	44	44	46	48	50	52	52	54	56	58	60	62
NY	082	26	28	28	30	30	30	32	32	34	34	34	36	38	40	40	42	44	44	46	48	50	52	52	54	56	58	60	60
NY	083	26	28	28	30	30	30	32	32	34	34	34	36	38	40	40	42	44	44	46	48	50	52	52	54	56	58	60	60
NY	084	26	28	28	30	30	30	32	32	34	34	34	36	38	40	40	42	44	44	46	48	50	52	52	54	56	58	60	60
NY	085	26	28	28	30	30	30	32	32	34	34	34	36	38	40	40	42	44	44	46	48	50	52	52	54	56	58	60	60
NY	086	28	28	28	30	30	30	32	32	34	34	34	36	38	40	40	42	44	44	46	48	50	52	52	54	56	58	60	60
NY	087	28	28	28	30	30	30	32	32	34	34	34	36	38	40	40	42	44	44	46	48	50	52	52	54	56	58	60	60
NY	088	28	28	28	30	30	30	32	32	34	34	34	36	38	40	40	42	44	44	46	48	50	52	52	54	56	58	60	60
NY	089	26	28	28	30	30	30	32	32	34	34	34	36	38	40	40	42	44	44	46	48	50	52	52	54	56	58	60	60
NY	090	28	28	28	30	30	30	32	32	34	34	34	36	38	40	40	42	44	44	46	48	50	52	52	54	56	58	60	60
NY	091	26	28	28	30	30	30	32	32	34	34	34	36	38	40	40	42	42	44	46	48	50	52	52	54	56	58	60	60
NY	092	26	28	28	30	30	30	32	32	34	34	34	36	38	40	40	42	44	44	46	48	50	52	52	54	56	58	60	60
NY	093	26	28	28	30	30	30	32	32	34	34	34	36	38	40	40	42	42	44	46	48	50	52	52	54	56	58	60	60
NY	094	26	28	28	30	30	30	32	32	34	34	34	36	38	40	40	42	44	44	46	48	50	52	52	54	56	58	60	60
NY	095	26	28	28	30	30	30	32	32	34	34	34	36	38	38	40	42	44	44	46	48	50	52	52	54	56	58	60	60
NY	096	26	28	28	30	30	30	32	32	34	34	34	36	38	40	40	42	42	44	46	48	50	52	52	54	56	58	60	60
NY	097	26	28	28	30	30	30	32	32	34	34	34	36	38	38	40	42	42	44	46	48	50	52	52	54	56	58	60	60
NY	098	26	28	28	30	30	30	32	32	34	34	34	36	38	38	40	42	42	44	46	48	50	52	52	54	56	58	60	60
NY	099	26	28	28	30	30	30	32	32	32	34	34	36	38	38	40	42	42	44	46	48	50	52	52	54	56	58	60	60
NY	100	26	28	28	30	30	30	32	32	32	34	34	36	38	38	40	42	42	44	46	48	50	52	52	54	56	58	60	60
NY	101	26	28	28	30	30	30	32	32	32	34	34	36	38	38	40	40	42	44	46	46	48	50	52	54	56	58	60	60
NY	102	26	28	28	28	30	30	32	32	32	34	34	36	38	38	40	40	42	44	46	46	48	50	52	54	56	58	60	60
NY	103	26	28	28	28	30	30	32	32	32	34	34	36	38	38	40	40	42	44	46	46	48	50	52	54	56	58	60	60
NY	104	26	28	28	28	30	30	32	32	32	34	34	36	38	38	40	40	42	44	46	48	48	50	52	54	56	58	60	60
NY	105	26	28	28	28	30	30	32	32	32	34	34	36	38	38	40	40	42	44	46	48	48	50	52	54	56	58	60	60
NY	106	26	28	28	28	30	30	32	32	32	34	34	36	38	38	40	40	42	44	46	46	48	50	52	54	56	58	60	60
NY	107	26	28	28	28	30	30	32	32	32	34	34	36	38	38	40	40	42	44	46	46	48	50	52	54	56	58	60	60
NY	108	26	28	28	28	30	30	32	32	32	34	34	36	38	38	40	40	42	44	46	46	48	50	52	54	56	58	60	60
NY	109	26	28	28	28	30	30	32	32	32	34	34	36	38	38	40	40	42	44	46	46	48	50	52	54	56	58	60	60
NY	110	26	28	28	28	30	30	32	32	32	34	34	36	38	38	40	40	42	44	46	46	48	50	52	54	56	58	60	60
NY	111	26	28	28	28	30	30	32	32	32	34	34	36	38	38	40	40	42	44	46	46	48	50	52	54	56	58	60	60
NY	112	26	28	28	28	30	30	32	32	32	34	34	36	38	38	40	40	42	44	46	46	48	50	52	54	56	58	60	60
NY	113	26	28	28	28	30	30	30	32	32	34	34	36	38	38	40	40	42	44	46	46	48	50	52	54	56	58	60	60
NY	114	26	28	28	28	30	30	32	32	32	34	34	36	38	38	40	40	42	44	46	48	48	50	52	54	56	58	60	60

STATE	Area	1951	1952	1953	1954	1955	1956	1957	1958	1959	1960	1961	1962	1963	1964	1965	1966	1967	1968	1969	1970	1971	1972	1973	1974	1975	1976	1977	78
NY	115	26	28	28	28	30	30	32	32	32	34	34	36	38	38	40	40	42	44	46	48	48	50	52	54	56	58	60	60
NY	116	26	28	28	28	30	30	30	32	32	34	34	36	38	38	40	40	42	44	46	46	48	50	52	54	56	58	60	60
NY	117	26	28	28	28	30	30	32	32	32	34	34	36	38	38	40	40	42	44	46	48	48	50	52	54	56	58	60	60
NY	118	26	28	28	28	30	30	32	32	32	34	34	36	38	38	40	40	42	44	46	46	48	50	52	54	56	58	60	60
NY	119	26	28	28	28	30	30	32	32	32	34	34	36	38	38	40	40	42	44	46	46	48	50	52	54	56	58	60	60
NY	120	26	28	28	28	30	30	32	32	32	34	34	36	38	38	40	40	42	44	46	46	48	50	52	54	56	58	60	60
NY	121	26	28	28	28	30	30	32	32	32	34	34	36	38	38	40	40	42	44	46	46	48	50	52	54	56	58	60	60
NY	122	26	26	28	28	30	30	32	32	32	34	34	36	38	38	40	40	42	44	46	46	48	50	52	54	56	58	58	60
NY	123	26	26	28	28	30	30	32	32	32	34	34	36	38	38	40	40	42	44	46	46	48	50	52	54	56	58	58	60
NY	124	26	26	28	28	30	30	30	32	32	34	34	36	38	38	40	40	42	44	46	46	48	50	52	54	56	58	58	60
NY	125	26	26	28	28	30	30	32	32	32	34	34	34	38	38	40	40	42	44	46	46	48	50	52	54	56	58	58	60
NY	126	26	26	28	28	30	30	30	32	32	34	34	34	38	38	40	40	42	44	44	46	50	52	54	54	54	58	58	60
NY	127	26	26	28	28	30	30	30	32	32	34	34	34	38	38	40	40	42	44	44	46	50	52	54	54	54	58	58	60
NY	128	26	26	28	28	30	30	30	32	32	34	34	34	38	40	40	40	42	44	44	46	50	52	54	54	54	58	58	60
NY	129	26	26	28	28	30	30	32	32	34	34	34	34	38	38	40	40	42	44	44	46	50	52	54	54	54	58	58	60
NY	130	26	26	28	28	30	30	30	32	32	34	34	34	38	38	40	40	42	44	44	46	50	52	54	54	54	58	58	60
NY	131	26	26	28	28	30	30	30	32	32	34	34	34	38	38	40	40	42	44	46	46	50	52	52	52	54	58	58	60
NY	132	26	26	28	28	30	30	32	32	32	34	34	36	38	38	40	40	42	44	44	46	50	52	52	52	54	58	58	60
NY	133	26	26	28	28	30	30	30	32	32	32	34	36	38	38	40	40	42	44	44	46	50	52	52	52	54	58	58	60
NY	134	26	26	28	28	30	30	30	32	34	34	34	34	36	38	40	40	42	44	44	46	48	52	52	52	54	58	58	60
NJ	135	26	28	28	30	30	32	32	32	34	34	36	36	38	40	42	44	46	46	48	50	52	56	58	58	62	64	66	68
NJ	136	26	28	28	30	30	32	32	32	34	34	36	36	38	40	42	44	46	46	48	50	52	56	58	58	62	64	66	68
NJ	137	26	28	28	30	30	30	32	32	34	34	36	36	40	40	42	44	46	46	48	50	52	56	58	58	62	64	66	68
NJ	138	26	28	28	30	30	30	32	32	34	34	36	36	38	40	42	44	44	46	48	50	52	56	58	58	62	64	66	68
NJ	139	26	28	28	28	30	30	32	32	34	34	34	36	38	40	42	44	44	46	48	50	52	56	58	58	62	64	66	68
NJ	140	26	28	28	28	30	30	32	32	34	34	34	36	38	40	42	44	44	46	48	50	52	56	58	58	60	64	66	68
NJ	141	26	28	28	28	30	30	32	32	34	34	34	36	38	40	42	44	44	46	48	50	52	56	58	58	60	64	66	68
NJ	142	26	28	28	28	30	30	32	32	32	34	34	36	38	40	42	42	44	46	48	50	52	56	58	58	60	64	66	68
NJ	143	26	28	28	28	30	30	32	32	32	34	34	36	38	40	42	42	44	46	48	50	52	56	58	58	60	64	66	66
NJ	144	26	26	28	28	30	30	32	32	32	34	34	36	38	40	42	42	44	46	48	50	52	56	58	58	60	64	66	66
NJ	145	26	26	28	28	30	30	32	32	32	34	34	36	38	40	40	42	44	46	48	50	52	56	58	58	60	64	66	66
NJ	146	26	26	28	28	30	30	32	32	32	34	34	36	38	40	40	42	44	46	48	50	52	56	58	58	60	64	66	66
NJ	147	26	26	28	28	30	30	32	32	32	34	34	36	38	40	40	42	44	46	48	48	52	56	58	58	60	64	66	66
NJ	148	26	26	28	28	30	30	32	32	32	34	34	36	38	40	40	42	44	46	48	50	52	56	58	58	60	62	66	66
NJ	149	26	26	28	28	30	30	30	32	32	34	34	36	38	40	40	42	44	46	48	48	52	56	58	58	60	62	66	66
NJ	150	26	26	28	28	30	30	30	32	32	34	34	36	38	40	40	42	44	46	48	48	52	56	58	58	60	62	66	66
NJ	151	26	26	28	28	28	30	30	32	32	34	34	36	38	38	40	42	44	46	46	48	50	52	56	58	60	62	64	66
NJ	152	26	26	28	28	28	30	30	32	32	34	34	36	38	38	40	42	44	46	46	48	50	52	56	58	60	62	64	66
NJ	153	26	26	28	28	28	30	30	32	32	32	34	34	38	38	40	42	44	46	48	48	50	52	54	58	60	62	64	66

STATE	Area	1951	1952	1953	1954	1955	1956	1957	1958	1959	1960	1961	1962	1963	1964	1965	1966	1967	1968	1969	1970	1971	1972	1973	1974	1975	1976	1977	78
NJ	154	24	26	26	28	28	30	30	32	32	32	34	34	38	38	40	42	44	46	48	48	50	52	54	58	60	62	64	66
NJ	155	24	26	26	28	28	30	30	32	32	32	34	34	38	38	40	42	44	46	46	48	50	52	54	58	60	62	64	66
NJ	156	26	26	26	28	28	30	30	32	32	32	34	34	38	38	40	42	44	44	46	48	50	52	54	58	60	62	64	66
NJ	157	26	26	26	28	28	30	30	30	32	32	34	34	38	38	40	42	44	44	46	48	50	52	54	58	60	62	64	66
NJ	158	26	26	26	28	28	30	30	30	32	32	34	34	38	38	40	42	44	44	46	48	50	52	54	56	60	62	64	66
PA	159	28	28	30	30	30	32	32	34	34	34	36	36	38	40	40	42	44	44	46	46	48	48	52	52	54	56	58	58
PA	160	28	28	30	30	30	32	32	34	34	34	36	36	38	40	40	42	44	44	46	46	48	48	52	52	54	56	58	58
PA	161	28	28	30	30	30	32	32	34	34	34	36	36	38	40	40	42	42	44	46	46	48	48	52	52	54	56	58	58
PA	162	28	28	30	30	30	32	32	34	34	34	36	36	38	40	40	42	42	44	46	46	48	48	52	52	54	56	58	58
PA	163	28	28	30	30	30	32	32	34	34	34	36	36	38	40	40	42	42	44	46	46	48	48	52	52	54	56	58	58
PA	164	28	28	30	30	30	32	32	34	34	34	36	36	38	40	40	42	42	44	46	46	48	48	52	52	54	56	58	58
PA	165	28	28	30	30	30	32	32	32	34	34	34	36	38	38	40	42	42	44	46	46	48	48	52	52	54	56	58	58
PA	166	28	28	30	30	30	32	32	32	34	34	36	36	38	38	40	42	42	44	46	46	48	48	52	52	54	56	58	58
PA	167	28	28	30	30	30	32	32	32	34	34	36	36	38	38	40	42	42	44	46	46	48	48	52	52	54	56	58	58
PA	168	28	28	30	30	30	32	32	32	34	34	34	36	38	38	40	42	42	44	46	46	48	48	52	52	54	56	58	58
PA	169	28	28	30	30	30	32	32	32	34	34	34	36	38	38	40	42	42	44	46	46	48	48	52	52	54	56	58	58
PA	170	28	28	30	30	30	32	32	32	34	34	34	36	38	38	40	42	42	44	46	46	48	48	52	52	54	56	58	58
PA	171	28	28	30	30	30	32	32	32	34	34	34	36	38	38	40	42	42	44	46	46	48	48	52	52	54	56	58	58
PA	172	28	28	28	30	30	32	32	32	34	34	34	36	38	38	40	42	42	44	46	46	48	48	52	52	54	56	58	58
PA	173	28	28	28	30	30	32	32	32	34	34	34	36	38	38	40	42	42	44	46	46	48	48	50	52	54	56	58	58
PA	174	28	28	28	30	30	32	32	32	34	34	34	36	38	38	40	42	42	44	44	46	48	48	50	52	54	56	58	58
PA	175	28	28	28	30	30	32	32	32	34	34	34	36	38	38	40	42	42	44	44	46	48	48	50	52	54	56	58	58
PA	176	28	28	28	30	30	32	32	32	34	34	34	36	38	38	40	42	42	44	46	46	48	48	50	52	54	56	58	58
PA	177	26	28	28	30	30	30	32	32	34	34	34	36	38	38	40	42	42	44	44	46	46	48	50	52	54	56	58	58
PA	178	26	28	28	30	30	30	32	32	34	34	34	36	38	38	40	42	42	44	46	46	48	48	50	52	54	56	58	58
PA	179	26	28	28	30	30	30	32	32	34	34	34	36	38	38	40	42	42	44	46	46	48	48	50	52	54	56	58	58
PA	180	26	28	28	30	30	32	32	32	34	34	34	36	38	38	40	42	42	44	44	46	48	48	50	52	54	56	58	58
PA	181	26	28	28	30	30	32	32	32	34	34	34	36	38	38	40	40	42	44	44	46	46	48	50	52	54	56	58	58
PA	182	26	28	28	30	30	32	32	32	34	34	34	36	38	38	40	40	42	44	44	46	46	48	50	52	54	56	58	58
PA	183	26	28	28	30	30	32	32	32	32	34	34	36	38	38	40	42	42	44	44	46	46	48	50	52	54	56	58	58
PA	184	26	28	28	30	30	30	32	32	34	34	34	36	38	38	40	40	42	44	44	46	46	48	50	52	54	56	58	58
PA	185	26	28	28	30	30	30	32	32	32	34	34	36	38	38	40	40	42	44	44	46	46	48	50	52	54	56	58	58
PA	186	26	28	28	30	30	30	32	32	32	34	34	36	38	38	40	40	42	44	44	46	46	48	50	52	54	56	58	58
PA	187	26	28	28	28	30	30	32	32	32	34	34	36	38	38	40	40	42	42	44	46	46	48	50	52	54	56	58	58
PA	188	26	28	28	28	30	30	32	32	32	34	34	36	38	38	40	40	42	44	44	46	46	48	50	52	54	56	58	58
PA	189	26	28	28	28	30	30	32	32	32	34	34	36	38	38	40	40	42	44	44	46	46	48	50	52	54	56	58	58
PA	190	26	28	28	28	30	30	32	32	32	34	34	34	36	38	40	40	42	42	44	46	46	48	50	52	54	56	58	58
PA	191	26	28	28	28	30	30	32	32	32	34	34	36	36	38	40	40	42	44	44	46	46	48	50	52	54	56	58	58
PA	192	26	28	28	28	30	30	32	32	32	34	34	34	36	38	40	40	42	42	44	46	46	48	50	52	54	56	58	58

STATE	Area	1951	1952	1953	1954	1955	1956	1957	1958	1959	1960	1961	1962	1963	1964	1965	1966	1967	1968	1969	1970	1971	1972	1973	1974	1975	1976	1977	78
PA	193	26	28	28	28	30	30	32	32	32	34	34	34	38	38	40	40	42	42	44	46	46	48	50	52	54	56	58	58
PA	194	26	28	28	28	30	30	32	32	32	34	34	34	36	38	40	40	42	42	44	46	46	48	50	52	54	56	58	58
PA	195	26	28	28	28	30	30	32	32	32	34	34	34	36	38	40	40	42	42	44	46	46	48	50	52	54	56	58	58
PA	196	26	28	28	28	30	30	32	32	32	34	34	34	38	38	40	40	42	42	44	46	46	48	50	52	54	56	58	58
PA	197	26	28	28	28	30	30	32	32	32	34	34	34	36	38	38	40	42	42	44	46	46	48	50	52	54	56	58	58
PA	198	26	28	28	28	30	30	32	32	32	34	34	34	36	40	38	40	42	42	44	46	46	48	50	52	54	56	58	58
PA	199	26	28	28	28	30	30	32	32	32	34	34	34	36	40	38	40	42	42	44	46	46	48	50	52	54	56	58	58
PA	200	26	28	28	28	30	30	32	32	32	32	34	34	36	40	38	40	42	42	44	44	46	48	50	52	54	56	58	58
PA	201	26	28	28	28	30	30	32	32	32	34	34	34	36	38	40	40	42	42	44	46	46	48	50	52	54	56	56	58
PA	202	26	28	28	28	30	30	30	32	32	32	34	34	36	38	38	40	42	42	44	44	46	48	50	52	54	56	56	58
PA	203	26	28	28	28	30	30	32	32	32	32	34	34	36	38	38	40	42	42	44	44	46	48	50	52	54	56	56	58
PA	204	26	26	28	28	30	30	30	32	32	32	34	34	38	38	38	40	42	42	44	44	46	46	50	52	54	54	56	58
PA	205	26	26	28	28	30	30	30	32	32	32	34	34	36	38	38	40	42	42	44	44	46	46	50	52	54	54	56	58
PA	206	26	26	28	28	30	30	30	32	32	32	34	34	36	38	38	40	42	42	44	44	46	46	50	52	54	54	56	58
PA	207	26	26	28	28	30	30	30	32	32	32	34	34	36	38	38	40	42	42	44	44	46	46	50	52	54	54	56	58
PA	208	26	26	28	28	30	30	30	32	32	32	34	34	36	38	38	40	42	42	44	44	46	46	50	52	54	54	56	56
PA	209	26	26	28	28	30	30	30	32	32	32	34	34	36	38	38	40	42	42	44	44	46	46	50	52	54	54	56	56
PA	210	26	26	28	28	28	30	30	32	32	32	34	34	36	38	38	40	42	42	44	44	46	46	50	52	54	54	56	56
PA	211	26	26	28	28	28	30	30	32	32	32	34	34	36	38	38	40	42	42	44	44	46	46	50	52	54	54	56	56
MD	212	32	34	34	36	36	38	40	40	42	42	44	46	50	52	54	56	58	62	64	66	70	72	76	80	82	86	90	92
MD	213	32	34	34	34	36	38	38	40	42	42	44	46	50	52	54	56	60	62	64	68	70	72	76	80	82	86	90	92
MD	214	32	34	34	34	36	38	38	40	40	42	44	46	50	52	54	56	58	62	64	66	70	72	76	80	82	86	00	92
MD	215	32	32	34	34	36	38	38	40	40	42	44	46	50	50	54	56	58	60	64	66	70	72	76	80	82	86	88	90
MD	216	32	32	34	34	36	36	38	40	40	42	42	44	48	50	54	56	58	60	64	66	70	72	76	78	82	86	88	90
MD	217	32	32	34	34	36	36	38	38	40	42	44	44	48	50	52	56	58	62	64	66	70	72	76	78	82	86	88	90
MD	218	32	32	34	34	36	36	38	40	40	42	42	44	48	50	52	56	58	60	64	66	70	72	76	78	82	86	88	90
MD	219	30	32	32	34	34	36	38	38	40	42	42	44	48	50	52	56	58	60	64	66	68	72	76	78	82	86	88	90
MD	220	30	32	32	34	34	36	38	38	40	40	42	44	48	50	52	56	58	60	62	66	68	72	76	78	82	84	88	90
DE	221	22	22	22	24	24	26	26	26	28	28	30	30	32	32	34	36	38	40	40	42	44	46	52	54	58	60	60	60
DE	222	20	20	22	22	24	24	24	26	26	26	28	28	30	32	34	34	36	38	40	42	44	46	52	54	56	58	60	60
VA	223	42	44	46	48	50	52	54	54	56	58	60	62	66	68	70	74	76	80	82	86	88	90	96	02	06	11	15	17
VA	224	40	44	46	48	50	52	52	54	56	58	60	62	66	68	70	74	76	80	82	84	88	90	96	02	06	11	15	17
VA	225	40	44	46	46	48	52	52	54	56	58	58	60	66	68	70	74	76	78	82	84	88	90	96	02	06	11	13	15
VA	226	42	44	46	46	48	50	52	54	56	56	58	60	66	68	70	74	76	78	82	84	88	90	96	02	06	11	13	15
VA	227	42	44	46	46	48	50	52	54	54	56	58	60	64	68	70	74	76	78	82	84	88	90	96	02	06	11	13	15
VA	228	42	44	46	46	48	50	52	54	54	56	58	60	64	68	70	74	76	78	82	84	86	90	96	02	06	11	13	15
VA	229	42	44	44	46	48	50	52	54	54	56	58	60	64	66	70	72	76	78	82	84	86	90	96	02	04	08	13	15

STATE	Area	1951	1952	1953	1954	1955	1956	1957	1958	1959	1960	1961	1962	1963	1964	1965	1966	1967	1968	1969	1970	1971	1972	1973	1974	1975	1976	1977	78
VA	230	42	42	44	46	48	50	52	52	54	56	58	60	64	66	70	72	76	78	80	84	86	90	96	02	04	08	13	15
VA	231	40	42	44	46	48	50	52	52	54	56	58	60	64	66	70	72	74	78	80	84	86	88	02	98	04	08	13	15
WV & NC	232	54	56	58	58	60	62	64	66	68	70	70	72	76	78	80	82	84	86	88	92	92	94	02	04	06	11	13	15
WV	233	54	54	56	58	60	62	64	66	66	68	70	72	76	76	80	82	84	86	88	90	92	94	98	04	06	11	13	15
WV	234	52	54	56	58	60	62	64	64	66	68	70	72	74	76	80	82	84	86	88	90	92	94	98	04	06	11	13	15
WV	235	52	54	56	58	60	62	64	64	66	68	70	70	74	76	78	82	84	86	88	90	92	94	98	02	06	08	13	13
WV	236	52	54	56	58	60	62	62	64	66	66	68	70	74	76	78	80	84	86	88	90	92	94	98	02	06	08	11	13
NC	237	50	52	54	56	58	60	62	66	66	70	72	74	76	80	82	86	90	92	94	98	02	04	11	15	19	23	27	29
NC	238	50	52	54	56	58	60	62	64	66	68	70	74	78	80	82	86	90	92	94	98	02	04	11	15	19	23	27	29
NC	239	48	52	54	54	58	60	62	64	66	68	70	72	76	80	82	86	90	92	94	98	02	04	11	15	19	23	25	29
NC	240	50	50	54	54	58	60	62	64	66	68	70	72	78	80	82	86	88	92	94	98	02	04	11	15	19	23	25	27
NC	241	48	50	52	54	58	60	62	64	66	68	70	72	76	80	82	86	88	92	94	98	02	04	11	15	19	23	25	27
NC	242	50	50	52	54	58	60	62	64	66	68	70	72	76	78	82	86	88	92	94	98	02	04	11	15	19	23	25	27
NC	243	48	50	52	54	56	60	62	64	66	68	70	72	76	78	82	86	88	90	94	96	02	04	11	15	19	23	25	27
NC	244	48	50	52	54	56	60	62	64	66	68	70	72	76	78	82	86	88	90	94	96	02	04	11	15	17	21	25	27
NC	245	48	50	52	54	56	60	62	64	66	68	70	72	76	78	82	84	88	90	94	96	02	04	11	15	17	21	25	27
NC	246	48	50	52	54	56	58	62	64	66	68	70	72	76	78	82	84	88	90	92	96	02	04	11	15	17	21	25	27
SC	247	54	52	58	58	62	64	66	68	70	74	76	78	82	84	88	94	96	98	04	06	11	13	19	25	31	33	37	39
SC	248	54	52	56	58	62	64	66	68	70	72	76	78	82	84	88	94	96	98	04	06	11	13	19	25	29	33	37	39
SC	249	52	52	56	58	62	64	66	68	70	72	74	78	82	84	88	92	96	98	02	06	08	13	19	25	29	33	37	39
SC	250	52	52	56	58	60	64	66	68	70	72	74	78	82	84	88	92	94	98	02	06	08	13	19	25	29	33	35	39
SC	251	52	54	56	58	60	64	66	68	70	72	74	76	82	84	88	94	94	96	02	06	08	13	19	25	29	33	35	39
GA	252	52	54	56	56	58	60	64	64	66	68	70	72	76	78	82	88	88	92	94	98	02	06	15	19	23	27	29	31
GA	253	52	54	54	56	58	60	62	64	66	68	70	72	76	78	82	88	88	92	94	96	02	06	15	19	23	27	29	31
GA	254	50	52	54	56	58	60	62	64	66	68	70	72	76	78	82	88	88	92	94	98	02	04	15	19	23	27	29	31
GA	255	52	52	54	56	58	60	62	64	66	68	70	72	76	78	82	88	88	92	94	96	02	04	15	19	23	27	29	31
GA	256	52	52	54	56	58	60	62	64	66	68	68	70	74	78	80	88	88	90	94	96	02	04	15	19	23	27	29	31
GA	257	52	52	54	56	58	60	62	64	64	66	68	70	74	76	80	88	88	90	94	96	02	04	17	21	23	27	29	31
GA	258	50	52	54	56	58	60	62	64	64	66	68	70	74	76	80	88	88	90	94	96	02	04	17	21	23	27	29	31
GA	259	50	52	54	56	58	60	62	62	64	66	68	70	74	76	80	86	86	90	92	96	02	04	17	21	25	27	27	29
GA	260	50	52	54	54	56	60	62	62	64	66	68	70	74	76	80	86	86	90	92	96	02	04	17	21	25	25	27	29
FL	261	48	50	52	54	58	60	62	64	68	70	74	78	88	94	98	13	13	19	23	31	35	39	51	61	67	75	81	87
FL	262	50	50	52	54	58	60	62	64	66	70	72	80	866	94	98	13	13	19	23	29	35	39	51	59	67	75	81	87
FL	263	48	50	52	54	56	60	62	64	66	70	72	78	88	92	98	13	13	17	23	29	35	39	51	59	67	75	81	85

STATE	Area	1951	1952	1953	1954	1955	1956	1957	1958	1959	1960	1961	1962	1963	1964	1965	1966	1967	1968	1969	1970	1971	1972	1973	1974	1975	1976	1977	78
FL	264	48	50	52	54	56	60	62	64	66	70	72	78	86	90	98	13	13	17	23	29	35	39	51	59	67	75	81	85
FL	265	48	50	52	54	56	60	62	64	66	68	72	76	86	92	98	13	13	17	23	29	35	39	51	59	67	73	81	85
FL	266	48	50	52	52	56	58	60	64	66	70	72	76	86	92	98	13	13	17	23	29	35	39	51	59	67	73	81	85
FL	267	48	50	50	54	56	58	60	62	66	68	72	76	86	92	98	11	11	17	23	29	33	39	49	59	67	73	79	85
OH	268	30	32	32	34	34	36	36	38	38	40	40	42	44	46	50	52	52	54	56	58	58	60	64	66	68	72	72	74
OH	269	30	32	32	34	34	36	36	38	38	40	40	42	44	46	50	52	52	54	54	56	58	60	64	66	68	72	72	74
OH	270	30	32	32	34	34	36	36	38	38	40	40	40	44	46	50	52	52	54	54	56	58	60	64	66	68	72	72	74
OH	271	30	32	32	34	34	36	36	38	38	38	40	40	44	46	50	52	52	54	54	56	58	60	64	66	68	72	72	74
OH	272	30	32	32	34	34	36	36	38	38	38	40	40	44	46	50	52	52	54	56	56	58	60	64	66	68	72	72	74
OH	273	30	32	32	34	34	36	36	36	38	38	40	40	44	46	50	52	52	54	54	56	58	60	64	66	68	72	72	74
OH	274	30	32	32	34	34	36	36	38	38	38	40	40	44	46	50	52	52	54	54	56	58	60	64	66	68	70	72	74
OH	275	30	32	32	34	34	36	36	36	38	38	40	40	44	46	50	52	52	52	54	56	58	60	64	66	68	70	72	74
OH	276	30	32	32	34	36	36	36	36	38	38	40	40	44	46	48	50	52	52	54	56	58	60	64	66	68	70	72	74
OH	277	30	32	32	32	36	36	36	36	38	38	40	40	44	46	48	50	52	52	54	56	58	60	64	66	68	70	72	74
OH	278	30	32	32	32	36	36	36	36	38	38	40	40	44	46	48	50	50	52	54	56	58	60	64	66	68	70	72	72
OH	279	30	32	32	32	34	34	36	36	38	38	40	40	44	46	48	50	50	52	56	56	58	60	64	66	68	70	72	72
OH	280	30	32	32	32	36	36	36	36	38	38	40	40	44	46	48	50	50	52	54	56	58	60	64	66	68	70	72	72
OH	281	30	32	32	32	36	36	36	36	38	38	40	40	44	46	48	50	50	52	54	56	58	60	64	66	68	70	72	72
OH	282	30	32	32	32	34	34	36	36	38	38	40	40	48	46	46	50	50	52	54	56	58	60	64	66	68	70	72	72
OH	283	30	30	32	32	34	34	36	36	38	38	40	40	48	46	48	50	50	52	54	56	58	60	64	66	68	70	72	72
OH	284	30	30	32	32	34	34	36	36	38	38	40	40	48	46	48	50	50	52	54	56	58	58	64	66	68	70	72	72
OH	285	30	30	32	32	34	34	36	36	38	38	38	40	48	46	48	50	50	52	54	56	58	58	64	66	68	70	72	72
OH	286	30	30	32	32	34	34	36	36	38	38	40	40	48	46	46	50	50	52	54	56	58	58	64	66	68	70	72	72
OH	287	30	30	32	32	34	34	36	36	38	38	38	40	48	46	46	48	50	52	54	56	58	58	64	66	68	70	72	72
OH	288	30	30	32	32	34	34	36	36	38	38	38	40	48	46	46	48	50	52	54	56	58	58	64	66	68	70	72	72
OH	289	30	30	32	32	34	34	36	36	38	38	38	40	48	44	46	48	50	52	54	56	58	58	64	66	68	70	72	72
OH	290	30	30	32	32	34	34	36	36	36	38	38	40	48	44	48	48	50	52	54	56	58	58	64	66	68	70	72	72
OH	291	30	30	32	32	34	34	36	36	36	38	38	40	48	44	48	48	52	52	54	56	56	58	64	66	68	70	72	72
OH	292	30	30	32	32	34	34	36	36	36	38	38	40	48	44	48	48	50	52	54	56	58	58	62	66	68	70	72	72
OH	293	30	30	32	32	34	34	36	36	36	38	38	40	42	44	48	48	50	52	54	56	56	58	62	66	68	70	72	72
OH	294	30	30	32	32	34	34	36	36	38	38	40	44	44	48	48	50	52	54	56	58	58	62	64	68	70	72	72	
OH	295	28	30	32	32	32	34	36	36	36	38	38	40	42	44	48	48	50	52	54	56	56	58	62	64	68	70	70	72
OH	296	28	30	32	32	34	34	34	36	36	38	38	40	44	44	48	48	50	52	54	56	56	58	62	64	68	70	70	72
OH	297	28	30	32	32	32	34	34	36	36	38	38	40	44	44	48	48	50	52	54	54	56	58	62	64	68	70	70	72
OH	298	28	30	32	32	32	34	34	36	36	38	38	40	44	44	48	48	50	52	54	54	56	58	62	64	66	70	70	72
OH	299	28	30	32	32	32	34	34	36	36	38	38	40	42	44	48	48	50	52	54	54	56	58	62	64	66	70	70	72
OH	300	30	30	30	32	32	34	34	36	36	38	38	40	44	44	48	48	50	52	54	54	56	58	62	64	66	70	70	72
OH	301	28	30	30	32	32	34	34	36	36	38	38	40	44	44	46	48	50	52	54	56	56	58	62	64	66	70	70	72
OH	302	28	30	30	32	32	34	34	36	36	38	38	40	44	44	46	48	50	52	54	54	56	58	62	64	66	70	70	72

STATE	Area	1951	1952	1953	1954	1955	1956	1957	1958	1959	1960	1961	1962	1963	1964	1965	1966	1967	1968	1969	1970	1971	1972	1973	1974	1975	1976	1977	78
IN	303	36	36	38	38	40	42	42	44	44	46	46	48	52	52	54	48	58	60	62	64	66	58	72	74	76	80	82	82
IN	304	34	36	38	38	40	42	42	44	44	46	46	48	52	52	54	56	58	60	62	64	66	68	72	74	76	80	82	82
IN	305	34	36	38	38	40	42	42	44	44	46	46	48	52	52	54	56	58	60	62	64	66	68	72	74	76	80	80	82
IN	306	34	36	36	38	40	40	42	42	44	46	46	48	50	52	54	56	58	60	62	64	66	68	72	74	76	80	80	82
IN	307	34	36	36	38	40	40	42	42	44	44	46	48	50	52	54	56	58	60	62	64	66	68	72	74	76	78	80	82
IN	308	34	36	36	38	40	40	42	42	44	44	46	48	50	52	54	56	58	60	62	64	66	68	72	74	76	78	80	82
IN	309	34	36	36	38	38	40	42	42	44	44	46	48	50	52	54	56	58	60	62	64	66	68	72	74	76	78	80	82
IN	310	34	36	36	38	38	40	42	42	44	44	46	48	50	52	54	56	58	60	62	64	66	68	72	74	76	78	80	82
IN	311	34	36	36	36	38	40	42	42	44	44	46	46	50	52	54	56	58	60	62	64	66	68	72	74	76	78	80	82
IN	312	34	34	36	38	38	40	42	42	44	44	46	46	50	52	54	56	58	58	62	64	66	68	70	74	76	78	80	82
IN	313	34	34	36	36	38	40	42	42	44	44	46	46	50	52	54	56	58	58	60	64	66	68	70	72	76	78	80	82
IN	314	34	34	36	36	38	40	40	42	42	44	46	46	50	52	54	54	56	58	60	62	66	68	70	72	74	78	80	82
IN	315	34	34	36	36	38	40	40	42	42	44	44	46	48	50	52	56	56	58	60	64	64	68	70	72	74	78	80	82
IN	316	34	34	36	36	38	40	40	42	42	44	44	46	50	50	52	54	56	58	60	62	64	66	70	72	74	78	80	80
IN	317	34	34	36	36	38	40	40	42	42	44	44	46	48	50	52	54	56	58	60	62	66	66	70	72	74	78	80	80
IL	318	28	30	30	32	32	34	34	34	36	36	38	38	40	42	44	46	46	48	50	52	54	54	58	60	62	64	66	66
IL	319	28	30	30	32	32	34	34	34	36	36	38	38	40	42	44	46	46	48	50	52	52	54	58	60	62	64	66	66
IL	320	28	30	30	30	32	34	34	34	36	36	38	38	40	42	44	44	46	48	50	52	52	54	58	60	62	66	66	66
IL	321	28	30	30	30	32	34	34	34	36	36	38	38	40	42	44	46	46	48	50	52	54	54	58	60	62	64	66	66
IL	322	28	30	30	30	32	32	34	34	36	36	38	38	40	42	44	44	46	48	50	52	54	54	58	60	62	64	66	66
IL	323	28	30	30	30	32	34	34	34	36	36	36	38	40	42	44	44	46	48	50	52	54	54	58	60	62	64	64	66
IL	324	28	30	30	30	32	34	34	34	36	36	36	38	40	42	44	44	46	48	50	52	52	54	58	60	62	64	64	66
IL	325	28	30	30	30	32	34	34	34	36	36	36	38	40	42	44	44	46	48	50	52	52	54	58	60	62	64	04	00
IL	326	28	30	30	30	32	32	34	34	36	36	36	38	40	42	44	44	46	48	50	52	54	54	58	60	62	64	64	66
IL	327	28	30	30	30	32	32	34	34	36	36	36	38	40	42	44	44	46	48	50	52	54	54	58	60	62	64	64	66
IL	328	28	30	30	30	32	32	34	34	36	36	36	38	40	42	42	44	46	48	50	52	52	54	58	58	60	64	64	66
IL	329	28	28	30	30	32	32	34	34	36	36	36	38	40	42	42	44	46	48	50	52	52	54	58	58	60	64	64	66
IL	330	28	28	30	30	32	32	34	34	36	36	38	40	42	44	44	46	48	50	50	52	54	54	58	58	60	64	64	66
IL	331	28	28	30	30	32	32	34	34	34	36	36	38	40	42	44	44	46	48	50	52	52	54	58	58	60	64	64	66
IL	332	28	28	30	30	32	32	34	34	34	36	36	38	40	42	42	44	46	48	50	52	52	54	58	58	60	64	64	66
IL	333	28	28	30	30	32	32	34	34	34	36	36	38	40	42	42	44	46	48	50	50	52	54	56	58	60	62	64	66
IL	334	28	28	30	30	32	32	34	34	34	36	36	38	40	42	42	44	46	48	50	50	52	54	56	58	60	62	64	66
IL	335	28	28	30	30	32	32	34	34	34	36	36	38	40	42	42	44	46	48	50	50	52	54	56	58	60	62	64	66
IL	336	28	28	30	30	32	32	34	34	34	36	36	38	40	42	42	44	46	48	50	50	52	54	56	58	60	62	64	66
IL	337	28	28	30	30	32	32	34	34	34	36	36	38	40	42	42	44	46	48	48	50	52	54	56	58	60	62	64	66
IL	338	28	28	30	30	32	32	34	34	34	36	36	38	40	42	42	44	46	48	50	50	52	54	56	58	60	62	64	66
IL	339	28	28	30	30	32	32	34	34	34	36	36	38	40	40	42	44	46	46	50	50	52	54	56	58	60	62	64	66
IL	340	28	28	30	30	32	32	34	34	34	36	36	38	40	40	42	44	46	46	48	50	52	54	56	58	60	62	64	66

STATE	Area	1951	1952	1953	1954	1955	1956	1957	1958	1959	1960	1961	1962	1963	1964	1965	1966	1967	1968	1969	1970	1971	1972	1973	1974	1975	1976	1977	78
IL	341	28	28	30	30	32	32	32	34	34	36	36	38	40	40	42	44	46	46	48	50	52	54	56	58	60	62	64	66
IL	342	28	28	30	30	32	32	32	34	34	36	36	38	40	40	42	44	46	46	48	50	52	54	56	58	60	62	64	66
IL	343	28	28	30	30	32	32	32	34	34	36	36	38	40	40	42	44	46	46	48	50	52	54	56	58	60	62	64	66
IL	344	28	28	30	30	30	32	32	34	34	36	36	38	40	40	42	44	46	48	48	50	52	54	56	58	60	62	64	66
IL	345	28	28	30	30	30	32	32	34	34	36	36	38	40	40	42	44	46	46	48	50	52	54	56	58	60	62	64	66
IL	346	28	28	30	30	30	32	32	34	34	36	36	38	40	40	42	44	46	46	48	50	52	54	56	58	60	62	64	66
IL	347	28	28	30	30	30	32	32	34	34	36	36	36	40	40	42	44	46	46	48	50	52	54	56	58	60	62	64	66
IL	348	28	28	30	30	30	32	32	34	34	36	36	36	40	40	42	44	46	46	48	50	52	54	56	58	60	62	64	66
IL	349	28	28	28	30	30	32	32	34	34	36	36	36	40	40	42	44	46	46	48	50	52	54	56	58	60	62	64	66
IL	350	26	28	28	30	30	32	32	34	34	34	36	36	40	40	42	44	46	46	48	50	52	52	56	58	60	62	64	66
IL	351	26	28	28	30	30	32	32	34	34	34	36	36	40	40	42	44	46	46	48	50	52	52	56	58	60	62	64	64
IL	352	28	28	28	30	30	32	32	34	34	34	36	36	38	40	42	44	46	46	48	50	52	52	56	58	60	62	64	64
IL	353	28	28	28	30	30	32	32	34	34	34	36	36	40	40	42	44	44	46	48	50	52	52	56	58	60	62	64	64
IL	354	26	28	28	30	30	32	32	34	34	34	36	36	40	40	42	44	44	46	48	50	52	52	56	58	60	62	64	64
IL	355	28	28	28	30	30	32	32	32	34	34	36	36	40	40	42	44	44	46	48	50	52	52	56	58	60	62	64	64
IL	356	26	28	28	30	30	32	32	32	34	34	36	36	40	40	42	44	44	46	48	50	52	52	56	58	60	62	64	64
IL	357	26	28	28	30	30	32	32	34	34	34	36	36	40	40	42	44	44	46	48	50	52	52	56	58	60	62	64	64
IL	358	26	28	28	30	30	32	32	32	34	34	36	36	38	40	42	44	44	46	48	50	52	52	56	58	60	62	64	64
IL	359	26	28	28	30	30	32	32	32	34	34	36	36	40	40	42	44	46	46	48	50	52	52	56	58	60	62	64	64
IL	360	26	28	28	30	30	32	32	32	34	34	36	36	38	40	42	44	44	46	48	50	52	52	56	58	60	62	64	64
IL	361	26	28	28	30	30	32	32	32	34	34	36	36	38	40	42	44	44	46	48	50	52	52	56	58	60	62	64	64
MI	362	34	36	36	38	38	40	42	42	44	44	44	46	48	50	54	56	56	60	62	62	64	66	72	74	76	80	82	84
MI	363	34	36	36	38	38	40	42	42	42	44	44	46	48	50	52	54	58	58	60	64	64	66	72	74	76	80	82	84
MI	364	34	36	36	38	38	40	42	42	42	44	44	46	48	50	52	54	56	60	60	62	64	66	72	74	76	80	82	84
MI	365	34	34	36	36	38	40	40	42	42	44	44	46	50	50	52	54	56	60	60	62	64	66	72	74	76	80	82	84
MI	366	34	34	36	38	38	40	40	42	42	44	44	46	48	50	52	54	56	58	60	62	64	66	70	74	76	80	82	84
MI	367	34	34	36	36	38	40	40	42	42	44	44	46	48	50	52	54	56	58	60	62	64	66	70	74	76	80	82	84
MI	368	34	34	36	36	38	40	40	42	42	44	44	46	48	50	52	54	56	58	60	62	64	66	70	74	76	80	82	84
MI	369	34	34	36	36	38	40	40	42	42	44	44	46	48	50	52	54	56	58	60	62	64	66	70	74	76	80	82	84
MI	370	34	34	36	36	38	40	40	42	42	44	44	46	48	50	52	54	56	58	60	62	64	66	70	74	76	78	82	84
MI	371	34	34	36	36	38	40	40	42	42	44	44	46	48	50	52	54	56	58	60	62	64	66	70	72	76	78	82	84
MI	372	32	34	36	36	38	40	40	42	42	44	44	46	48	50	52	54	56	58	60	62	64	66	70	72	76	78	82	84
MI	373	32	34	36	36	38	40	40	42	42	44	44	46	48	50	52	54	56	58	60	62	64	66	70	72	74	78	82	82
MI	374	34	34	36	36	38	40	40	40	42	44	44	46	48	50	52	54	56	58	60	62	64	66	70	72	74	78	82	82
MI	375	34	34	36	36	38	40	40	40	42	44	44	46	48	50	52	54	56	58	60	62	64	66	70	72	74	78	82	82
MI	376	32	34	36	36	38	40	40	40	42	44	44	46	48	50	52	54	56	58	60	62	64	66	70	72	74	78	82	82
MI	377	32	34	36	36	38	38	40	40	42	42	44	46	48	50	52	54	56	58	60	62	64	66	70	72	74	78	80	82
MI	378	32	34	36	36	38	38	40	40	42	42	44	46	48	50	52	54	56	58	60	62	64	64	70	72	74	78	80	82
MI	379	32	34	36	36	38	38	40	40	42	42	44	44	48	50	52	54	56	58	60	62	64	64	70	72	74	78	80	82

STATE	Area	1951	1952	1953	1954	1955	1956	1957	1958	1959	1960	1961	1962	1963	1964	1965	1966	1967	1968	1969	1970	1971	1972	1973	1974	1975	1976	1977	78
MI	380	32	34	34	36	38	38	40	40	42	42	44	44	48	50	52	54	56	58	60	62	64	64	70	72	74	78	80	80
MI	381	32	34	34	36	38	38	40	40	42	42	44	44	48	50	52	54	56	58	60	62	64	64	70	72	74	78	80	80
MI	382	32	34	34	36	38	38	40	40	42	42	44	44	48	50	52	54	56	58	60	62	64	64	70	72	74	78	80	80
MI	383	32	34	34	36	38	38	40	40	42	42	44	44	48	50	52	54	56	58	60	62	64	64	70	72	74	78	80	80
MI	384	32	34	34	36	36	38	40	40	42	42	44	44	48	50	52	54	56	58	60	60	64	64	70	72	74	78	80	80
MI	385	32	34	34	36	36	38	40	40	42	42	44	44	48	50	50	54	54	58	60	60	62	64	70	72	74	78	80	80
MI	386	32	34	34	36	36	38	40	40	40	42	44	44	48	48	52	54	54	58	60	60	64	64	70	72	74	78	80	80
WI	387	32	34	34	36	36	38	40	40	42	42	44	44	48	50	52	54	56	58	60	62	64	66	70	74	76	80	82	80
WI	388	32	32	34	34	36	38	40	40	42	42	44	44	48	50	52	54	56	58	60	62	64	66	70	74	76	80	82	80
WI	389	32	32	34	34	36	38	40	40	42	42	44	44	48	50	52	54	56	58	60	62	64	66	70	74	76	80	82	80
WI	390	32	32	34	34	36	38	40	40	40	42	44	44	48	50	52	54	56	58	60	62	64	66	70	74	76	80	80	80
WI	391	32	32	34	34	36	38	38	40	40	42	44	44	48	50	52	54	56	58	60	62	64	66	70	74	76	78	80	80
WI	392	32	32	34	34	36	38	38	40	40	42	44	44	48	50	52	54	56	58	60	62	64	66	70	72	76	78	80	80
WI	393	32	32	34	34	36	38	38	40	40	42	44	44	48	50	52	54	56	58	60	62	64	66	70	72	76	78	80	80
WI	394	32	32	32	34	36	38	38	40	40	42	44	44	48	50	52	54	56	58	60	62	64	66	70	72	76	78	80	80
WI	395	30	32	32	34	36	36	38	40	40	42	44	44	48	50	52	54	56	58	60	62	64	64	70	72	76	78	80	80
WI	396	30	32	32	34	36	38	38	38	40	42	44	44	48	50	50	54	56	58	58	60	64	64	70	72	74	78	80	80
WI	397	30	32	32	34	36	36	38	38	40	42	44	44	46	48	50	54	56	56	58	60	62	64	70	72	74	78	80	80
WI	398	30	32	32	34	34	36	38	38	40	40	44	44	48	48	50	52	54	58	60	60	62	64	70	72	74	78	80	80
WI	399	30	32	32	34	34	36	38	38	40	40	44	44	48	48	50	54	54	56	58	60	64	64	70	72	74	78	80	80
KY	400	44	46	48	50	52	54	56	56	58	60	60	62	66	68	72	74	76	78	82	84	86	88	94	98	04	06	08	11
KY	401	44	46	48	48	52	54	56	56	58	58	60	62	66	68	70	74	76	78	80	84	86	88	94	98	04	06	08	11
KY	402	44	46	48	48	50	54	54	56	58	58	60	62	66	68	70	74	76	78	80	84	86	88	92	96	04	06	00	11
KY	403	42	46	46	48	50	54	54	56	56	58	60	62	66	66	70	72	76	78	80	82	86	88	92	96	02	06	08	11
KY	404	44	44	46	48	50	52	54	56	56	58	60	62	64	66	70	72	74	78	80	82	86	88	92	96	02	06	08	11
KY	405	44	44	46	48	50	52	54	54	56	58	60	62	64	66	70	72	76	78	80	82	86	88	92	96	02	06	08	11
KY	406	42	44	46	48	50	52	54	56	56	58	60	62	64	66	70	72	74	76	80	82	84	88	92	96	02	06	08	11
KY	407	42	44	46	48	50	52	54	54	56	58	58	60	64	66	68	72	74	76	78	82	84	86	92	96	02	04	08	08
TN	408	54	56	58	58	62	64	66	66	68	70	72	74	78	80	84	86	90	92	96	98	02	06	15	19	23	27	08	29
TN	409	54	54	54	58	60	64	66	66	68	70	72	74	78	80	84	88	90	92	94	98	04	06	15	19	23	27	29	29
TN	410	54	54	54	58	62	64	66	66	68	70	72	74	78	80	84	88	90	92	94	98	02	04	13	19	23	25	27	29
TN	411	52	54	54	58	60	62	64	66	68	70	72	74	78	80	84	88	90	92	94	98	02	04	13	19	21	25	27	29
TN	412	52	54	54	58	60	62	64	66	68	70	72	74	78	80	84	86	88	92	94	98	02	04	13	17	21	25	27	29
TN	413	52	54	54	58	60	62	64	66	68	70	70	74	76	80	82	86	88	92	94	96	02	04	13	17	21	25	27	29
TN	414	52	54	54	58	60	62	64	66	68	70	72	72	76	80	84	86	88	92	94	96	02	04	13	17	21	25	27	29
TN	415	52	54	54	58	60	62	64	66	68	68	70	72	76	78	82	86	88	90	94	96	02	04	13	17	21	25	27	29

STATE	Area	1951	1952	1953	1954	1955	1956	1957	1958	1959	1960	1961	1962	1963	1964	1965	1966	1967	1968	1969	1970	1971	1972	1973	1974	1975	1976	1977	78
AL	416	44	46	46	48	50	52	54	54	56	58	60	62	64	66	70	72	74	76	78	80	82	84	90	94	96	02	04	06
AL	417	44	44	44	48	50	52	54	54	56	58	60	60	64	66	70	72	74	76	78	80	82	84	90	94	96	02	04	04
AL	418	42	44	44	48	50	52	54	54	56	58	60	60	64	66	68	72	74	76	78	80	82	84	90	94	96	98	02	04
AL	419	44	44	44	48	50	52	52	54	56	58	58	60	64	66	70	72	74	74	78	80	82	84	90	94	96	98	02	04
AL	420	44	44	44	48	50	52	52	54	56	58	58	60	64	66	68	70	72	76	76	80	82	84	90	92	96	98	02	04
AL	421	42	44	44	48	50	50	52	54	56	58	58	60	64	64	68	70	74	74	76	78	80	82	90	92	96	98	02	04
AL	422	42	44	44	46	48	50	52	54	56	56	58	60	62	64	68	72	74	74	76	78	80	82	90	92	96	98	02	04
AL	423	42	44	44	46	48	50	52	54	54	56	58	60	62	64	68	70	72	74	76	78	80	84	88	92	94	98	02	04
AL	424	42	44	44	46	48	50	52	54	54	56	58	60	62	64	68	70	72	74	76	78	80	82	88	92	94	98	02	04
MS	425	62	64	64	70	74	78	82	84	86	88	90	94	98	98	98	98	98	98	98	02	08	11	17	21	25	29	31	33
MS	426	60	64	68	70	74	78	80	82	86	88	90	92	98	98	98	98	98	98	98	02	06	11	17	21	25	29	31	33
MS	427	60	64	66	68	74	78	80	82	84	88	90	92	96	98	98	98	98	98	98	02	06	11	15	21	25	29	29	31
MS	428	62	64	66	68	74	76	80	82	84	86	90	92	96	98	98	98	98	98	98	02	06	11	15	19	23	29	29	31
AR	429	62	62	66	66	70	74	74	76	78	80	82	86	88	90	96	98	02	04	08	11	15	17	25	29	33	35	39	41
AR	430	60	62	64	66	70	72	74	76	78	80	82	84	88	90	96	98	02	04	06	11	13	17	23	27	31	35	37	39
AR	431	60	62	64	66	70	72	74	76	78	80	82	84	88	90	94	98	02	04	06	11	13	17	23	27	31	35	37	39
AR	432	60	62	64	66	68	72	74	76	76	78	82	84	88	90	94	98	02	04	06	11	13	15	23	27	31	35	37	39
LA	433	48	50	52	54	56	58	60	60	62	64	66	68	72	74	80	84	86	90	94	98	02	06	15	19	25	29	33	35
LA	434	48	50	52	52	54	56	58	60	62	64	64	68	72	74	78	82	86	90	92	98	02	06	15	19	25	29	33	35
LA	435	48	50	52	52	54	56	58	60	62	64	66	66	72	74	78	82	86	88	92	96	02	06	13	19	25	29	31	35
LA	436	48	50	52	52	54	56	58	60	62	62	64	66	72	74	76	82	86	88	92	96	02	06	13	19	23	29	31	35
LA	437	48	48	50	52	54	56	58	60	60	62	64	66	72	74	78	82	84	88	92	96	02	06	13	19	23	29	31	35
LA	438	48	48	50	52	54	56	58	60	60	62	64	68	70	74	78	82	86	88	92	96	02	06	13	19	23	27	31	33
LA	439	48	48	50	52	54	56	58	58	60	62	64	66	70	74	78	82	84	88	92	96	02	04	13	17	23	27	31	33
OK	440	34	36	36	38	38	40	42	42	44	44	46	46	48	50	52	54	54	56	58	60	62	62	66	68	70	72	74	74
OK	441	34	34	36	36	38	40	40	42	42	44	44	46	48	50	52	54	54	56	58	60	62	62	66	68	70	72	74	74
OK	442	32	34	36	36	38	40	40	42	42	44	44	46	48	50	52	54	54	56	58	60	60	62	66	68	70	72	74	74
OK	443	34	34	36	36	38	40	40	42	42	44	44	46	48	48	50	52	54	56	58	58	60	62	66	68	70	72	74	74
OK	444	32	34	36	36	38	40	40	42	42	42	44	46	48	48	50	52	54	56	56	58	60	62	66	68	70	72	72	74
OK	445	34	34	36	36	38	38	40	40	42	42	44	46	46	48	50	52	54	56	56	58	60	62	66	68	70	72	72	74
OK	446	34	34	34	36	38	38	40	40	42	42	44	44	46	48	50	52	54	54	56	58	60	62	64	68	70	72	72	74
OK	447	32	34	34	36	38	38	40	40	42	42	44	44	46	48	50	52	54	54	56	58	60	62	64	66	70	72	72	74
OK	448	32	34	34	36	36	38	40	40	42	42	44	44	46	48	50	52	52	54	56	58	58	60	64	66	70	70	72	74
TX	449	54	56	58	58	62	64	66	68	70	72	74	76	80	84	88	92	96	98	06	08	13	15	25	29	35	39	41	45
TX	450	52	56	58	58	62	64	66	68	70	72	74	76	80	84	88	92	94	98	04	06	13	15	23	29	35	39	41	45

STATE	Area	1951	1952	1953	1954	1955	1956	1957	1958	1959	1960	1961	1962	1963	1964	1965	1966	1967	1968	1969	1970	1971	1972	1973	1974	1975	1976	1977	78
TX	451	54	56	58	58	62	64	66	68	70	72	74	76	82	84	88	92	96	98	04	08	13	15	23	29	33	39	41	45
TX	452	52	56	58	58	62	64	66	68	70	72	74	76	80	84	88	92	96	98	04	08	11	15	23	29	33	39	41	45
TX	453	54	54	56	58	62	64	66	68	70	72	74	76	80	84	88	92	94	98	04	08	13	15	23	29	33	39	41	43
TX	454	52	56	56	58	62	64	66	68	70	72	72	76	80	82	88	92	94	98	04	06	13	15	23	29	33	39	41	43
TX	455	54	54	56	58	60	64	66	68	68	72	72	76	80	84	88	92	94	98	04	08	13	15	23	29	33	37	41	43
TX	456	54	54	56	58	60	64	66	68	68	70	74	76	80	84	88	92	94	98	04	06	13	15	23	29	33	37	41	43
TX	457	52	54	56	58	60	64	66	68	68	70	72	76	80	82	88	90	94	98	04	06	13	15	23	29	33	37	41	43
TX	458	52	54	58	58	60	64	66	66	68	70	72	76	80	82	88	92	94	98	04	06	11	15	23	29	33	37	41	43
TX	459	52	54	56	58	60	64	66	66	68	70	72	76	80	82	86	92	94	96	04	06	11	15	23	29	33	37	41	43
TX	460	52	54	56	58	60	64	66	66	68	70	72	74	80	82	86	92	94	98	04	06	11	13	23	29	33	37	41	43
TX	461	52	54	56	58	60	62	66	66	68	70	72	74	80	82	86	90	94	98	02	06	11	13	23	29	33	37	39	43
TX	462	52	54	56	58	60	62	64	66	68	70	72	74	80	82	86	90	94	98	02	06	11	13	23	29	33	37	39	43
TX	463	52	54	56	58	60	62	64	66	68	70	72	74	80	82	88	90	94	98	02	06	11	13	23	27	33	37	39	43
TX	464	52	54	56	58	60	64	64	66	68	70	72	76	80	82	86	90	94	96	02	06	11	13	23	27	33	37	39	43
TX	465	52	54	56	58	60	62	64	66	68	70	72	74	80	82	86	90	92	96	02	06	11	13	23	27	33	37	39	43
TX	466	52	54	56	58	60	62	64	66	68	70	72	74	80	82	86	90	94	98	02	06	08	13	23	27	33	37	39	43
TX	467	52	54	56	56	60	44	64	66	68	70	72	74	78	82	84	90	94	96	02	06	11	13	23	27	33	37	39	43
MN	468	36	38	38	40	42	44	46	46	48	48	50	52	56	56	58	62	64	66	68	70	72	74	80	82	84	84	90	90
MN	469	36	36	38	40	42	44	46	46	48	48	50	52	56	56	58	62	64	66	68	70	72	74	78	82	84	84	90	90
MN	470	34	36	38	40	42	44	44	46	48	48	50	52	54	56	58	62	64	64	68	70	72	74	78	82	84	84	88	90
MN	471	36	36	38	38	42	44	44	46	46	48	50	50	54	56	58	60	62	64	66	70	70	72	78	82	84	84	88	90
MN	472	34	36	38	38	42	44	44	46	46	48	50	52	54	56	58	60	62	64	66	68	70	72	78	82	84	84	88	90
MN	473	34	36	38	38	40	44	44	46	46	48	50	50	54	56	58	60	62	64	66	68	70	72	78	80	84	84	88	90
MN	474	36	36	38	38	40	42	44	44	46	48	48	50	54	56	58	60	62	64	66	68	70	72	78	80	84	84	88	90
MN	475	34	36	36	38	40	42	44	44	46	48	48	50	54	56	58	60	62	64	66	68	70	72	78	80	84	84	88	90
MN	476	34	36	36	38	40	42	44	44	46	48	48	50	54	56	58	60	62	64	66	68	70	72	78	80	84	84	88	90
MN	477	34	36	36	38	40	42	44	44	46	46	48	50	52	56	56	60	62	64	66	68	70	72	78	80	82	82	88	90
IA	478	36	38	40	42	46	48	50	50	52	52	54	56	62	62	66	68	70	72	74	76	78	78	84	86	88	88	94	94
IA	479	36	38	40	42	44	48	48	50	52	52	54	56	58	62	66	68	70	72	74	74	78	78	84	86	88	88	94	94
IA	480	38	38	40	40	44	48	48	50	50	52	54	56	60	62	64	66	68	70	72	74	76	78	82	86	88	88	94	94
IA	481	38	38	40	40	44	48	48	50	50	52	54	54	58	62	64	66	68	72	72	74	76	78	82	86	88	88	92	94
IA	482	38	38	40	40	44	48	48	50	50	52	54	54	58	62	64	66	68	70	72	74	76	78	82	86	88	88	92	94
IA	483	36	38	40	40	44	48	48	48	50	52	52	54	58	62	64	66	68	70	72	74	76	78	82	86	88	88	92	94
IA	484	36	38	38	40	44	46	48	48	50	52	52	54	58	62	64	66	68	70	72	74	76	78	82	84	88	88	92	94
IA	485	34	38	38	40	42	46	48	48	50	52	52	54	58	60	64	66	68	70	72	74	76	78	82	84	88	88	92	94
MO	486	38	38	40	40	42	44	44	46	46	48	48	50	52	54	56	56	58	60	62	64	66	66	70	72	74	74	80	80
MO	487	38	38	40	40	42	44	44	46	46	48	48	50	52	54	54	58	58	60	62	64	66	66	70	72	74	74	80	80

STATE	Area	1951	1952	1953	1954	1955	1956	1957	1958	1959	1960	1961	1962	1963	1964	1965	1966	1967	1968	1969	1970	1971	1972	1973	1974	1975	1976	1977	78
MO	488	36	38	40	40	42	44	44	46	46	48	48	50	52	52	56	56	58	60	62	64	66	66	70	72	74	74	80	80
MO	489	36	38	40	40	42	44	44	44	46	46	48	50	52	52	56	56	58	60	62	64	66	66	70	72	74	74	80	80
MO	490	36	38	38	40	42	44	44	44	46	46	48	50	52	52	54	56	58	60	62	64	64	66	70	72	74	74	78	80
MO	491	36	38	38	40	42	42	44	44	46	46	48	48	52	52	54	56	58	60	62	62	64	66	70	72	74	74	78	80
MO	492	36	38	38	40	42	44	44	44	46	46	48	48	52	52	54	56	58	60	62	62	64	66	70	72	74	74	78	80
MO	493	36	38	38	40	42	42	44	44	46	46	48	48	50	52	54	56	58	60	62	62	64	66	70	72	74	74	78	80
MO	494	36	38	38	40	42	42	44	44	46	48	48	52	52	54	56	58	60	60	62	64	66	70	72	74	74	78	80	80
MO	495	36	38	38	40	40	42	44	44	46	46	48	48	50	52	54	56	58	58	60	62	64	66	70	72	74	74	78	80
MO	496	36	36	38	38	40	42	44	44	44	46	48	48	50	52	54	56	58	58	60	62	64	66	68	72	74	74	78	80
MO	497	36	36	38	38	40	42	44	44	44	46	46	48	50	52	54	56	58	58	60	62	64	66	68	72	74	74	78	80
MO	498	36	36	38	38	40	42	44	44	44	46	46	48	50	52	54	56	58	58	60	62	64	66	68	70	74	74	78	80
MO	499	36	36	38	38	40	42	42	44	44	46	46	48	50	52	54	56	56	58	60	62	64	66	68	70	74	74	78	80
MO	500	36	36	38	38	40	42	42	44	44	46	46	48	50	52	54	56	56	58	60	62	64	66	68	70	72	72	78	78
ND	501	30	32	34	34	40	42	44	44	46	48	48	50	54	54	56	60	56	64	68	70	74	78	84	88	90	90	92	92
ND	502	32	32	32	34	36	40	42	44	44	46	48	50	52	54	56	58	56	62	66	70	72	76	84	86	88	88	92	92
SD	503	34	34	36	38	42	46	46	48	48	50	52	54	58	60	60	64	66	68	70	72	76	78	86	88	90	90	94	94
SD	504	32	34	36	36	40	44	46	46	48	50	50	54	56	58	60	62	64	66	68	72	74	76	84	86	90	90	92	92
NE	505	40	42	42	44	48	52	52	54	54	56	58	60	62	64	66	70	72	74	76	78	82	84	88	92	94	94	98	02
NE	506	38	40	42	44	46	50	52	52	54	56	56	58	64	64	66	70	72	74	76	78	80	84	88	92	94	94	98	02
NE	507	32	40	42	42	46	50	52	52	54	54	56	58	62	64	66	68	70	74	76	78	80	82	88	90	94	94	98	98
NE	508	32	40	40	42	46	50	50	52	54	54	56	58	62	64	66	68	70	72	74	78	80	82	88	90	94	94	96	98
KS	509	32	34	36	36	38	40	42	42	44	44	46	46	52	52	54	56	56	58	60	62	64	66	72	74	76	78	78	80
KS	510	32	34	34	36	38	40	42	42	44	44	46	46	50	52	54	54	56	58	60	62	64	66	70	74	76	78	78	80
KS	511	32	34	34	36	38	40	40	42	42	44	46	46	50	52	52	54	56	58	60	62	64	66	70	72	74	76	78	78
KS	512	32	32	34	36	38	40	40	42	42	44	44	46	50	50	52	54	56	58	60	62	64	66	70	72	74	76	78	78
KS	513	30	32	34	34	38	40	40	42	42	44	44	46	48	50	52	54	56	58	60	62	64	64	70	72	74	76	78	78
KS	514	32	32	34	34	36	40	40	40	42	42	44	46	50	50	52	54	56	58	60	62	64	64	70	72	74	76	76	78
KS	515	32	32	34	34	36	38	40	40	42	42	44	46	48	50	52	54	56	56	58	60	62	64	70	72	74	76	76	78
MT	516	36	38	40	40	42	46	46	48	48	50	52	54	56	58	60	64	66	66	70	72	74	76	86	88	90	94	94	94
MT	517	36	36	38	40	42	44	46	46	48	50	50	52	56	58	60	62	64	66	68	70	72	74	84	88	90	92	92	92
ID	518	38	38	40	40	42	44	46	48	48	50	52	54	58	58	60	64	66	68	70	72	74	76	86	88	92	94	94	94
ID	519	36	36	38	40	42	44	44	46	48	50	52	54	56	56	60	62	64	66	70	72	74	76	84	88	90	92	94	94
WY	520	36	36	38	40	42	44	44	46	46	48	50	52	56	56	58	60	62	64	66	68	70	72	80	84	86	88	90	90

STATE	Area	1951	1952	1953	1954	1955	1956	1957	1958	1959	1960	1961	1962	1963	1964	1965	1966	1967	1968	1969	1970	1971	1972	1973	1974	1975	1976	1977	78
CO	521	42	42	46	48	50	52	52	54	56	58	60	62	66	68	72	76	78	80	84	88	90	94	02	08	13	17	21	23
CO	522	42	42	46	46	48	50	52	54	54	56	58	60	66	68	72	74	78	80	84	86	90	94	02	06	13	17	21	23
CO	523	42	42	44	46	58	50	52	52	54	56	58	60	66	68	70	74	76	80	82	86	90	94	02	06	11	17	19	23
CO	524	42	42	44	46	58	50	52	52	54	56	58	60	64	66	72	74	76	80	84	86	90	94	98	06	11	15	19	21
NM	525	74	74	80	84	86	92	96	98	98	98	98	98	98	98	98	98	98	98	98	98	98	98	08	15	19	23	25	27
AZ	526	44	44	46	48	52	54	56	60	62	64	68	72	78	80	86	90	96	02	08	17	21	27	41	51	59	65	71	75
AZ	527	42	44	46	48	50	54	56	58	60	64	66	70	74	82	84	92	96	02	08	15	21	27	41	49	57	65	69	75
UT	528	44	44	46	48	50	52	54	56	58	60	62	64	68	70	72	76	80	84	88	90	92	94	06	13	17	21	23	25
UT	529	42	44	46	48	50	52	52	54	56	58	60	64	68	70	72	76	80	84	86	88	92	94	06	11	15	19	21	25
NV	530	20	22	22	24	24	26	26	28	28	30	30	32	36	36	38	42	44	46	50	52	56	58	70	74	78	82	84	84
WA	531	32	34	34	34	38	38	40	40	40	42	44	44	48	50	52	54	56	58	60	62	64	64	70	72	74	78	80	82
WA	532	32	34	34	34	36	38	38	40	40	42	42	44	48	50	52	54	56	58	60	62	64	64	68	72	74	78	80	82
WA	533	32	32	34	34	36	38	38	40	40	42	42	44	48	48	50	54	56	58	60	60	64	64	68	72	74	78	80	82
WA	534	32	32	34	34	36	38	38	40	40	42	42	44	48	48	50	54	56	56	58	60	64	64	68	70	74	78	80	82
WA	535	32	32	32	34	36	38	38	38	40	40	42	44	46	48	50	52	54	56	60	60	62	64	68	70	74	76	80	82
WA	536	35	32	32	34	36	36	38	38	40	40	42	44	46	48	50	52	54	56	58	60	62	64	68	70	74	76	80	82
WA	537	30	32	32	34	36	36	38	38	40	42	42	44	46	48	50	52	54	56	58	60	62	64	68	70	74	76	80	82
WA	538	30	30	32	34	36	36	38	38	40	40	42	44	46	48	50	52	54	56	58	60	62	64	68	70	72	76	78	80
WA	539	30	32	32	34	36	36	38	38	40	40	42	42	46	48	50	52	54	56	58	60	62	64	68	70	72	76	78	80
OR	540	36	38	40	40	44	46	46	48	48	50	50	52	56	58	60	62	64	66	68	70	74	76	80	84	88	90	92	94
OR	541	36	38	40	40	44	44	46	46	48	48	50	52	56	58	60	62	64	66	68	72	74	76	80	84	88	90	92	94
OR	542	36	38	38	40	42	44	46	46	48	48	50	52	56	56	60	62	64	66	68	72	74	74	80	84	86	90	92	94
OR	543	36	36	38	38	42	44	44	46	46	48	50	52	54	56	58	60	64	64	68	72	74	74	80	84	86	90	92	94
OR	544	36	36	38	40	42	44	44	46	46	48	50	50	54	56	58	60	64	64	66	72	74	74	80	82	86	90	90	92
CA	545	46	48	50	50	52	54	56	58	60	62	64	68	72	76	80	86	88	92	98	04	11	19	27	33	39	45	49	53
CA	546	44	48	48	50	52	54	56	58	60	62	64	68	74	76	80	84	88	92	96	04	11	19	27	33	39	45	49	53
CA	547	44	46	48	50	52	54	56	58	60	62	64	66	72	76	80	84	88	92	98	02	08	19	27	33	39	45	49	53
CA	548	46	46	48	50	52	54	56	58	60	62	64	66	72	76	80	84	88	92	96	04	11	19	27	33	39	45	49	53
CA	549	46	46	48	50	52	54	56	58	60	62	64	68	72	76	80	84	88	92	96	02	08	19	27	33	39	45	49	53
CA	550	46	46	48	50	52	54	56	58	60	62	64	68	72	76	80	84	88	92	96	04	11	19	27	33	39	45	49	53
CA	551	46	46	48	50	52	54	56	58	60	62	64	68	72	76	78	84	88	92	96	02	11	17	27	33	39	45	49	53
CA	552	46	46	48	50	52	54	56	58	60	62	64	66	72	76	78	84	88	92	96	02	08	19	27	33	39	45	49	53

STATE	Area	1951	1952	1953	1954	1955	1956	1957	1958	1959	1960	1961	1962	1963	1964	1965	1966	1967	1968	1969	1970	1971	1972	1973	1974	1975	1976	1977	78
CA	553	46	46	48	50	52	54	56	58	60	60	64	66	72	76	80	82	88	92	96	02	11	19	27	33	39	43	49	53
CA	554	44	46	48	50	52	54	56	58	58	62	64	66	72	76	80	84	88	92	96	04	11	19	27	33	39	43	49	53
CA	555	44	46	48	50	52	54	56	56	58	62	64	66	72	76	80	84	88	92	96	04	11	19	27	33	37	43	49	53
CA	556	44	46	48	50	52	54	56	56	58	62	64	66	72	74	80	84	88	92	96	04	11	17	27	33	37	43	49	53
CA	557	44	46	48	50	52	54	56	56	58	62	64	66	72	74	80	82	88	92	96	02	11	17	27	33	37	43	49	53
CA	558	44	46	48	50	52	54	56	56	58	60	62	66	72	74	80	84	88	92	96	02	11	19	27	33	37	43	49	53
CA	559	44	46	48	50	52	54	56	56	58	60	64	68	70	74	80	84	86	92	96	02	08	19	27	33	37	43	49	53
CA	560	44	46	48	50	52	54	56	56	58	60	64	66	72	74	80	82	88	90	96	04	08	19	27	33	37	43	49	53
CA	561	46	46	48	50	52	54	54	56	58	60	62	66	70	74	561	82	86	92	96	02	11	19	27	33	37	43	49	53
CA	562	44	46	48	50	50	54	54	56	58	60	62	66	70	74	561	82	86	92	96	02	08	17	27	33	37	43	49	53
CA	563	44	46	48	48	50	52	54	56	58	60	62	66	70	74	80	82	86	92	94	02	08	17	27	33	37	43	49	53
CA	564	44	46	48	48	50	54	54	56	58	60	62	66	72	74	78	82	86	92	96	02	08	17	27	33	37	43	49	53
CA	565	44	46	48	48	50	52	54	56	58	60	62	66	70	74	78	82	86	90	96	02	08	17	27	33	37	43	49	53
CA	566	44	46	48	48	50	54	54	56	58	60	62	66	72	74	80	84	86	90	96	02	08	17	27	33	37	43	49	53
CA	567	44	46	48	48	50	52	54	56	58	60	62	66	72	74	78	82	88	92	96	02	08	17	27	33	37	43	49	53
CA	568	44	46	48	48	50	54	54	56	58	60	62	66	72	74	78	82	86	92	96	02	08	17	27	31	37	43	49	53
CA	569	44	46	48	48	50	52	54	56	58	60	62	66	70	74	78	82	86	92	96	02	08	17	27	31	37	43	49	53
CA	570	44	46	48	48	50	52	54	56	58	60	62	66	72	74	78	82	88	90	96	02	08	17	27	31	37	43	49	53
CA	571	44	46	46	48	50	52	54	56	58	60	62	66	72	74	78	82	86	90	96	98	08	17	27	31	37	43	47	53
CA	572	44	46	46	48	50	52	54	56	58	60	62	66	70	74	78	82	86	90	96	02	08	17	27	31	37	43	47	53
CA	573	44	46	46	48	50	52	54	56	58	60	62	66	70	74	78	82	86	90	94	02	08	17	25	31	37	43	47	53
AK	574	10	10	12	12	12	12	14	14	14	14	16	18	18	18	20	22	24	24	26	28	30	32	52	54	56	58	58	60
HI	575	32	36	36	36	36	38	40	40	42	44	46	48	50	52	56	58	64	64	68	72	76	78	88	92	96	04	06	06
HI	576	30	32	32	36	36	38	38	40	42	44	44	48	50	52	54	58	60	64	66	72	74	76	88	92	96	02	04	04
DC	577	46	48	50	52	52	52	54	56	56	58	60	60	64	64	66	68	72	74	74	76	78	80	86	88	92	96	96	98
DC	578	48	46	48	50	52	52	54	54	56	56	58	60	62	64	66	68	70	74	74	76	78	80	86	88	92	94	96	96
DC	579	30	48	48	48	50	52	54	54	54	56	58	60	62	64	66	68	70	72	74	76	78	80	84	88	90	94	96	96
Virgin Islands	580	28	40	48	54	62	66	72	78	82	86	92	96	98	98	98	98	98	98	98	98	98	98	02	04	06	06	08	08
Puerto Rico	581	28	40	48	52	60	68	74	78	80	86	92	96	98	98	98	98	98	98	98	98	98	98	11	19	23	41	55	63
Puerto Rico	582		40	48	52	60	66	72	76	80	86	92	98	98	98	98	98	98	98	98	98	98	98	11	17	23	41	55	61
Puerto Rico	583													07	10	22	34	46	54	64	74	84	94	11	17	23	39	55	61
Puerto Rico	584													03	10	18	34	40	50	62	74	84	92	08	17	23	39	55	61
NM	585								01	05	09	12	18	26	30	38	44	50	58	66	78	88	94	08	13	19	23	25	27

STATE	Area	1951	1952	1953	1954	1955	1956	1957	1958	1959	1960	1961	1962	1963	1964	1965	1966	1967	1968	1969	1970	1971	1972	1973	1974	1975	1976	1977	78
Guam	586						01	01	01	01	01	01	03	03	03	03	03	05	05	07	07	07	09						
Amrican Samoa							20	20	20	20	20	20	20	20	20	22	22	22	22	22	22	24	24						
Phillipine							30	30	30	30	30	30	30	30	30	30	30	30	30	30	30	30	30						
Islands							60	60	60	60	60	60	60	60	60	60	60	60	60	60	60	60	62	62	64	66	68	68	70
(see above)	587														05	26	46	58	74	92	98	98	98	15	19	23	27	29	31
RR	700	18	18	18	18	18	18	18	18	18	18	18	18	18	18	18	18	18	18	18	18	18	18	18	18	18	18	18	18
RR	701	18	18	18	18	18	18	18	18	18	18	18	18	18	18	18	18	18	18	18	18	18	18	18	18	18	18	18	18
RR	702	18	18	18	18	18	18	18	18	18	18	18	18	18	18	18	18	18	18	18	18	18	18	18	18	18	18	18	18
RR	703	18	18	18	18	18	18	18	18	18	18	18	18	18	18	18	18	18	18	18	18	18	18	18	18	18	18	18	18
RR	704	18	18	18	18	18	18	18	18	18	18	18	18	18	18	18	18	18	18	18	18	18	18	18	18	18	18	18	18
RR	705	18	18	18	18	18	18	18	18	18	18	18	18	18	18	18	18	18	18	18	18	18	18	18	18	18	18	18	18
RR	706	18	18	18	18	18	18	18	18	18	18	18	18	18	18	18	18	18	18	18	18	18	18	18	18	18	18	18	18
RR	707	18	18	18	18	18	18	18	18	18	18	18	18	18	18	18	18	18	18	18	18	18	18	18	18	18	18	18	18
RR	708	18	18	18	18	18	18	18	18	18	18	18	18	18	18	18	18	18	18	18	18	18	18	18	18	18	18	18	18
RR	709	18	18	18	18	18	18	18	18	18	18	18	18	18	18	18	18	18	18	18	18	18	18	18	18	18	18	18	18
RR	710	18	18	18	18	18	18	18	18	18	18	18	18	18	18	18	18	18	18	18	18	18	18	18	18	18	18	18	18
RR	711	18	18	18	18	18	18	18	18	18	18	18	18	18	18	18	18	18	18	18	18	18	18	18	18	18	18	18	18
RR	712	18	18	18	18	18	18	18	18	18	18	18	18	18	18	18	18	18	18	18	18	18	18	18	18	18	18	18	18
Railroad	713	18	18	18	18	18	18	18	18	18	18	18	18	18	18	18	18	18	18	18	18	18	18	18	18	18	18	18	18
Retirement	714	18	18	18	18	18	18	18	18	18	18	18	18	18	18	18	18	18	18	18	18	18	18	18	18	18	18	18	18
RR	715	18	18	18	18	18	18	18	18	18	18	18	18	18	18	18	18	18	18	18	18	18	18	18	18	18	18	18	18
RR	716	18	18	18	18	18	18	18	18	18	18	18	18	18	18	18	18	18	18	18	18	18	18	18	18	18	18	18	18
RR	717	18	18	18	18	18	18	18	18	18	18	18	18	18	18	18	18	18	18	18	18	18	18	18	18	18	18	18	18
RR	718	18	18	18	18	18	18	18	18	18	18	18	18	18	18	18	18	18	18	18	18	18	18	18	18	18	18	18	18
RR	719	18	18	18	18	18	18	18	18	18	18	18	18	18	18	18	18	18	18	18	18	18	18	18	18	18	18	18	18
RR	720	18	18	18	18	18	18	18	18	18	18	18	18	18	18	18	18	18	18	18	18	18	18	18	18	18	18	18	18
RR	721	18	18	18	18	18	18	18	18	18	18	18	18	18	18	18	18	18	18	18	18	18	18	18	18	18	18	18	18
RR	722	18	18	18	18	18	18	18	18	18	18	18	18	18	18	18	18	18	18	18	18	18	18	18	18	18	18	18	18
RR	723	18	18	18	18	18	18	18	18	18	18	18	18	18	18	18	18	18	18	18	18	18	18	18	18	18	18	18	18
RR	724	18	28	28	28	28	28	28	28	28	28	28	28	28	28	28	28	28	28	28	28	28	28	28	28	28	28	28	28
RR	725	18	28	18	18	18	18	18	18	18	18	18	18	18	18	18	18	18	18	18	18	18	18	18	18	18	18	18	18
RR	726	18	18	18	18	18	18	18	18	18	18	18	18	18	18	18	18	18	18	18	18	18	18	18	18	18	18	18	18
RR	727	10	10	10	10	10	10	10	10	10	10	10	10	10	10	10	10	10	10	10	10	10	10	10	10	10	10	10	10
RR	728	09	09	18	12	12	14	14	14	14	14	14	14	14	14	14	14	14	14	14	14	14	14	14	14	14	14	14	14
RR	729	09																											

APPENDIX 3: Private Detective Licensure

Here is a copy of the Massachusetts Private Detective Licensing law (MGL Chapter 147), which was current as of this writing. I've included it as a sample of what PI licensing laws are like in the states that have them. The exact details and requirements will, of course, vary from state to state. Some states have testing and educational requirements, which will not be reflected in the Massachusetts law. As always, consult your own attorney regarding the laws in your jurisdiction before making any life-changing career choices.

GENERAL LAWS OF MASSACHUSETTS
PART I
ADMINISTRATION OF THE GOVERNMENT

TITLE XX
PUBLIC SAFETY AND GOOD ORDER

CHAPTER 147 STATE AND OTHER POLICE, AND CERTAIN POWERS AND DUTIES OF THE DEPARTMENT OF PUBLIC SAFETY

Chapter 147: Section 22. Definitions.
Section 22. In this section and in sections twenty-three to thirty, inclusive, the following words shall have the following meanings unless a different meaning is clearly required by the context:

"Licensee", any person licensed under section twenty-five.

"Private detective business", the business of private detective or private investigator, and the business of watch, guard or patrol agency.

"Private detective" or "private investigator", a person engaged in business as a private detective or private investigator, including any person who, for hire, fee, reward or other consideration, (1) uses a lie-detector for the purpose of obtaining information with reference to the conduct, integrity, efficiency, loyalty or activities of any person or (2) engages in the business of making investigations for the purpose of obtaining information with reference to any of the following matters, whether or not other functions or services are also performed for hire, fee, reward or other consideration, or other persons are employed to assist in making such investigations:

(a) Crime or other acts committed or threatened against the laws or government of the United States or any state of the United States;

(b) The identity, habits, conduct, movements, whereabouts, affiliations, associations, transactions, reputation or character of any person;

(c) Libels, fires, losses, accidents, or damage to, or loss or theft of, real or personal property;

(d) Evidence to be used before any investigating committee, board of award, or board of arbitration, or in the trial of civil or criminal cases.

"Watch, guard or patrol agency", the business of watch, guard or patrol agency, including the furnishing, for hire or reward, of watchmen, guards, private patrolmen or other persons to protect persons or property, to prevent the theft or the unlawful taking of goods, wares or merchandise, or the misappropriation or concealment thereof or of money, bonds, stocks, notes or other valuable documents, papers or articles of value, or to procure the return thereof, whether or not other functions or services are also performed for hire or reward, or other persons are employed to assist therein.

Chapter 147: Section 23. Necessity of license for private detective business; exceptions.

Section 23. No person shall engage in, advertise or hold himself out as being engaged in, nor solicit private detective business or the business of watch, guard or patrol agency, notwithstanding the name or title used in describing such business, unless licensed for such purpose as provided in section twenty-five.

The provisions of this section shall not apply to an agent, employee or assistant of a licensee, to any corporation, if its resident manager, superintendent or official representative is a licensee, nor to the following:

1. A person employed by or on behalf of the commonwealth, including the general court or either of its branches, any committee of the general court or either of its branches, any special commission required to report to the general court, any political subdivision of the commonwealth or any public instrumentality, while such person is engaged in the discharge of his official duties.

2. A charitable, philanthropic or law enforcement agency, duly incorporated under the laws of the commonwealth, or any agent thereof while he is engaged in the discharge of his duties as such agent; provided, that such agency is promoted and maintained for the public good and not for private profit.

3. A person employed as an investigator, detective, watchman, guard, patrolman, or employed or assigned to perform any of the activities described in the definition "watch, guard or patrol agency" or whose duties include an inquiry into the fitness of an applicant for employment, in connection with the regular and customary business of his employer and whose services are not let out to another for profit or gain, but only while so acting for his employer.

4. A credit reporting bureau or agency whose business is principally the furnishing of information as to business and financial standing and credit responsibility.

5. Investigations as to the personal habits and financial responsibility of applicants for insurance or indemnity bonds, provided, such investigations do not include other activities described in section twenty-two.

6. An attorney at law in the practice of his profession.

7. Investigations with respect to, or the compilation or dissemination of, any data or statistics pertaining to any business or industry, by any trade or business association, board or organization, incorporated or unincorporated, not operated for profit, representing persons engaged in such business or industry, or by any agent of any such trade or business association while he is engaged in the discharge of his duties as such agent.

8. An insurance adjuster or investigator while acting in such capacity as an employee.

9. Any trade or business association, board or organization, incorporated or unincorporated, which furnishes as a service to members thereof, information pertaining to the business and financial standing, credit responsibility or reputation of persons with whom such members consider doing business; provided, that an investigation conducted by such association, board or organization shall be no more extensive than is reasonably required to determine the

business and financial standing, credit responsibility or reputation of such person.

10. A person engaged in earning his livelihood by genealogical work and the compilation of family history while so engaged.

11. A person hired by the owner of a residential dwelling for the limited purpose of inspecting the exterior of an unoccupied residential dwelling for storm damage.

Whoever violates any provision of this section shall be punished by a fine of not less than two hundred nor more than one thousand dollars or by imprisonment for not more than one year, or by both such fine and imprisonment.

12. Individuals who are independently and currently licensed by the commonwealth in a profession or field of expertise, whereby they are exclusively utilized and confined in conducting an investigation to that profession or field of expertise, inasmuch as the context and extent of their inquiry and investigation does not exceed the particular area of their profession or field of expertise in which they are independently licensed within the commonwealth.

Chapter 147: Section 24. Applications; qualifications of applicants.

Section 24. An application for a license to engage in the private detective business or a license to engage in the business of watch, guard or patrol agency shall be filed with the colonel of the state police on forms furnished by him, and statements of fact therein shall be under oath of the applicant. Such application shall include a certification by each of three reputable citizens of the commonwealth residing in the community in which the applicant resides or has a place of business, or in which the applicant proposes to conduct his business, that he has personally known the applicant for at least three years, that he has read the application and believes each of the statements made therein to be true, that he is not related to the applicant by blood or marriage, and that the applicant is honest and of

good moral character. The applicant, or, if the applicant is a corporation, its resident manager, superintendent or official representative, shall be of good moral character, and, unless such application is for a license to engage in the business of watch, guard or patrol agency, shall have been regularly employed for not less than three years as a detective doing investigating work, a former member of an investigative service of the United States, a former police officer, of a rank or grade higher than that of patrolman, of the commonwealth, any political subdivision thereof or an official police department of another state, or a police officer in good standing formerly employed for not less than ten years with the commonwealth, or any political subdivision thereof or with an official police department of another state.

Chapter 147: Section 25. License; disqualification of convicts; duration; posting; name of licensee and approval; renewal and revocation.

Section 25. The colonel of the state police may grant to an applicant complying with the provisions of section twenty-four a license to engage in the private detective business or a license to engage in the business of watch, guard or patrol agency; provided, however, that no such license shall be granted to any person who has been convicted in any state of the United States of a felony. No person convicted of a violation of section ninety-nine or ninety-nine A of chapter two hundred and seventy-two of the general laws shall be granted a license and any license previously granted to such person shall be revoked.

Such license shall be for one year, shall state the name under which the licensed business is to be conducted and the address of its principal office, and shall be posted by the licensee in a conspicuous place in such office. Such name shall be subject to the approval of the colonel of the state police; provided that such name shall not contain the words "police", "fire", nor any name which denotes or implies any association with agencies of the governments of the United

States, the commonwealth or any of its political subdivisions. Failure to comply with the provisions of this paragraph shall constitute cause for revocation of such license.

The colonel of the state police; may annually renew and may at any time for cause, after notice and a hearing, revoke, any such license. An application for a renewal shall be on a form furnished by the colonel.

Chapter 147: Section 25A. Repealed, 1960, 802, Sec. 1.

Chapter 147: Section 25B. Repealed, 1954, 544, Sec. 1.

Chapter 147: Section 25C. Repealed, 1960, 802, Sec. 1.

Chapter 147: Section 26. License fees; bond.
Section 26. The fee for an original license and for a renewal of any license shall be determined annually by the commissioner of administration under the provision of section three B of chapter seven for the filing thereof. If a person fails to apply for a renewal of a license within six months after the expiration thereof he shall pay for a renewal the fee herein provided for an original license.

Each licensee shall give to the commissioner a bond in the sum of five thousand dollars, executed by the applicant as principal and by a surety company authorized to do business as such in the commonwealth as surety. Such bond shall be in such form as the commissioner may prescribe, conditioned upon the honest conduct of the business of the licensee and the right of any person including the officer of any aggrieved labor union or association, whether or not incorporated, injured by the wilful, malicious or wrongful act of the licensee to bring in his own name an action on the bond.

Chapter 147: Section 27. Employment to determine labor conditions or disseminate propaganda; penalty.

Section 27. No licensee shall enter, or cause any person to enter, any place of employment for any purpose having to do with the organizing or organization of employees in said establishment, or any purpose having to do with hours of labor, wages or salaries paid, or conditions of employment in such establishment or its branches or subsidiaries or related units, or to disseminate propaganda of any sort among employees in such establishment, or to be concerned with labor conditions of employees as a group, nor shall any licensee or agent or employee of a licensee pose as an employee in any such establishment for any of the aforementioned purposes.

Violation of any provision of this section shall be cause for the suspension of such license for not less than one year, after a public hearing by the colonel of the state police, on written complaint of any aggrieved person, or the officer of any aggrieved labor union or association, whether incorporated or otherwise.

Chapter 147: Section 28. Assistants; employment; divulgence of information or false report; penalty.

Section 28. A licensee may employ to assist him in his business as many persons as he may deem necessary but shall not knowingly employ in connection with his business in any capacity any person who has been convicted of a felony or any former licensee whose license has been revoked.

If a licensee falsely states or represents that a person is or was in his employ, such false statement or representation shall be cause for revocation of his license. Whoever falsely states or represents that he has been a licensee or employed by a licensee shall be punished by a fine of not less than fifty nor more than five hundred dollars.

No person shall be employed by any licensee until he shall have executed and furnished to such licensee a statement under oath setting forth his full name, date of birth and residence; his parents' names and places of birth; the business or occupation in which he has been engaged for the three years immediately preceding the date of filing his statement; and that he has not been convicted of a felony or of any offence involving moral turpitude. Such statements shall be kept on file by the licensee and furnished to the colonel of the state police on demand.

Any person who is or has been an employee of a licensee and any licensee who divulges to anyone other than to his employer or as his employer shall direct, except before an authorized tribunal, any information acquired by him during such employment in respect to any of the work to which he has been assigned by such employer, and any such employee who wilfully makes a false report to his employer in respect to any such work, shall be punished by a fine of not more than five hundred dollars or by imprisonment for not more than one year, or both.

No minor shall be employed as an investigator or guard by a licensee if the use of firearms is required in the performance of his duties.

Chapter 147: Section 29. Badges, identification cards, weapons, equipment and vehicles.

Section 29. No licensee or employee or agent of a licensee shall use a badge of any kind for identification purposes except a guard or watchman in uniform who shall wear any such badge on the left breast of his uniform. Such badge shall not contain the word "Police" or any part of the seal of the Commonwealth of Massachusetts or of any political subdivision thereof. A licensee or his employee or agent shall carry only such weapons and equipment as are authorized by the colonel of the state police; provided, however, that if said licensee, employee or agent, is authorized to carry a firearm, as defined in section one hundred and twenty-one of chapter one hundred and forty, said firearm shall be loaded while in the performance of his duties. A licensee, or his employee or agent, while in the performance of his duties, shall not carry an imitation firearm as defined in said section one hundred and twenty-one of said

chapter one hundred and forty. A licensee or his employee or agent may use as identification a card, approved as to form by the colonel of the state police, which shall bear the signature of the licensee and, if such card is used as identification by an employee or agent, the signature of such employee or agent.

No motor vehicle used in the business of a licensee shall have displayed therein or thereon the words "police" or "emergency", and no such motor vehicle shall be deemed to be a special purpose motor vehicle assigned to emergency disaster services under the provisions of section seven I of chapter ninety.

Whoever violates any provision of this section shall be punished by a fine of not more than fifty dollars.

Chapter 147: Section 29A. Daily records concerning guards carrying guns required.

Section 29A. Any watch, guard or patrol agency shall maintain daily records which shall include the names of guards and other employees carrying guns in the performance of their duties, the purpose of their carrying such guns and whether such guns are the personal property of the guards and other employees or issued by such agency.

Chapter 147: Section 30. Prohibited acts; penalty.

Section 30. No licensee nor any of his employees shall knowingly:

1. Incite, encourage or aid any person who has become a party to any strike to commit any unlawful act against any person or property.

2. Incite, stir up, create or aid in the inciting of discontent, or dissatisfaction among the employees of any person with the intention of having them strike.

3. Interfere with or prevent lawful and peaceful picketing during strikes.

4. Interfere with, restrain or coerce employees in the exercise of their right to form, join or assist any labor organization of their own choosing.

5. Interfere with or hinder lawful or peaceful collective bargaining between employers and employees.

6. Pay, offer or give any money, gratuity, consideration or other thing of value, directly or indirectly, to any person for any verbal or written report of the lawful activities of employees in the exercise of their right to organize, form or assist any labor organization and to bargain collectively through representatives of their own choosing.

7. Advertise for, recruit, furnish or replace, or offer to furnish or replace for hire or reward, within or without the commonwealth, any skilled or unskilled help or labor, armed guards, other than armed guards theretofore regularly employed for the protection of payrolls, property or premises, for service upon property which is being operated in anticipation of or during the course or existence of a strike.

8. Furnish armed guards upon the highways for persons involved in labor disputes.

9. Furnish or offer to furnish to employers or their agents, any arms, munitions, tear gas implements or any other weapons.

10. Send letters or literature to employers offering to eliminate labor unions.

11. Advise any person of the membership of an individual in a labor organization for the purpose of preventing such individual from obtaining or retaining employment.

Whoever violates any provision of this section shall be punished by a fine of not less than two hundred nor more than one thousand dollars or by imprisonment for not less than six months nor more than one year, or both.

Chapter 147: Section 31. Names of police officers sent to criminal justice training council; failure to send names.

Section 31. The clerk of each town in which a chief of police or city marshal is appointed shall, within one week after such appointment, notify the executive director of the municipal police training committee of the name of the person so appointed; and the clerk of each town not having a chief of police shall annually, on October first, send to the executive director of the municipal police training committee the names of all the police officers and constables in such town. If he neglects or refuses so to do, he shall be punished by a fine of fifty dollars.

ABOUT THE AUTHOR

Bud Jillett is a licensed private detective in the Commonwealth of Massachusetts, license number P-210. He has worked in the field most of his adult life. Though his specialty and most rewarding pursuit has been heir finding, he has also worked numerous missing persons, domestic, insurance fraud, and other investigations. Please send any inquiries regarding this text to pica@jillett.com.